Uneasy ELIXIRS

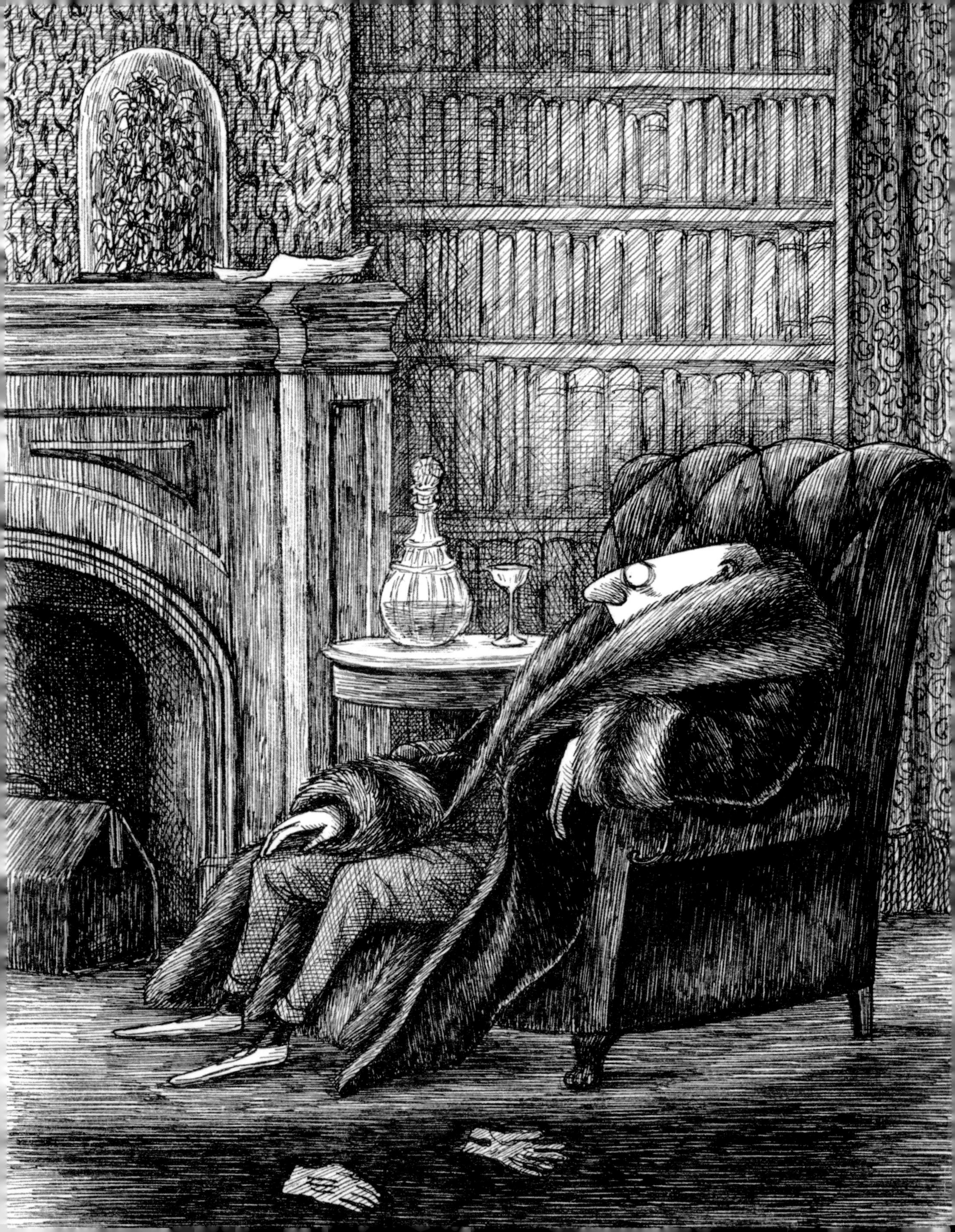

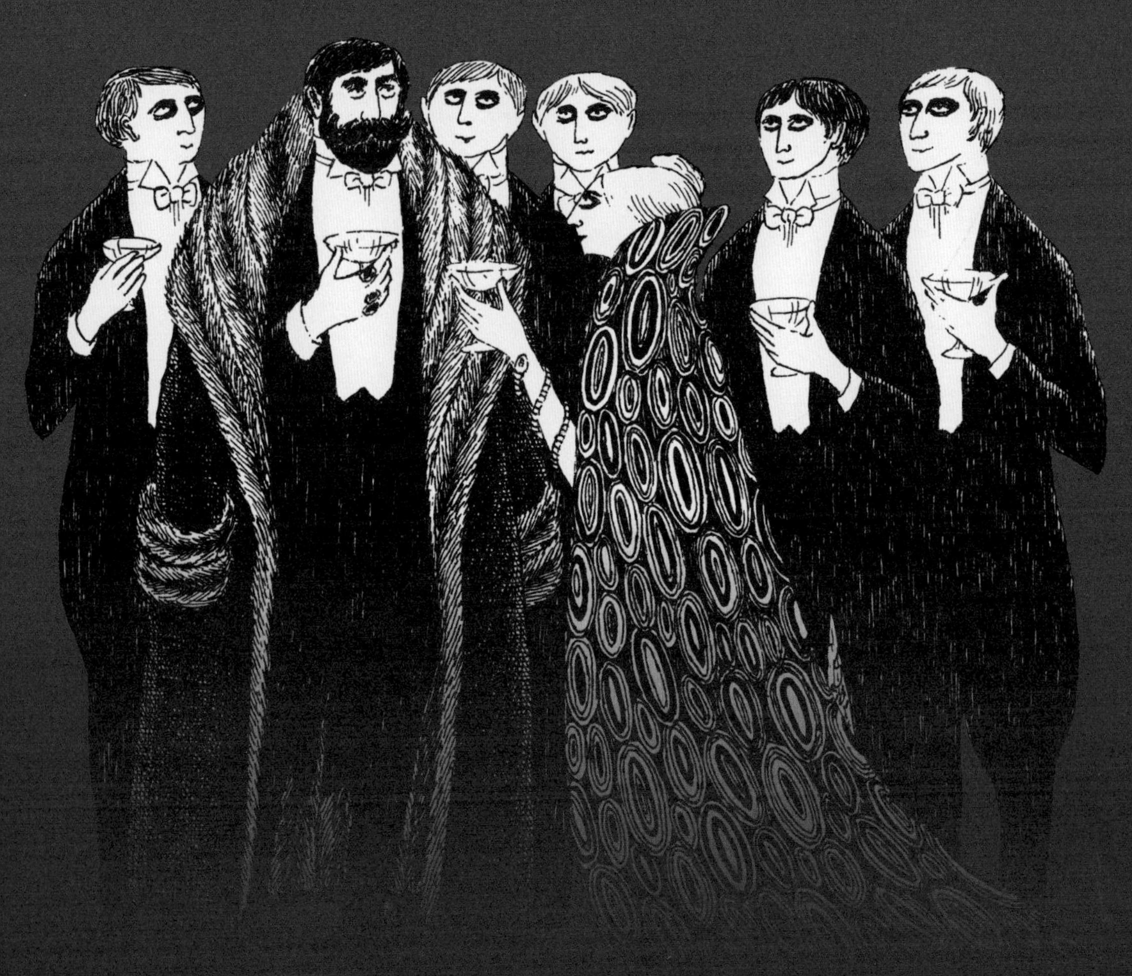

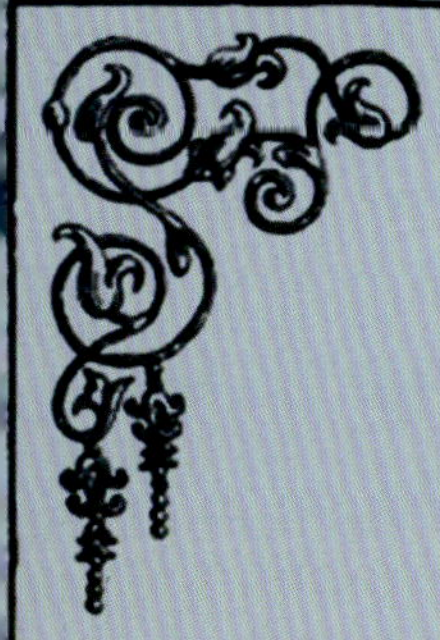

Uneasy ELIXIRS

50 Curious Cocktails
Inspired by the Works of
EDWARD GOREY

Virginia Miller

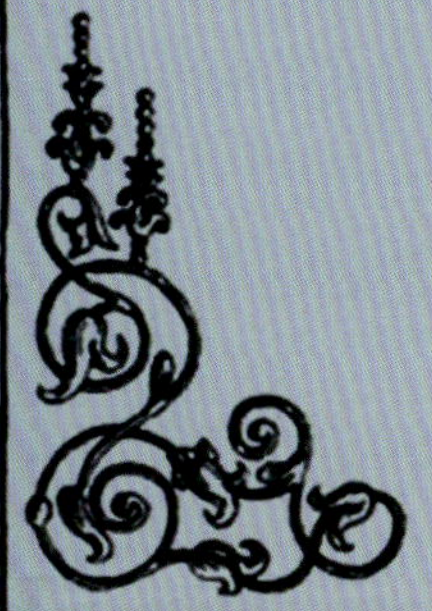
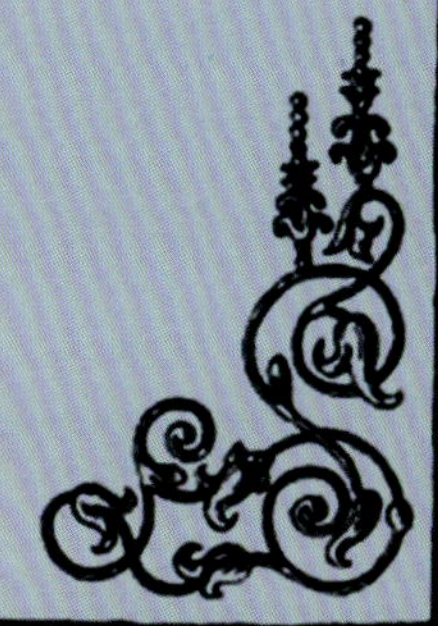

weldonowen

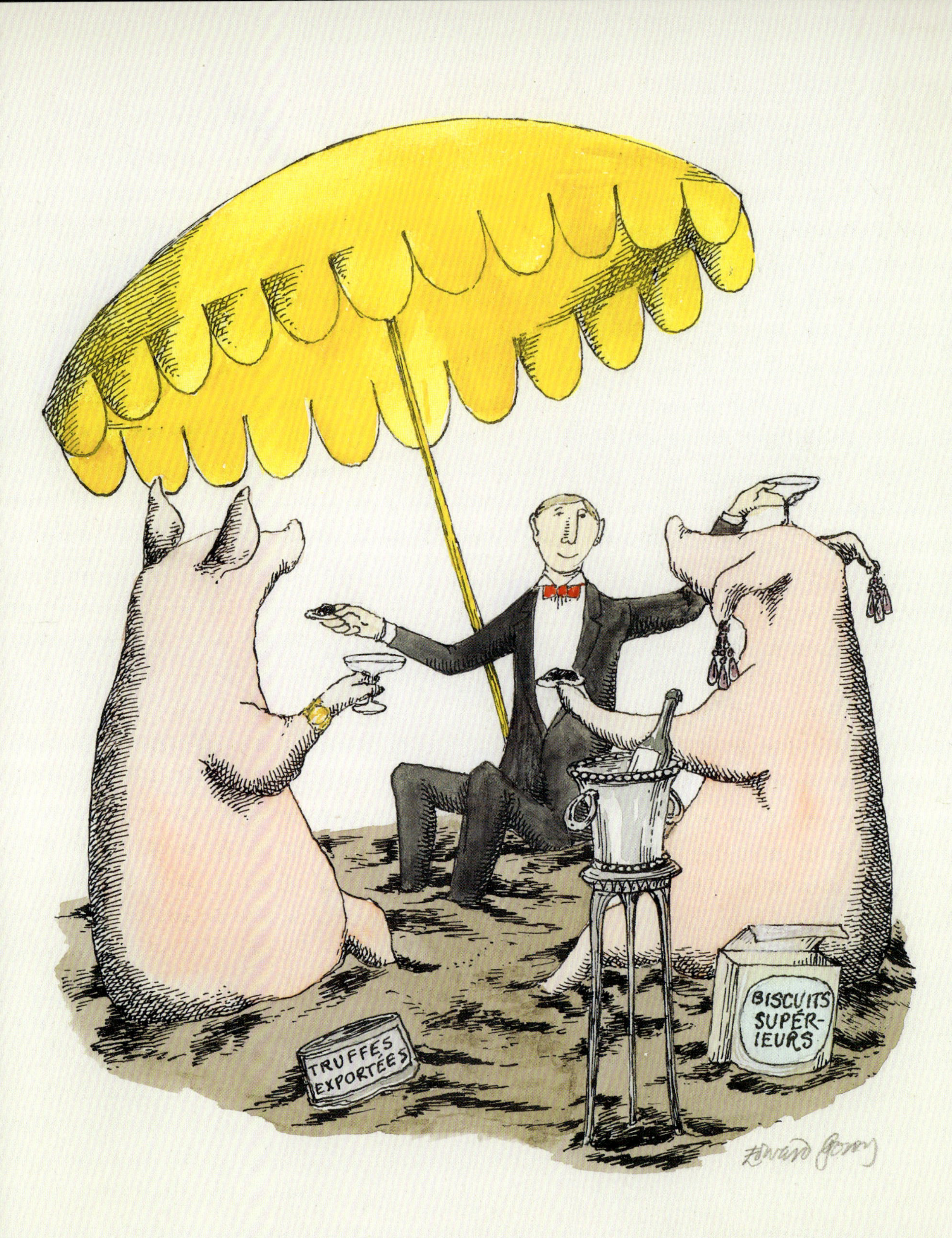
TRUFFES EXPORTÉES
BISCUITS SUPÉRIEURS
Edward Gorey

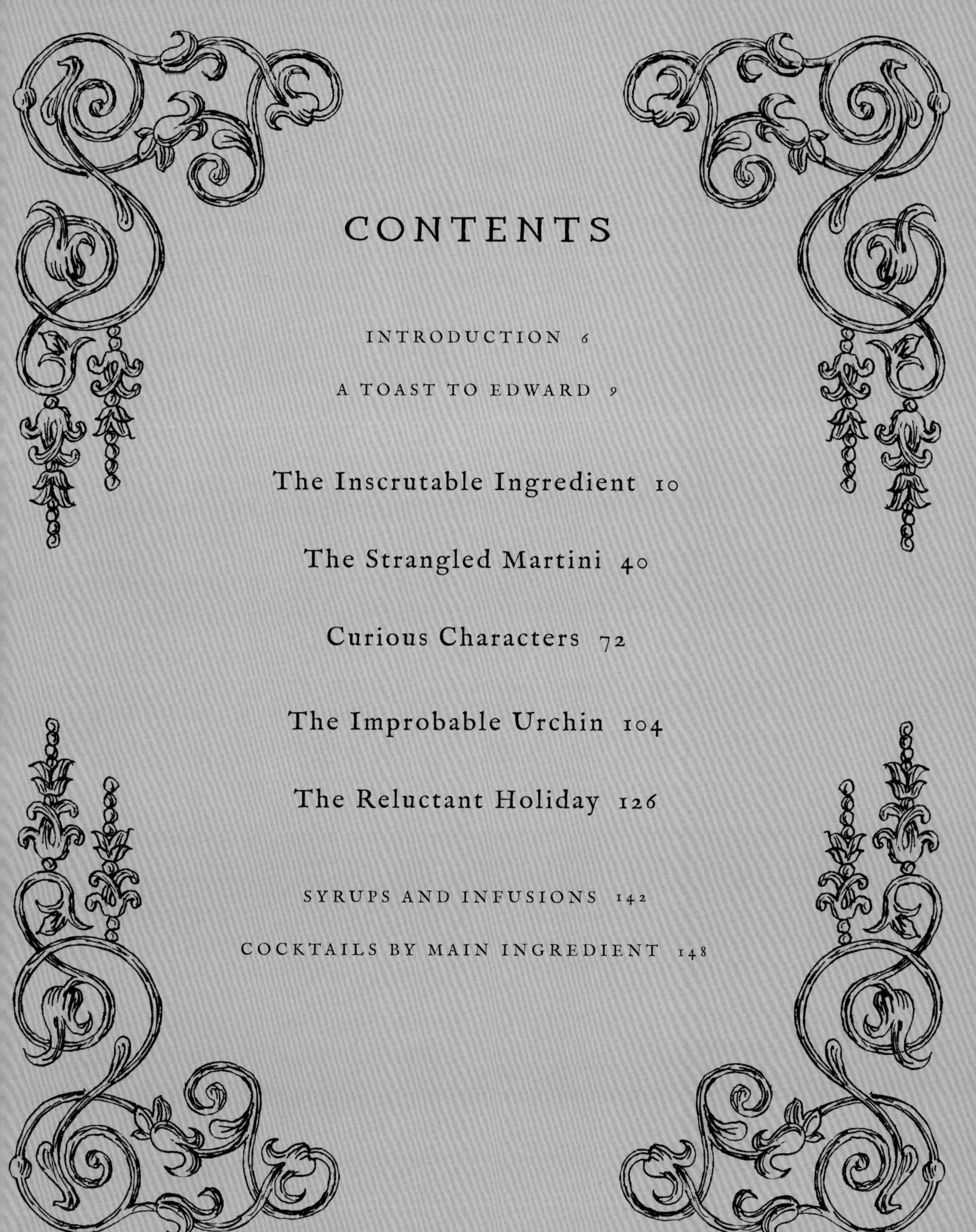

CONTENTS

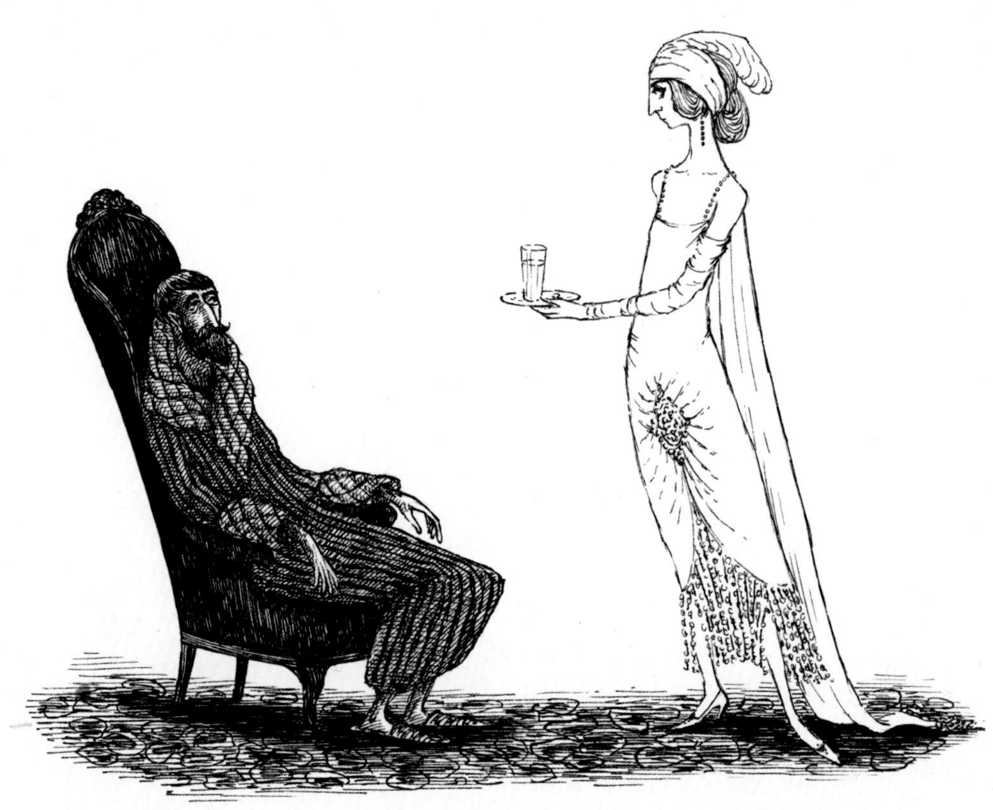

INTRODUCTION

Like many of us, I was first introduced to the work of Edward St. John Gorey with *The Gashlycrumb Tinies*, his 1963 opus of twenty-six children representing the alphabet as he creatively details their untimely deaths. As a geeky, incessant reader, I was homeschooled and grew up on both coasts with a few years in the Midwest. Spending many long, lonely, and rich hours studying at home, I was drawn to the gothic, the moody, and the ethereal, with books like *Wuthering Heights* being a favorite book since age seven and the films of Tim Burton resonating deeply with me as a girl. So I was immediately drawn to Gorey's dark yet whimsical art, his humorous gloom, his moody take on Victorian and Edwardian eras, and his unique perspective in art and verse.

As George R. Bodmer wrote in *The Post-Modern Alphabet: Extending the Limits of the Contemporary Alphabet Book, from Seuss to Gorey*, this best known of Gorey's books is a "sarcastic rebellion against a view of childhood that is sunny, idyllic, and instructive." Gorey showed us a rarified world that millions related to. Born in Chicago with degrees from the likes of Harvard, he was an artist, writer, and Tony Award–winning costume designer. In the 1950s, he lived in Manhattan and worked there for the art department of Doubleday Anchor, illustrating renowned books by legends like Charles Dickens and T. S. Eliot. Beginning with *The Unstrung Harp* in 1953, his own singular work unfolded in drawings and books, gaining a cult following then, as he continues to draw even now since his death in 2000. He wrote and illustrated an estimated five hundred or more books.

While we have only glimpses of Gorey's own drink preferences (see our Toast to Edward, page 9), from his iconic characters, like *Gashlycrumb*'s Zillah, who really loved her gin, to Gorey glassware for collectors, his delightfully ominous tales partner well with all types of cocktails. Each drink in this book is inspired in some way by Gorey's incomparable stories. From the Wuggly Ump to the Deranged Cousins, I celebrate his strange characters and quirky stories with a wide range of spirits—from vodka, whiskies, and gin to agave, brandies, and herbal liqueurs. Some are classic cocktail variations, low-proof sippers, or nonalcoholic imbibements, while others take culinary inspiration from the seasons and ingredients that play well together. But all of them are very much Gorey.

Spending time revisiting all of his books and drawings over this year has been a joy of fanciful, haunted proportions, returning me to my youth but in adult form. Gorey's uncommon stories invigorate this collection of cocktails energized by his unparalleled vision.

As in Gorey's *The Bug Book*, may we celebrate and adventure together as the bugs did, with no giant black bug to break up our parties. Like his colorful bugs, may you read, create, drink, and "enjoy yourself immensely."

Cheers,

Virginia Miller

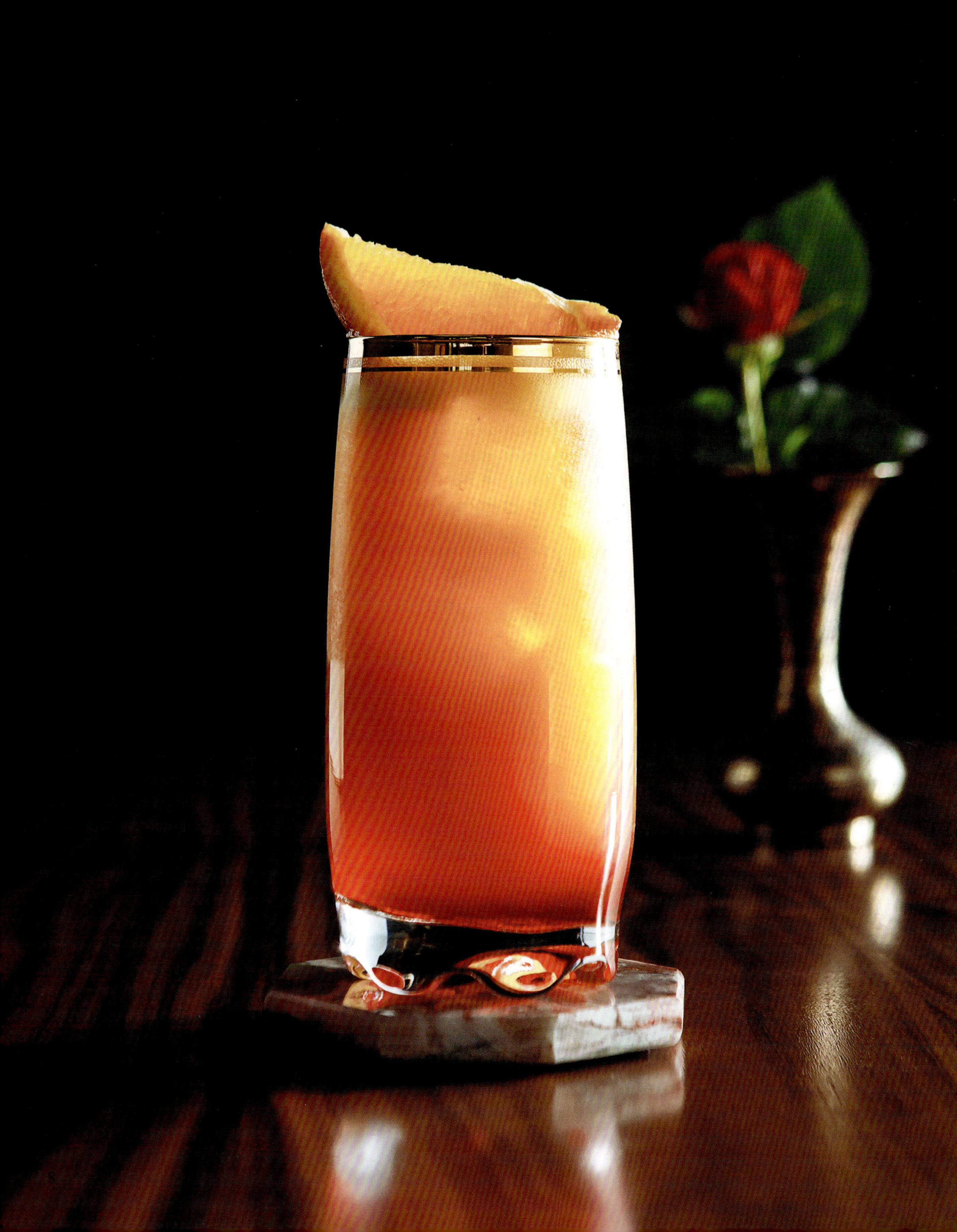

THE ROSALIE DARLING

· MAKES 1 COCKTAIL · GLASS: COLLINS ·

Edward, whose nickname was Ted, was dear friends with Rosalie Lewis, the head of the New York City Ballet (NYCB) gift shop, managing their merchandise development for years. At the bar O'Neal's Balloon, Ted and Rosalie, dance writer Robert Greskovic, and other friends in their artistic circles would go—along with the ballerinas—for drinks post-NYCB performances. Ted often greeted Rosalie with a hearty, "Rosalie, darling!" And thus, the two of them would drink Campari and orange juice, which they'd call The Rosalie Darling, a rosy, fresh, bitter imbibement.

In reality, this is a classic cocktail, the Garibaldi. This rosy-orange cocktail was named after Italian revolutionary general Giuseppe Garibaldi. Purportedly, his supporters wore red shirts, inspiring the drink's fiery color, while Campari is an Italian spirits staple. Sweet oranges play nicely with Campari's bitter.

Thanks to Robert Greskovic, senior dance writer for *The Wall Street Journal* and Gorey's closest still-living friend and one of two recipients of Gorey's estate in his will, for this story of Ted and Rosalie and The Rosalie Darling.

1½ oz (45 ml) Campari
4–6 oz (120–180 ml) fresh orange juice
Pinch of salt
Garnish: Orange wedge

Half fill a Collins glass with ice, then add the Campari. Blend the orange juice and salt in an electric juicer or blender until frothy. Add a bit of juice to the glass, then stir to combine. Add another ice cube or two and the rest of the orange juice. Garnish with an orange wedge.

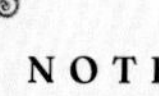

NOTE

Fresh-squeezed oranges make all the difference, adding a fluffy "foam" when frothed just before drinking, ideally with a high-speed juicer, blender, or Vitamix. Use Aperol if you prefer a softer bitter than the more bracing bittersweet of Campari. You can also vary the types of oranges for different flavor profiles (e.g., mandarins, blood oranges, navel, Valencia, etc.). A pinch of salt sharpens and enhances flavors.

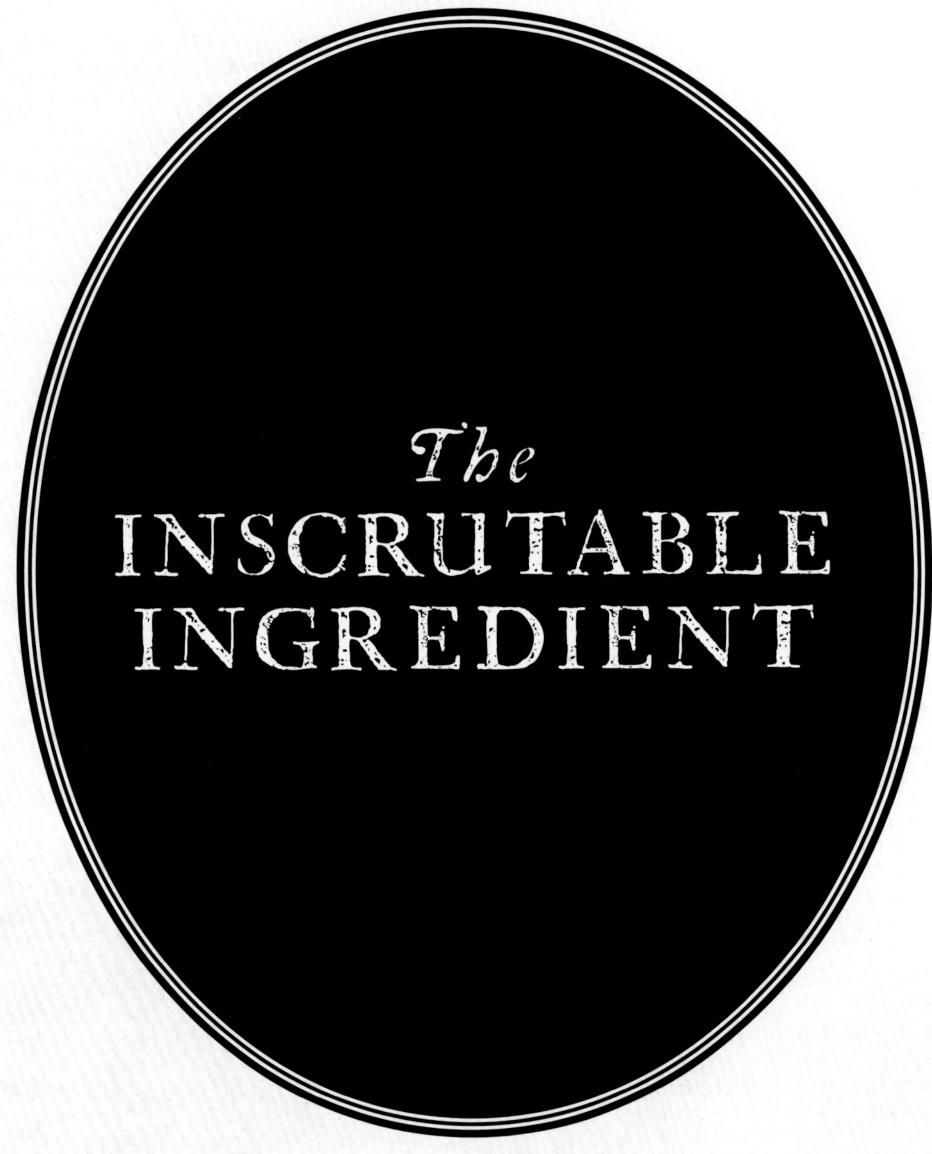

The INSCRUTABLE INGREDIENT

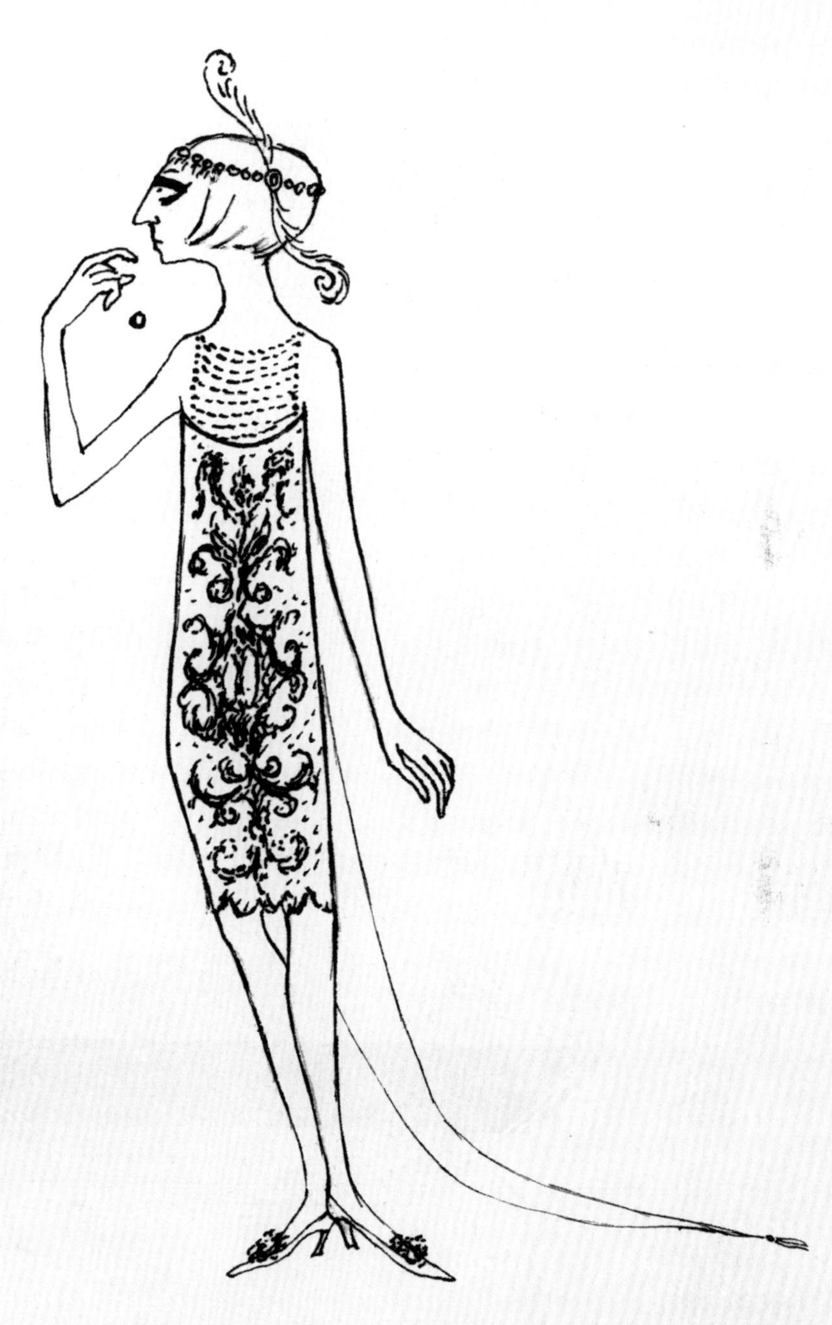

THE ROSY MARSH

• MAKES 1 COCKTAIL • GLASS: NICK AND NORA OR MARTINI •

The Deranged Cousins is a darkly delightful little tale of death centered around three cousins, cleverly named Rose Marshmary, Mary Rosemarsh, and Marsh Maryrose, who live in a rose-covered house at the edge of a marsh. While Mary murders Rose with a doorknob and buries her in a field known as the Rabbits' Restroom, Marsh perilously downs the dregs of a bottle of vanilla extract he found in the mud and dies in agony. Mary completes the deranged tale by being carried off by a high tide, never to be seen again.

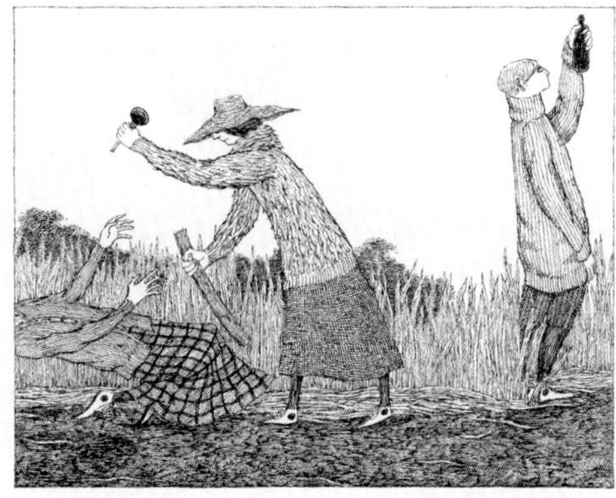

Decidedly less sinister, The Rosy Marsh is a martini variation with vanilla bean–infused vodka instead of deadly vanilla extract and pure rose water to honor the trio's marshy, rose-covered house. The crème de framboise (raspberry liqueur) adds a rosy, tart-sweet tinge to this bracing martini. If desired, a splash of soda water rounds out the rose and liqueur intensity, adding a touch of lean dryness.

2½ oz (75 ml) Vanilla Bean–Infused Vodka (page 146)

½ oz (15 ml) crème de framboise (raspberry or other berry liqueur)

2–3 drops pure rose water

1 oz (30 ml) soda water

Garnish: ½ vanilla bean

In a mixing glass with ice, combine the vodka, crème de framboise, and rose water. Stir with a barspoon for 20–30 seconds, until well chilled. Pour into a Nick and Nora or martini glass. Top with a splash of soda water. Garnish with half a vanilla bean.

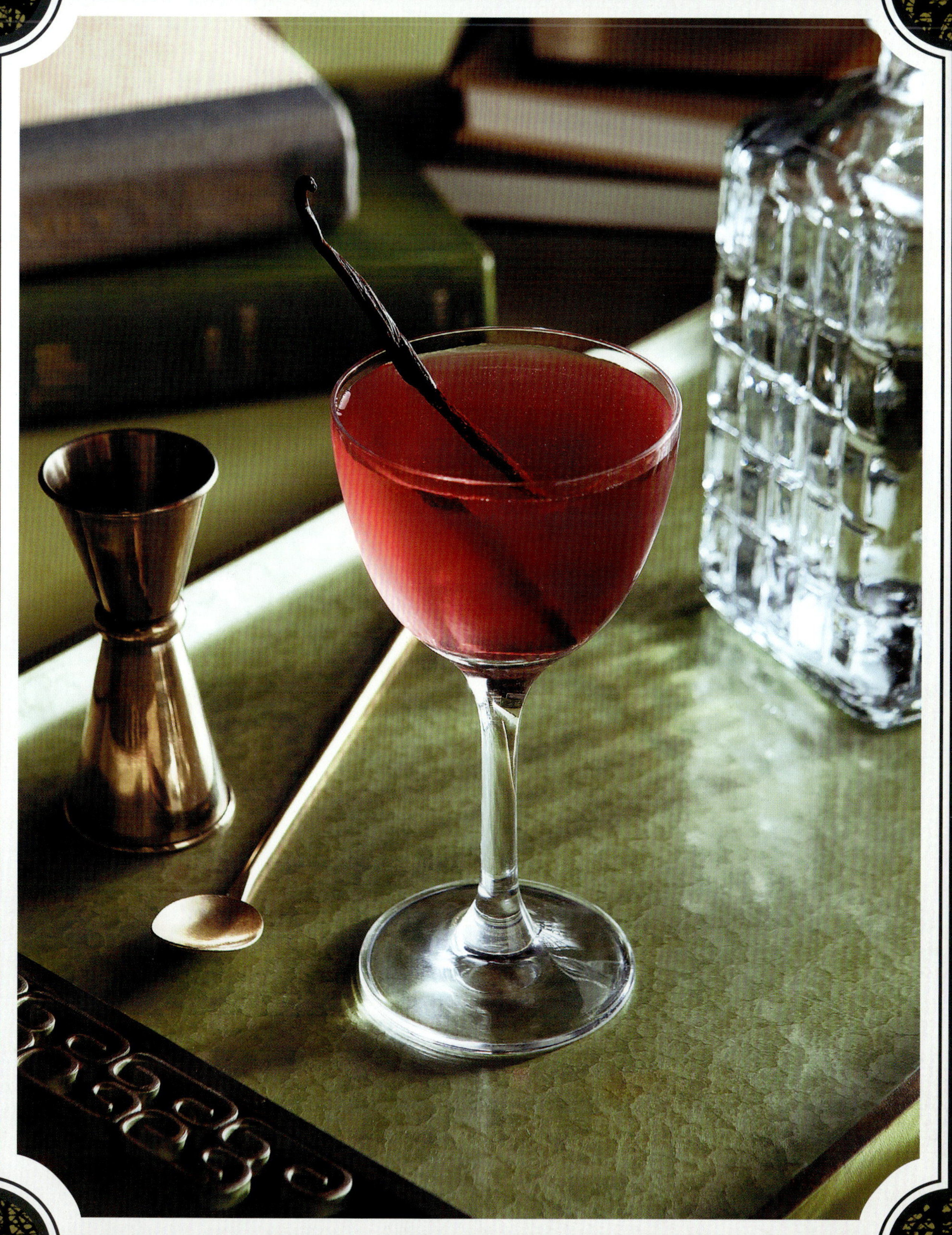

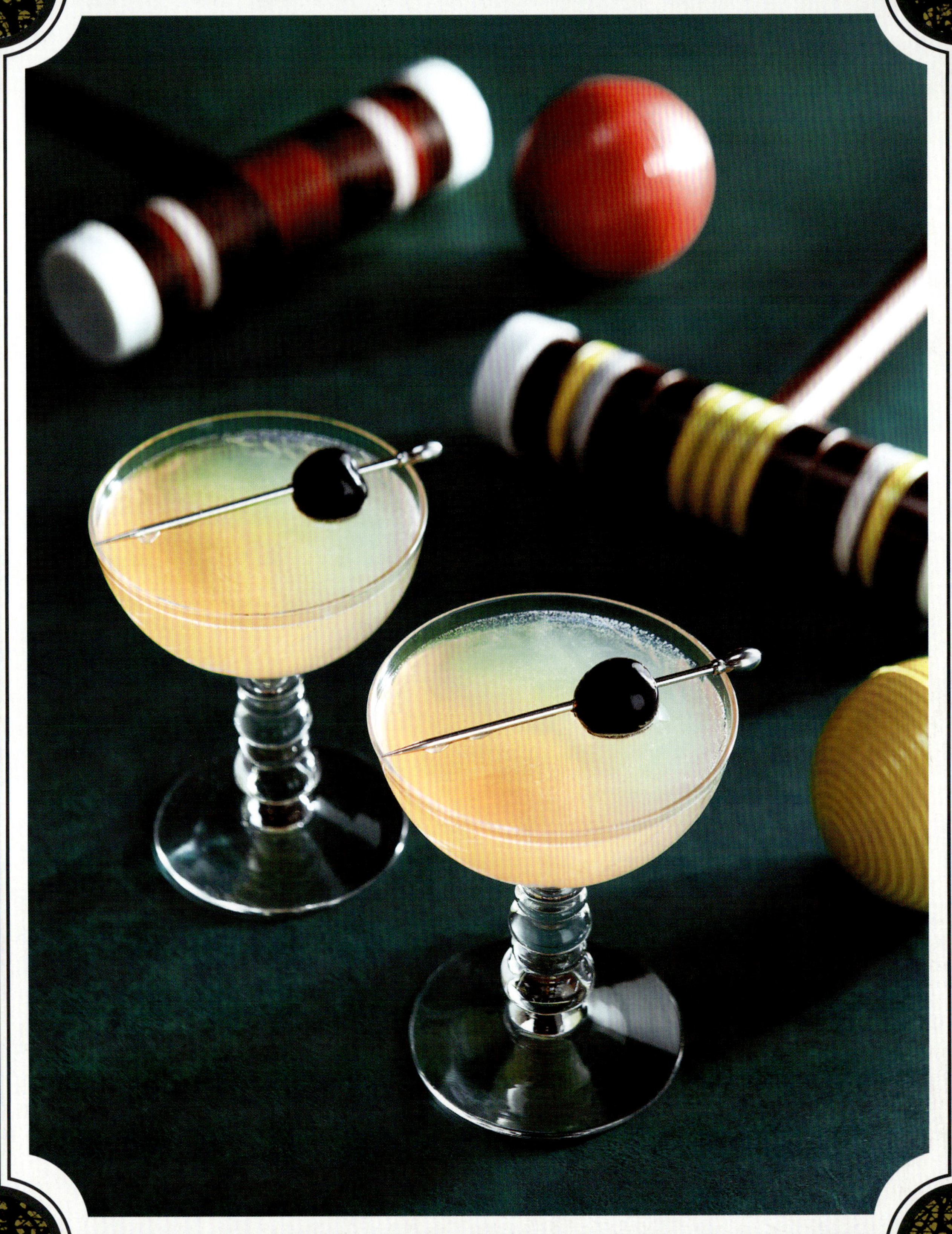

EMBLEY AND YEWBERT'S SPARKLING REVIVER

• MAKES 1 COCKTAIL • GLASS: COUPE •

A 1930s Corpse Reviver No. 2 cocktail already has Gorey-esque synergy in its name, purported to be a hangover cure bracing enough to "revive a corpse." Here, we revive the collapsed, "exhausted" Embley and Yewbert from *The Epiplectic Bicycle* with a bubbly version of the cocktail classic. Today's version of Lillet no longer includes quinine, so it changes the flavor profile of the cocktail. Thus we suggest Cocchi Americano Italian aperitif as one alternative that comes a bit closer to Kina Lillet's quinine bitterness.

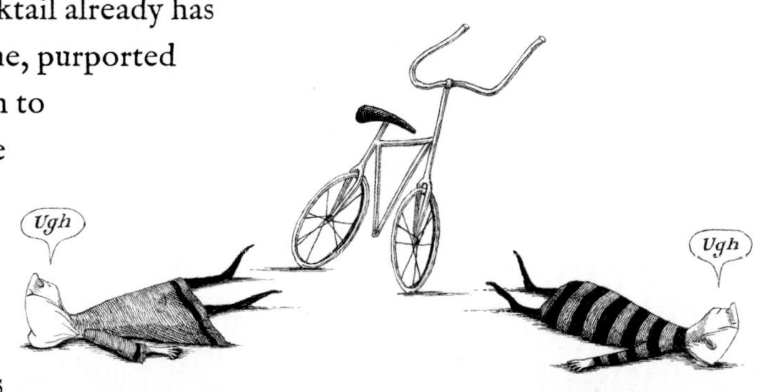

As a Prohibition-era cocktail, the Corpse Reviver No. 2 was lost to time until the cocktail renaissance of the aughts. It has been fully revived, is often popular at brunch, and is true to its revivifying "wake the dead" namesake roots. The drink initially is a classic sour-style cocktail, but add club soda for a bubbly perk, watching the absinthe slightly luge, turning cloudy and milky in the glass.

¾ oz (20 ml) gin
¾ oz (20 ml) fresh lemon juice
¾ oz (20 ml) Cocchi Americano or Lillet
¾ oz (20 ml) orange liqueur or orange curaçao
2 dashes absinthe
1 oz (30 ml) club soda
Garnish: Luxardo maraschino cherry

Place a coupe glass in the freezer to chill completely. In a cocktail shaker with ice, combine the gin, lemon juice, Cocchi Americano, orange liqueur, and absinthe. Cover and shake vigorously for 20–30 seconds, until well chilled. Strain into the chilled glass. Top with the club soda. Garnish with a maraschino cherry.

HENRY'S DEMISE

MAKES 1 COCKTAIL • GLASS: COUPE

The Water Flowers is Gorey's visually striking tale of resourcefulness, replete with moments that linger in the memory: making food last in an intense snowstorm, death on Christmas Eve, and getting lost in a good book. Jane's white sauce feeds a full household of men in fur coats as it's poured over everything, from soda crackers to "some ill-mashed turnips," leading to the demise of one of the fur-clad gents.

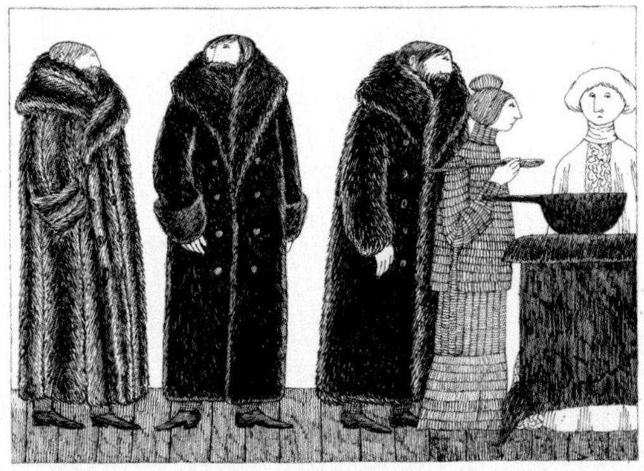

The classic Army & Navy gin cocktail—a tart, nutty combination of gin, lemon juice, and orgeat—is linked to Washington, DC's members-only Army and Navy Club, where a daiquiri was first served in the United States, and first appeared in print in 1948. As with many gin classics, you can substitute Scandinavian aquavit for gin to gain unexpected surprises in flavor. Like gin, aquavit (or akvavit) is distilled from grain or potatoes with a neutral grain base, flavored with a range of herbs and botanicals. Aquavit is the "secret ingredient," beguiling with garden-fresh savoriness, the kind of cocktail that makes you crave a Reuben sandwich, cured fish, or even something drenched in a white sauce.

---

2 oz (60 ml) aquavit
1 oz (30 ml) fresh lemon juice
¾ oz (20 ml) orgeat
1 dash Angostura bitters
Garnish: Grapefruit twist

Place a coupe glass in the freezer to chill completely. In a cocktail shaker with ice, combine the aquavit, lemon juice, orgeat, and Angostura bitters. Cover and shake for 20–30 seconds, until well chilled. Strain into the chilled glass. Garnish with a grapefruit twist.

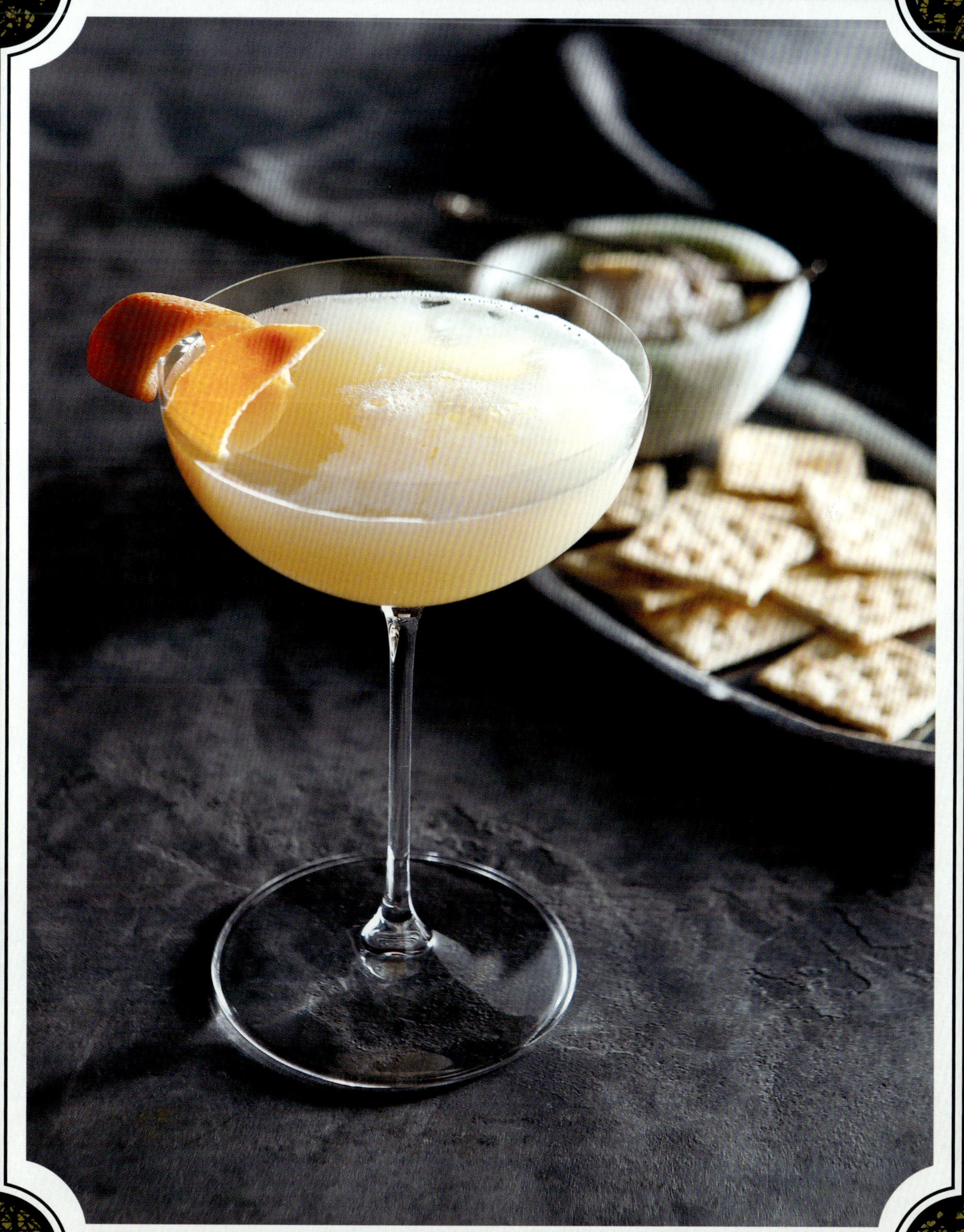

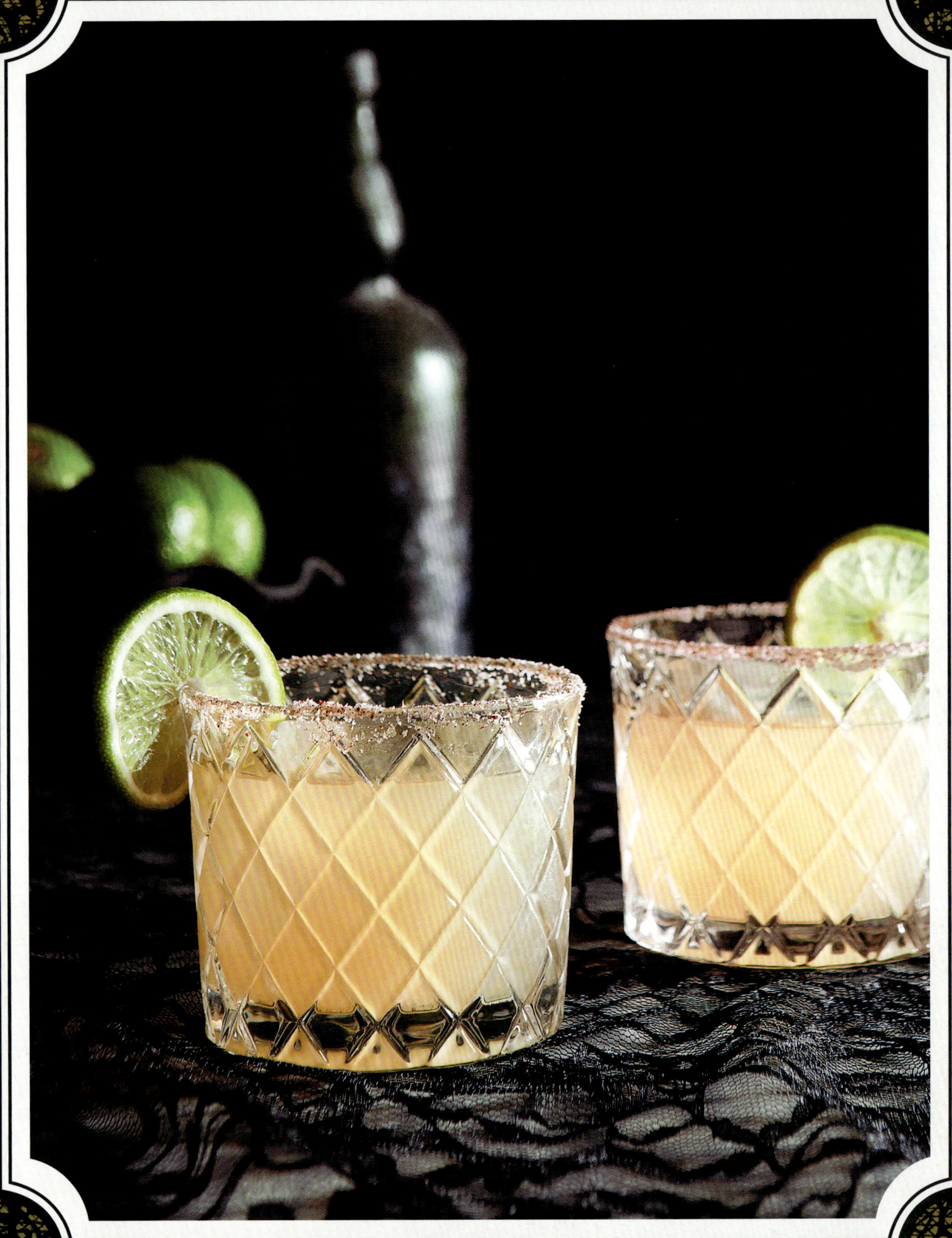

INSPIRED BY *The Curious Sofa*

THE THUMBFUMBLE

MAKES 1 COCKTAIL • GLASS: ROCKS

Charmingly risqué, *The Curious Sofa* is a playfully naughty series of drawings and encounters. Gorey gets particularly creative with the likes of a "most amusing game of 'Thumbfumble'" and a questionable pool party, where Alice puts on "an ingeniously constructed bathing slip." This spicy little story is a wild romp, rife with innuendo. And in true Gorey fashion, it includes an unexpected death.

This Gorey-for-grown-ups tale calls for a drink with an element of roguish surprise. In this case, it is a vegetal-fresh variation on a classic margarita, which also gains intrigue from smoky-slatey mezcal. Ancho Reyes Verde is made with ancho chiles that are picked while still green in color, then fire-roasted. The liqueur exudes verdant, fresh flavors that sing with the slate notes that show up in mezcals made with the most common agave plant, espadin. A rim of chili powder and sea salt ups the savory elements with a hit of salty heat. Go for half a rim if you wish to regulate the amount of chili and salt in each sip.

Rim: Chili powder, sea salt, lime wedge
1 oz (30 ml) mezcal
1 oz (30 ml) Ancho Reyes Verde
1 oz (30 ml) fresh lime juice
½ oz (15 ml) 1:1 Simple Syrup (page 142)
Garnish: Lime wheel

On a small plate, mix equal parts chili powder and salt and spread in an even layer. Gently rub the lime wedge around the rim of a rocks glass. Holding the base of the glass, dip the rim into the mixture. Set the glass aside.

In a cocktail shaker with ice, combine the mezcal, Ancho Reyes Verde, lime juice, and simple syrup. Cover and shake vigorously for 20–30 seconds, until well chilled. Double-strain into the glass over ice. Garnish with the lime wheel.

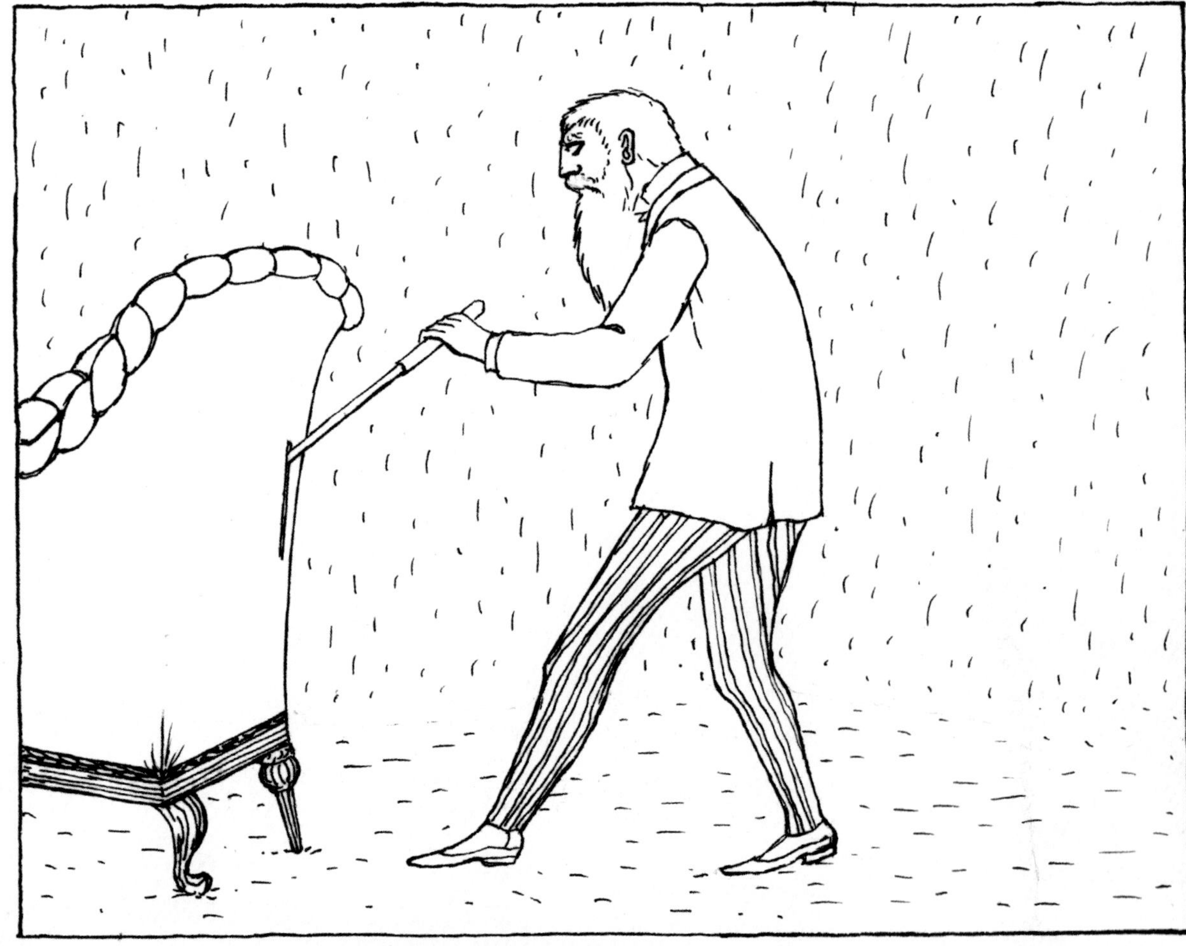

As soon as everybody had crowded into the room, Sir Egbert fastened shut the door, and started up the machinery inside the sofa.

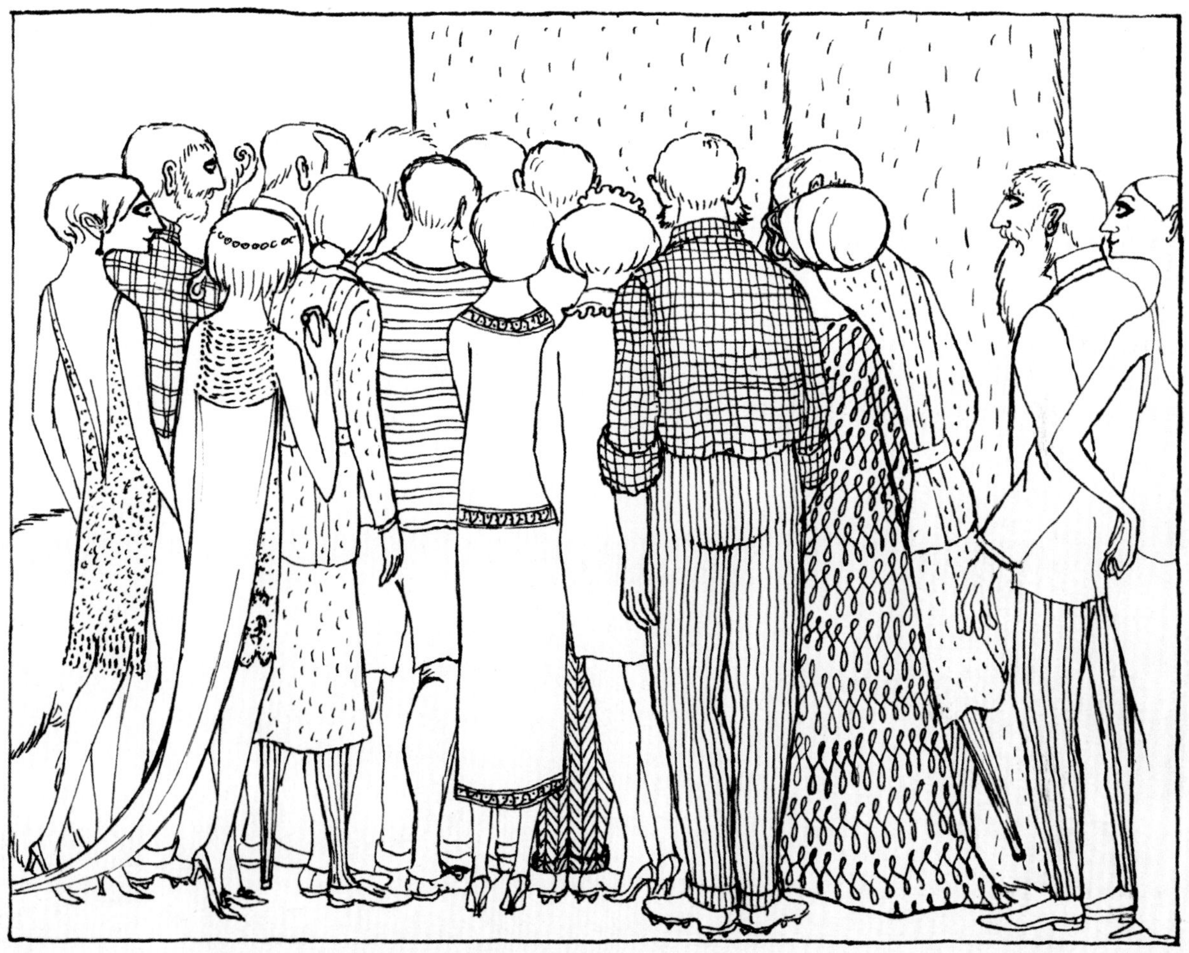

It stood in a windowless room lined with polar bear fur and otherwise empty; it was upholstered in scarlet velvet, and had nine legs and seven arms.

THE TRIPLE TIPPLE

• MAKES 1 COCKTAIL • GLASS: COUPE •

The Salt Herring tells a tale of a man with a ladder, pointy tools, and . . . a herring. This nonsensical story of a swinging salt herring claims to "make all serious men mad, mad, mad" but would "amuse children little, little, little."

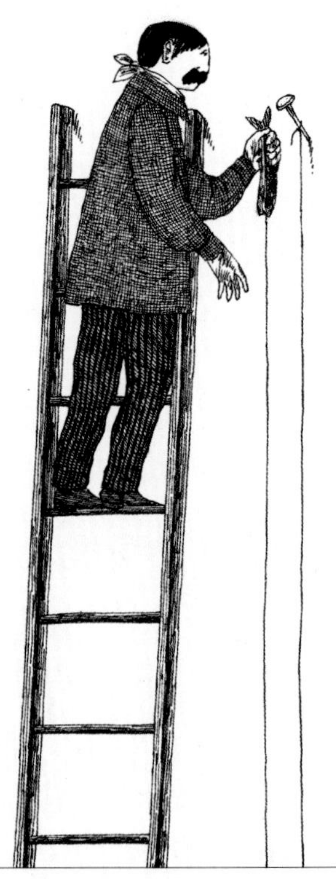

It may not be a dry, swinging salt herring, but we got a bit salty with this agave sipper that takes distant tropical Tiki inspiration from drinks like a classic Jungle Bird, a drink with elements ranging from bittersweet Campari to nutty, spiced velvet falernum. Falernum is a staple of classics like a mai tai with its notes of lime, almond, vanilla, ginger, and clove. The salty part comes in the form of saline solution. A couple of dashes add a sharpened balance to the bitter-sweet-nutty-spiced-tart drink.

1½ oz (45 ml) blanco tequila
½ oz (15 ml) velvet falernum
½ oz (15 ml) Aperol
¾ oz (20 ml) fresh lime juice
1 dash Saline Solution (page 147)

Place a coupe glass in the freezer to chill completely. Pour the tequila, falernum, Aperol, lime juice, and saline solution into a cocktail shaker. Cover and shake vigorously for 20–30 seconds, until well chilled. Strain into the chilled glass.

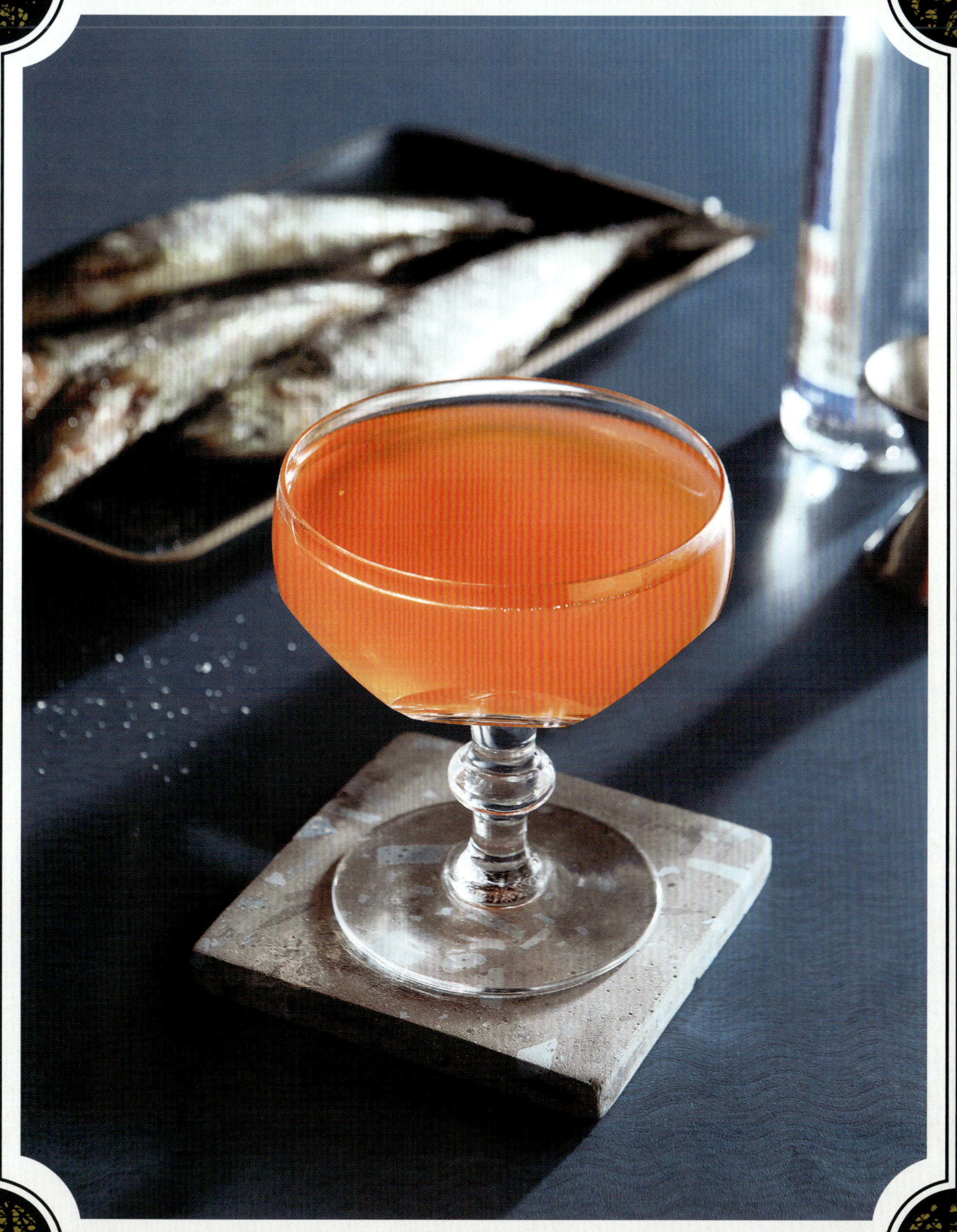

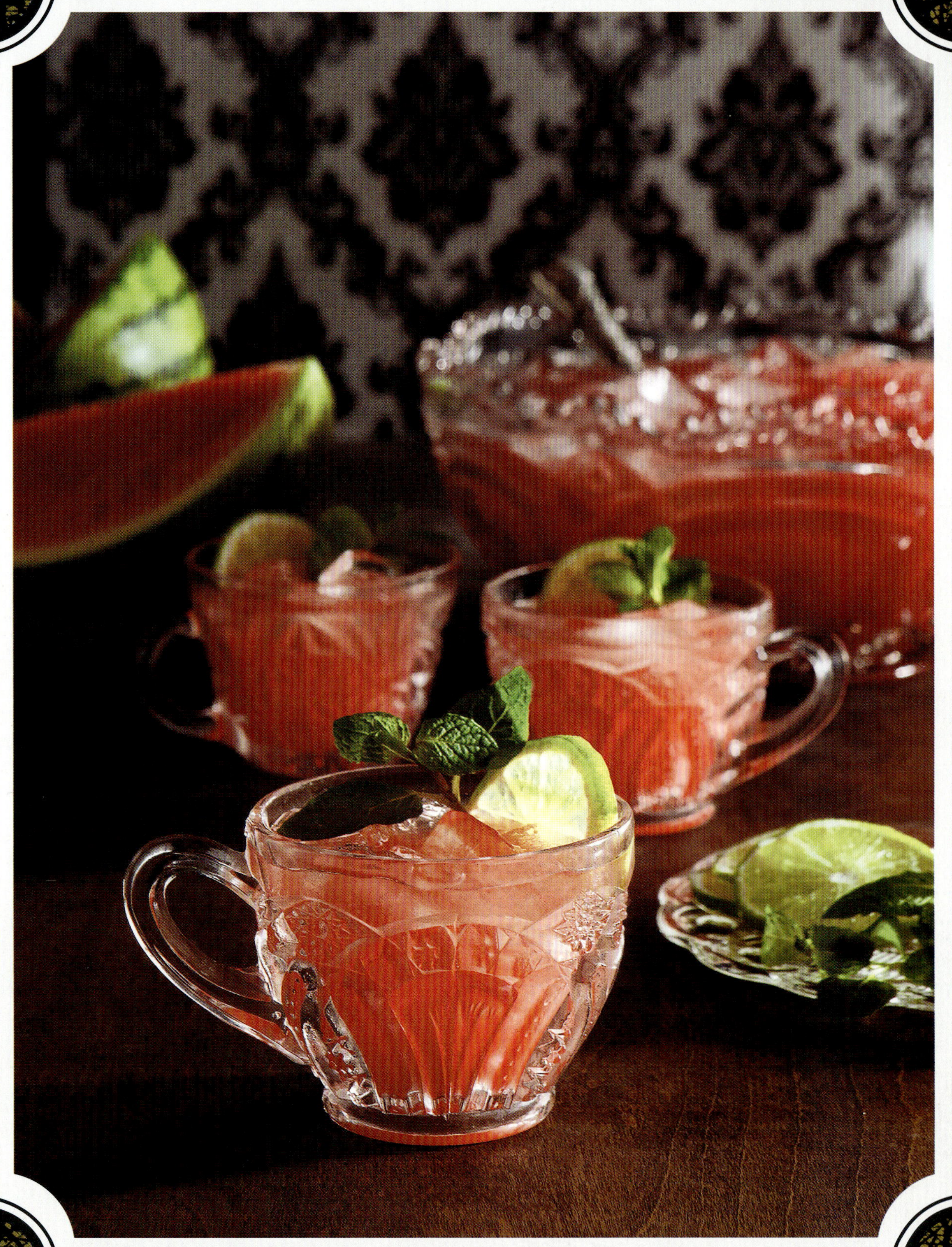

INSPIRED BY *The West Wing*

THE WEST WING

• MAKES 12 COCKTAILS • PUNCH BOWL OR PITCHER AND PUNCH GLASSES •

Wordless and atmospheric, Gorey's enigmatic *The West Wing* invites your imagination to run wild, as it contains various rooms inside an old house hinting at floods and other damage. People inhabit few of the drawings, while ghostly spirits center others. This moody pictorial may not be an obvious partner with sunny watermelon and tequila, but elderflower liqueur's ethereal floral whisper mirrors the spirits that haunt The West Wing.

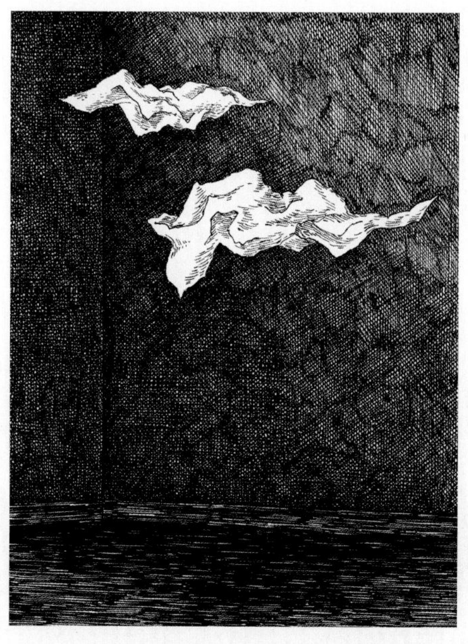

Blanco tequila is the most refreshing option. But try a reposado tequila if you prefer a richer, slightly woody note. This punch can easily be made without elderflower liqueur. But do you want to be without that floral intrigue?

6- to 8-pound (3- to 4-kg) seedless watermelon

12 oz (360 ml) fresh lime juice

2½ oz (75 ml) 1:1 Simple Syrup (page 142)

16 oz (480 ml) blanco tequila

6 oz (180 ml) elderflower liqueur

Garnish: Lime wheels, fresh mint leaves

Using a large knife, cut both ends off the watermelon and stand it upright. Use a sharp knife to cut the green peel and white pith away from the flesh, rotating the watermelon as you go. Cut the watermelon into roughly 2-inch (5-cm) chunks. Transfer half the watermelon chunks to a blender and blend on high speed until smooth. Strain the blended watermelon through a fine-mesh sieve into a large bowl. Repeat with the remaining watermelon chunks. You should have about 8 cups (1.9 l) of watermelon purée.

Add the lime juice, simple syrup, tequila, and elderflower liqueur to the watermelon purée bowl. Stir until combined. Transfer to a punch bowl or pitcher and chill for 30 minutes. Pour into ice-filled glasses. Garnish each glass with lime wheels and mint leaves.

C IS FOR CHARTREUSE

MAKES 1 COCKTAIL • GLASS: COUPE OR NICK AND NORA

Gorey's *The Nursery Frieze* is a small oblong book showcasing a procession of hippopotamus-like creatures parading in single file. Each is exclaiming words as random as clavicle, wax, thunder, and dismemberment. Food ingredient words show up, too: cardamom, turmeric, aspic, vanilla, amaranth, salsify. But there are also obscure, rarely seen words, like velleity, etui, ganosis, and thurible. It all sounds like nonsense, but it's not. These are real words, whimsically chosen by Gorey. To add complexity, large letters scattered underfoot of the hippos spell *The Nursery Frieze* when strung together. Laid out end to end, each page would form a wallpaper long enough to encircle a room, like a nursery. But this frieze is all about unusual words and strange syllables.

This cocktail takes inspiration from a classic Last Word cocktail, a revered gin and green Chartreuse classic first served at the Detroit Athletic Club in 1915, likely created by a bartender named Frank Fogarty. We add Southeast Asian intrigue to this industry favorite in the form of makrut lime, although the drink works just as beautifully with lemongrass as with makrut lime.

¾ oz (20 ml) gin
¾ oz (20 ml) green Chartreuse
¾ oz (20 ml) Makrut Lime Simple Syrup (page 142)
¾ oz (20 ml) fresh lime juice
Garnish: Makrut lime leaf

Place a coupe or Nick and Nora glass in the freezer to chill completely. In a cocktail shaker filled with ice, combine the gin, green Chartreuse, makrut simple syrup, and lime juice. Cover and shake vigorously for 20–30 seconds, until well chilled. Strain into the chilled glass. Garnish with a makrut lime leaf.

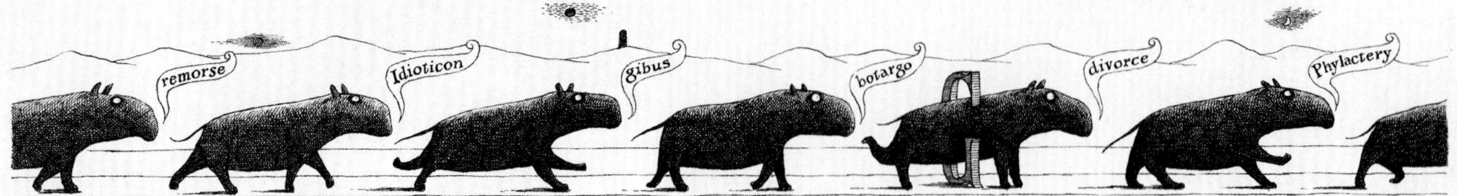

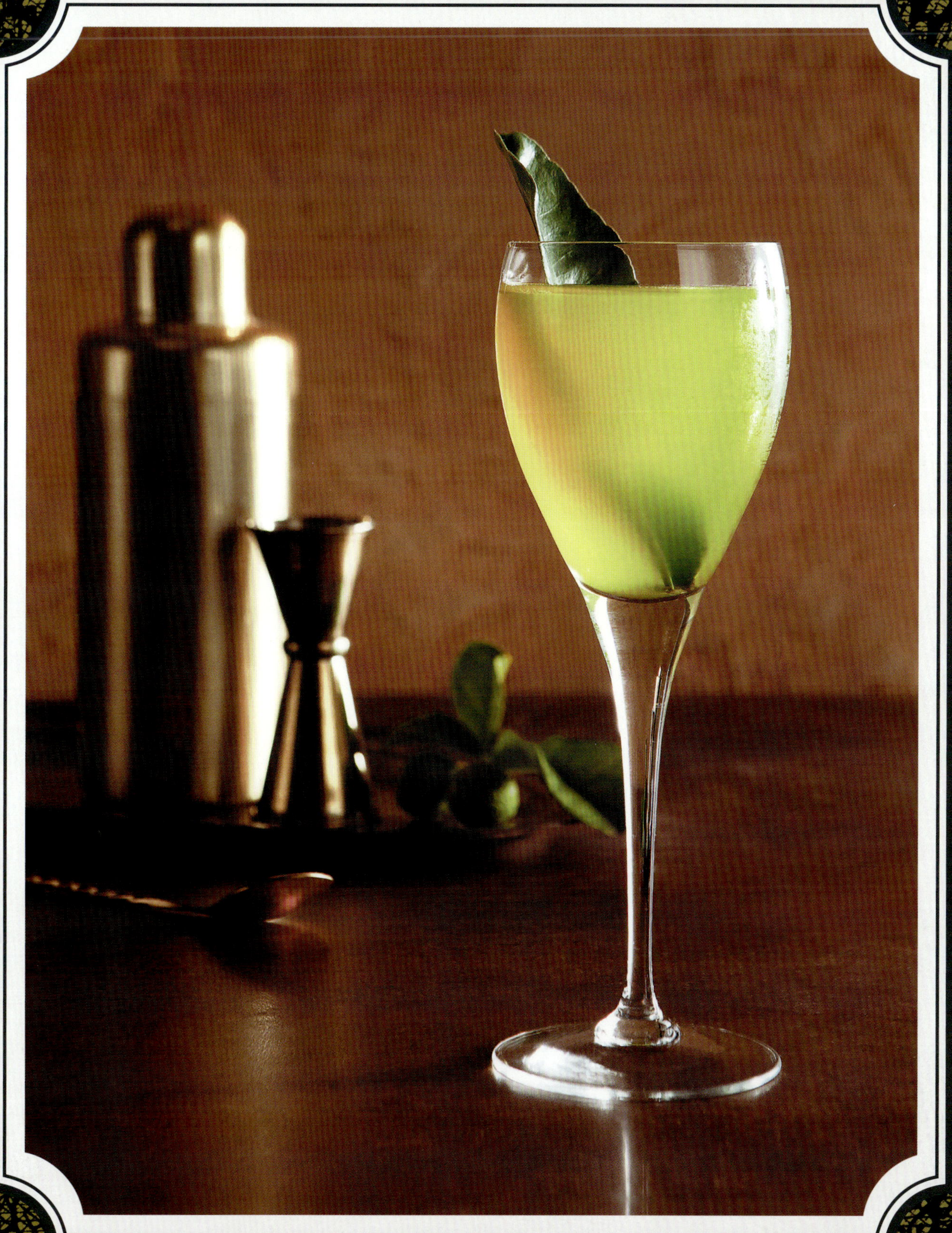

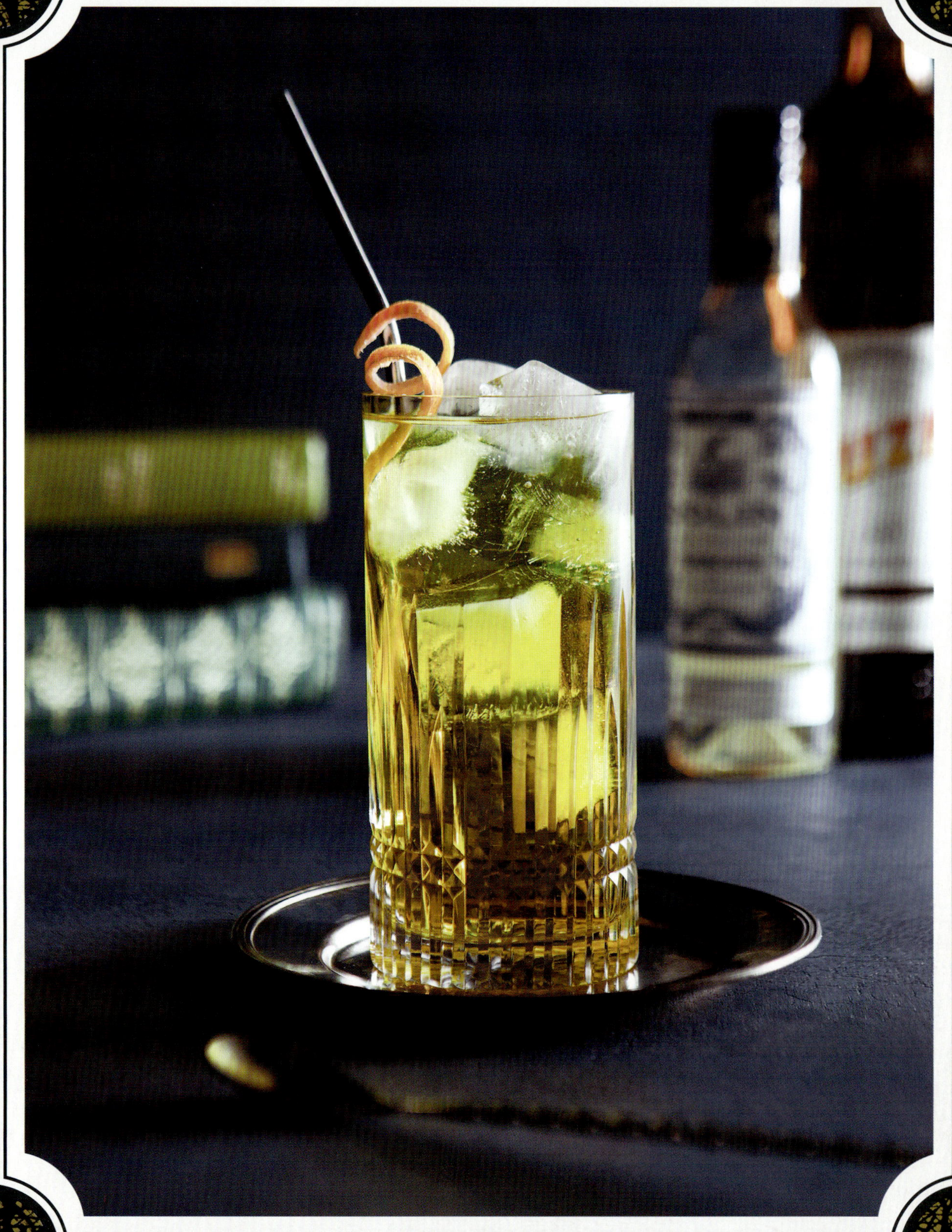

THE MORAL SUZE

• **MAKES 1 COCKTAIL** • **GLASS: COLLINS** •

Not unlike Gorey's character in *Frivolity, at the Edge of a Moral Swamp*, who "hears Hymn Singing in the Distance and dons the Galoshes of Remorse," this seemingly simple drink of Suze and soda wades in with galoshes. Herbaceous, bittersweet, almost neon yellow Suze is a classic French liqueur made since the 1800s, originally by distiller Fernand Moureaux. It is essentially an aperitif, or lower-proof liqueur, featuring gentian root, which imparts subtle bitter notes.

Spritzy bubbles make a happy partner to Suze's bold, herbaceous bitterness. Add a layer of white vermouth, whether floral Lillet or the citrusy mineral hit of Carpano bianco vermouth. The vermouth draws out the citrus notes of Suze, smoothing and rounding out the drink, while not drowning Suze's welcome bitterness and herbal hits of anise, tarragon, citrus, and stone fruit. Although Suze is also lovely with the quinine bitter of tonic water, this easy interplay of soda and vermouth imparts a lightheartedness. The breezy bitters mirror the character of Frivolity, who is bravely wearing vivid orange gloves at the edge of that gray-blue Moral Swamp.

---

1 oz (30 ml) Suze
1 oz (30 ml) bianco (white) vermouth
Club soda to top
Garnish: Grapefruit twist

Add the Suze and bianco vermouth to a Collins glass filled with ice and stir. Top with soda water. Garnish with a grapefruit twist.

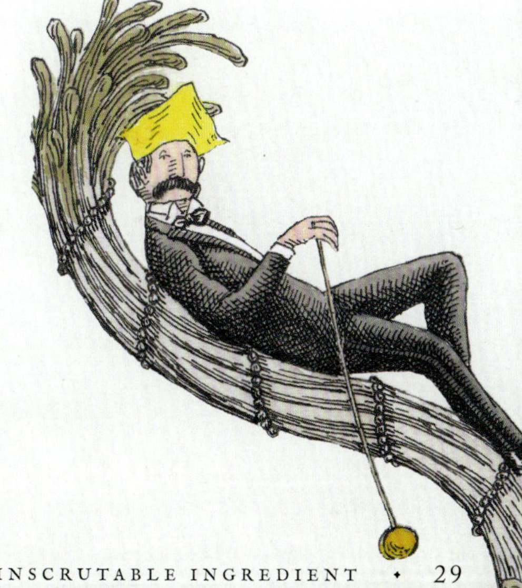

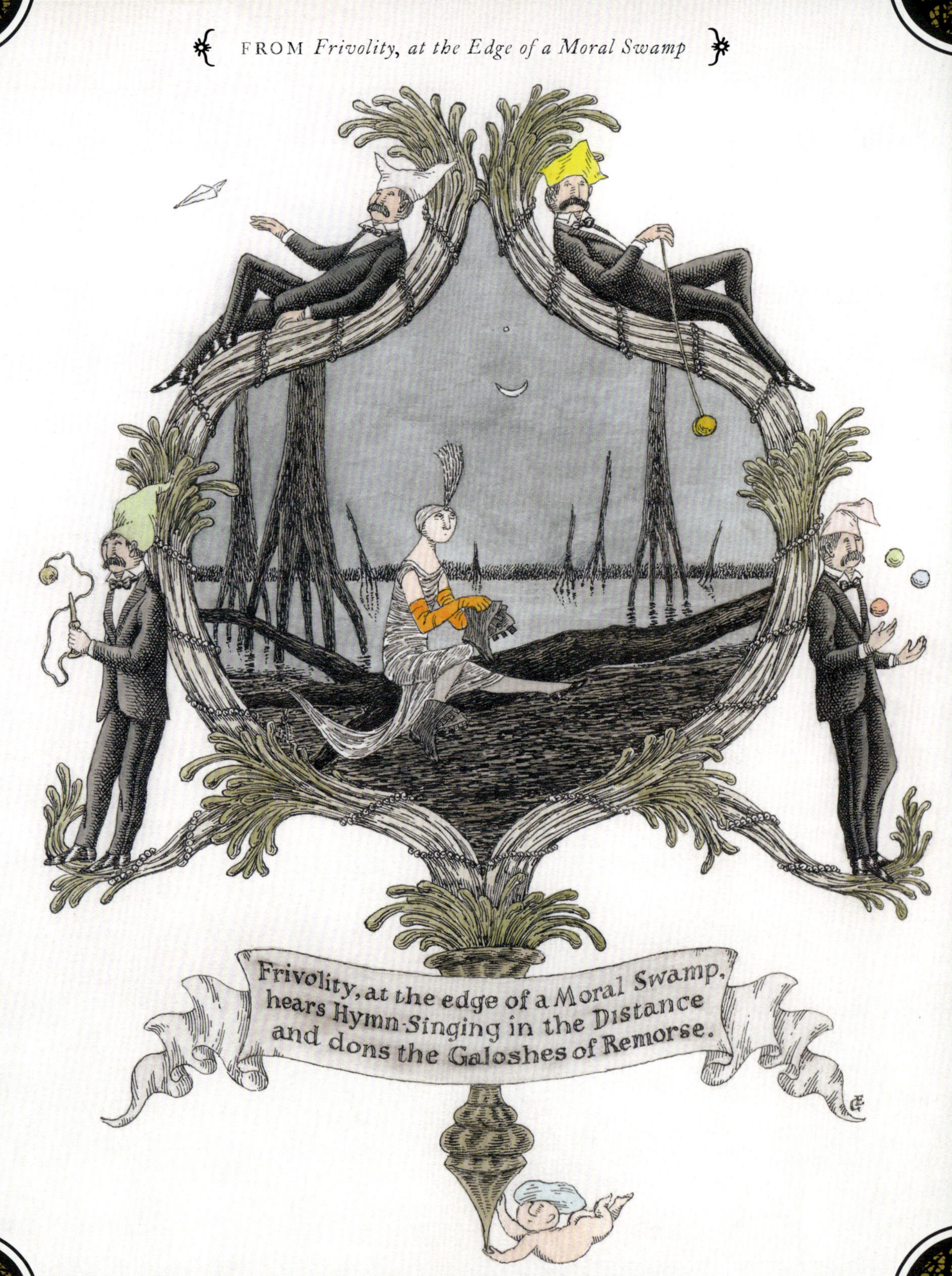
Frivolity, at the edge of a Moral Swamp,
hears Hymn-Singing in the Distance
and dons the Galoshes of Remorse.

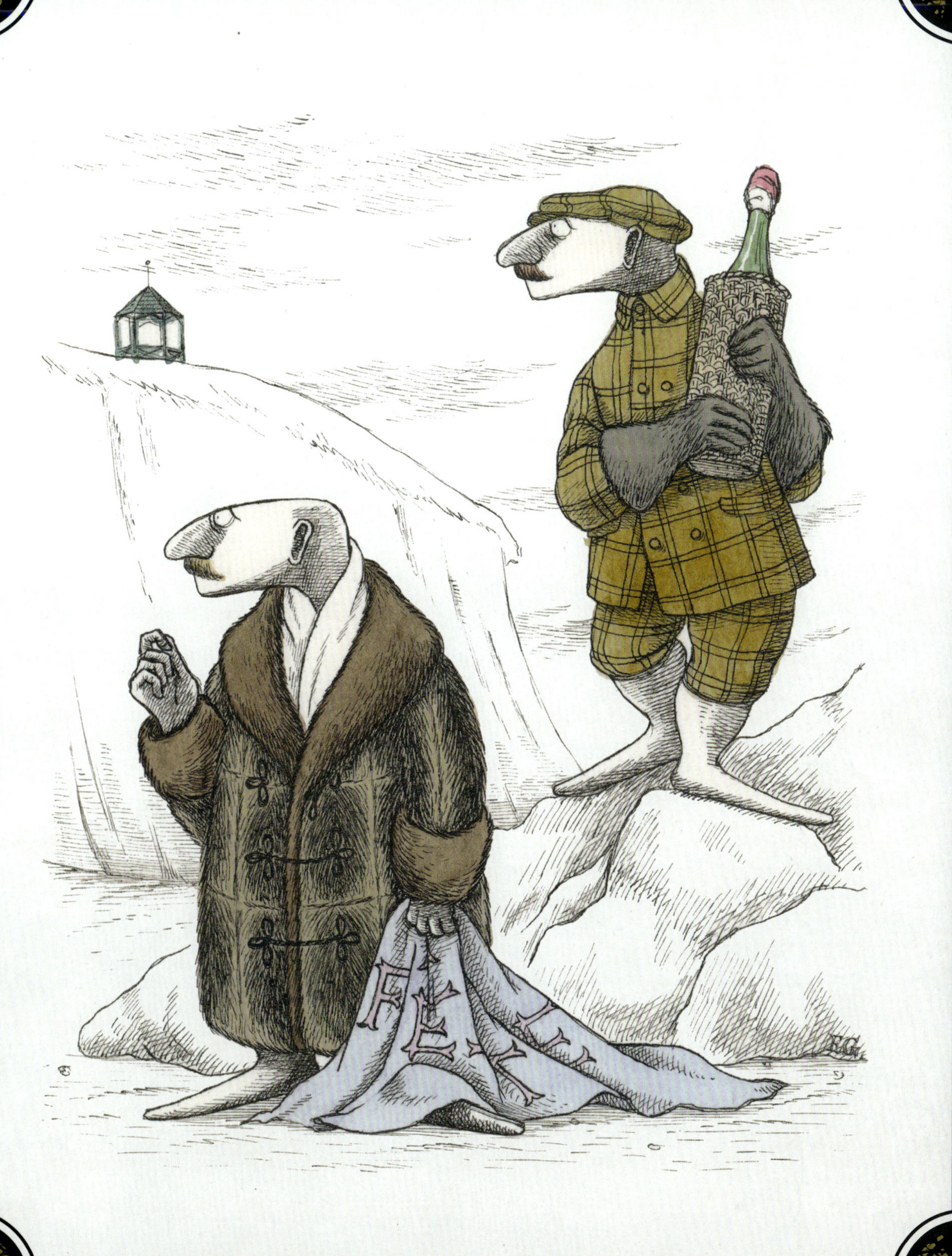

THE UNKNOWN VEGETABLE

• MAKES 1 COCKTAIL • GLASS: COUPE •

In this cocktail, *The Unknown Vegetable* refers to the dominant artichoke in Cynar, an Italian amaro or a bitter liqueur made with thirteen botanicals, including the mighty 'choke. It's also the name of Gorey's fable of Filda, who heard a sound while out strolling "that came from underneath the ground." She watches a stalk grow, then wrenches it out of the ground, takes it home, and eats it. As you can imagine, her encounter with the unknown vegetable does not lead to a good end.

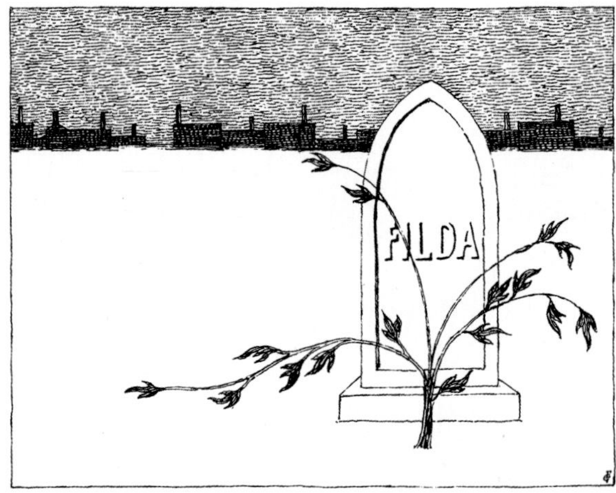

But this twist on a Paper Plane does. This modern-day classic was created by New York bartender Sam Ross in 2008 and takes its inspiration from a Last Word, with equal parts and a touch of citrus. This twist plays with Cynar instead of sweeter, milder Amaro Nonino. Cynar adds vegetal, earthy, bitter depths to the cocktail, meeting softer bitter layers from Aperol, balanced by tart lemon and sweet bourbon.

- ¾ oz (20 ml) bourbon
- ¾ oz (20 ml) Aperol
- ¾ oz (20 ml) Cynar
- ¾ oz (20 ml) fresh lemon juice

In a cocktail shaker with ice, combine the bourbon, Aperol, Cynar, and lemon juice. Cover and shake for 20–30 seconds, until well chilled. Strain into a coupe glass.

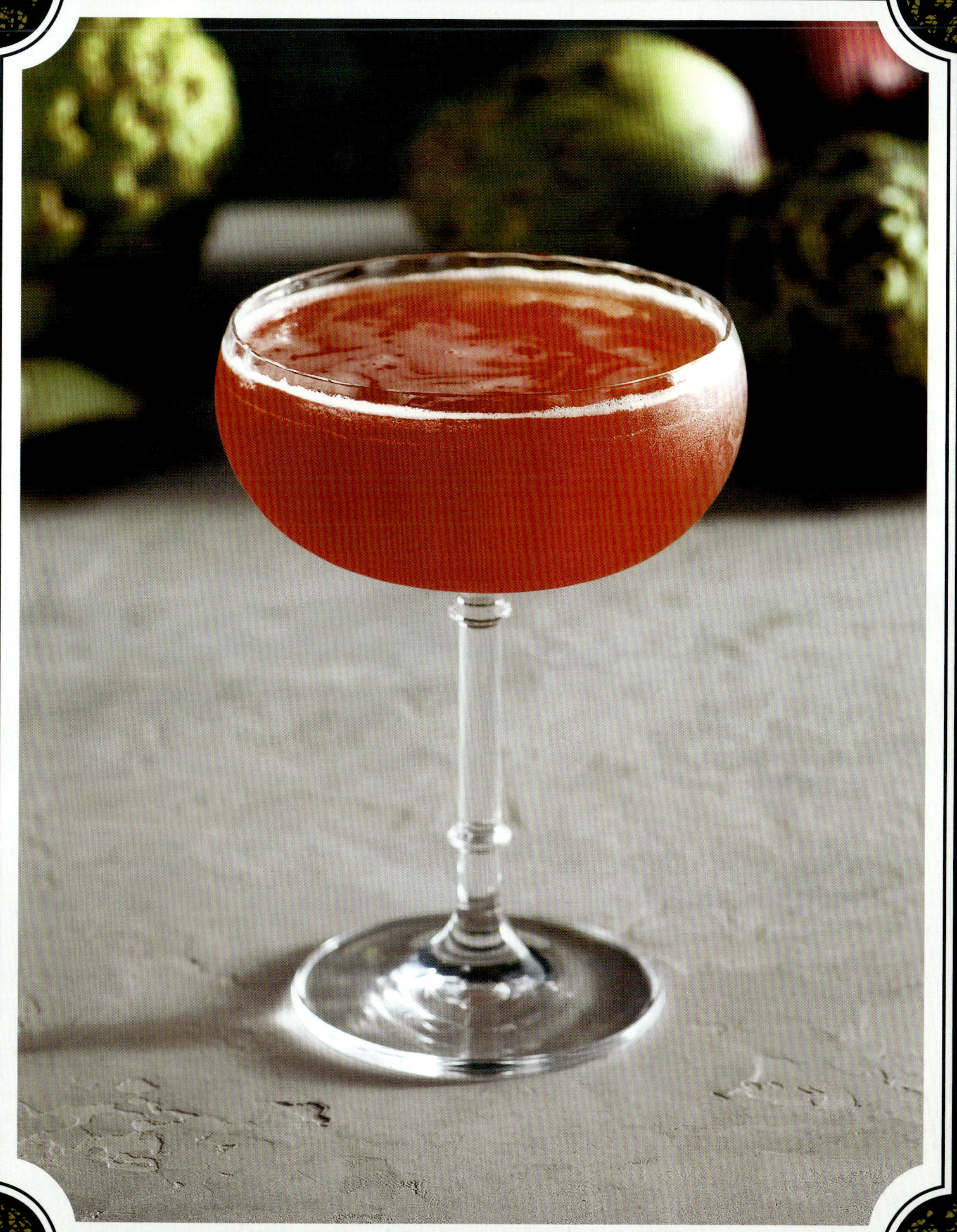

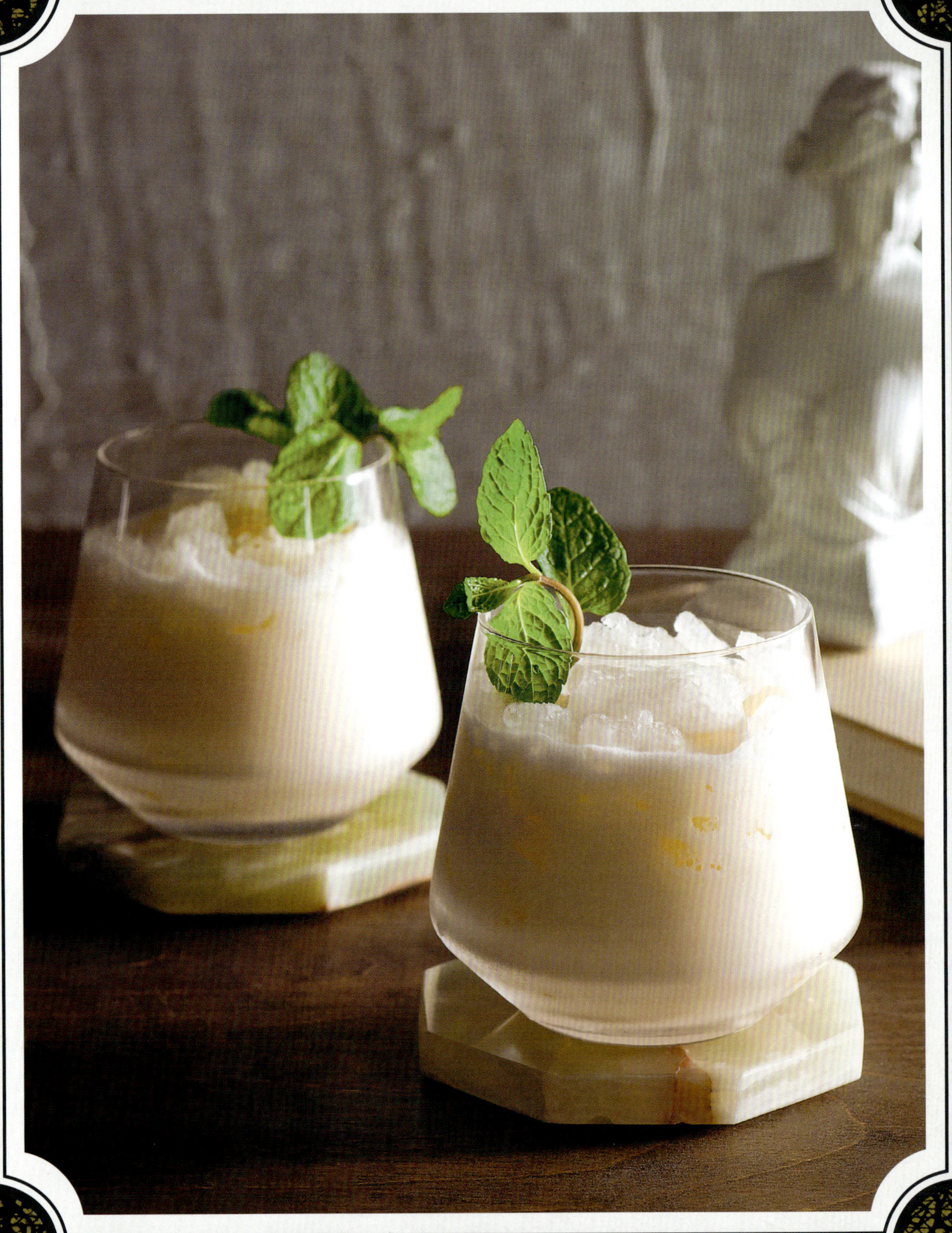

{ INSPIRED BY *The Just Dessert* }

THE JUST DESSERT

• MAKES 1 COCKTAIL • GLASS: ROCKS •

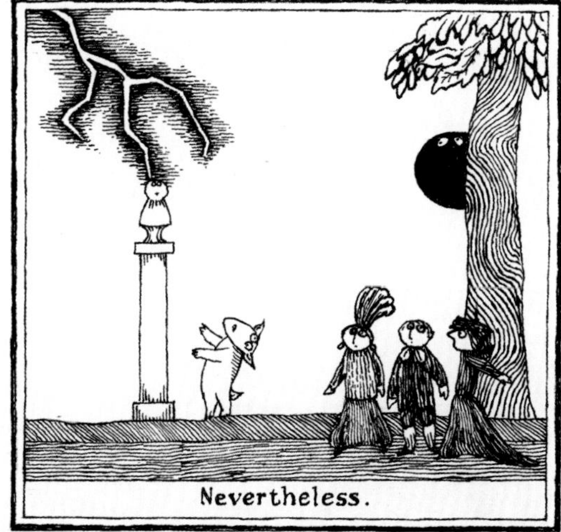

Though this is far from zabaglione, an Italian dessert of whipped egg yolks, sugar, and sweet wine, a classic Absinthe Suissesse is *The Just Dessert*, as Gorey's little tale is titled. This illogical series of drawings is captioned by single words and little commands and phrases, like "take umbrage" or "keep laughing mechanically." As three bug-eyed, well-heeled people talk, argue, and gaze at a dog and a statue, the meaning of this cryptic story is cloaked.

So are the riches of this classic New Orleans cocktail, created in the 1890s but still unsung outside of Nola. This should not be so. This beauty is rightfully a brunch cocktail favorite in Nola but also cools any hot, steamy day with its crushed ice creaminess. You can use all absinthe or balance that with an anise-flavored liqueur like Herbsaint. The word *Suissesse* means "Swiss," acknowledging Switzerland's historic role in absinthe production, alongside France.

---

1 oz (30 ml) absinthe
½ oz (15 ml) Herbsaint
¾ oz (20 ml) heavy cream
½ oz (15 ml) orgeat
¼ oz (7.5 ml) white crème de menthe
1 egg white
Garnish: Fresh mint sprig

In a cocktail shaker with ice, combine the absinthe, Herbsaint, heavy cream, orgeat, crème de menthe, and egg white. Cover and shake vigorously for 30–40 seconds, until well chilled. Strain and pour over tightly packed crushed ice. Garnish with a sprig of fresh mint.

THE TROUBLED ADVERB

• MAKES 1 COCKTAIL • GLASS: CHAMPAGNE FLUTE •

Gorey's *The Glorious Nosebleed* is yet another dark, playful romp through the alphabet. From doorbells ringing Ominously to a gent in a motorcar who "struck her down Wilfully," there is all sorts of mischief to be had. We play off our blood-red theme with strawberry.

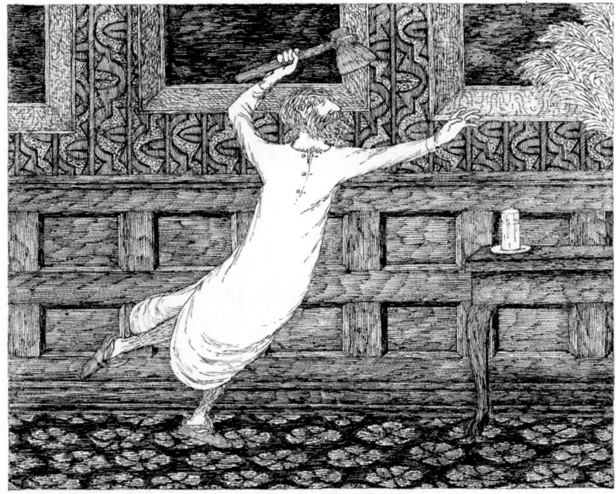

He ran through the hall Maniacally.

Our drink is a play on one of Ernest Hemingway's favorite cocktails, Death in the Afternoon, titled for his 1932 novel of the same name. While a classic Death in the Afternoon's ingredient proportions vary, Hemingway himself went for broke. In *So Red the Nose, or Breath in the Afternoon* (1935), he states, "Pour one jigger absinthe into a champagne glass. Add iced Champagne until it attains the proper opalescent milkiness. Drink three to five of these slowly." This is excessive by any standards, so we go with restraint and a splash of strawberry purée. If you desire more absinthe, go lighter on the Champagne. If you want it more effervescent, add a bit more sparkling wine. If you want it sweeter, add a few drops of simple syrup.

½ oz (15 ml) absinthe

1 oz (30 ml) strawberry purée, such as The Perfect Purée

3–4 oz (90–120 ml) chilled Champagne or dry sparkling wine

Pour the absinthe and strawberry purée into a champagne flute. Stir briefly. Slowly top with the desired amount of chilled Champagne.

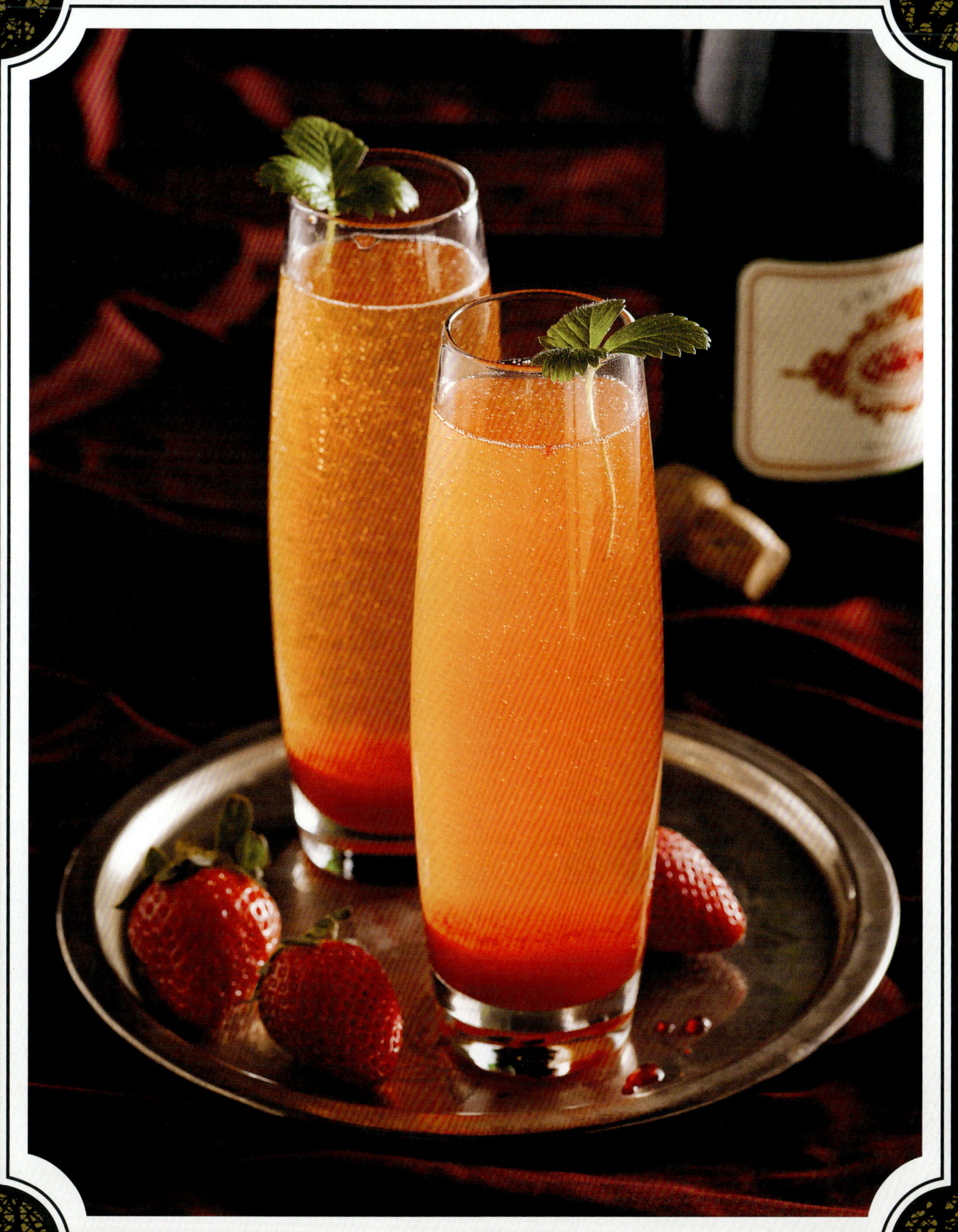

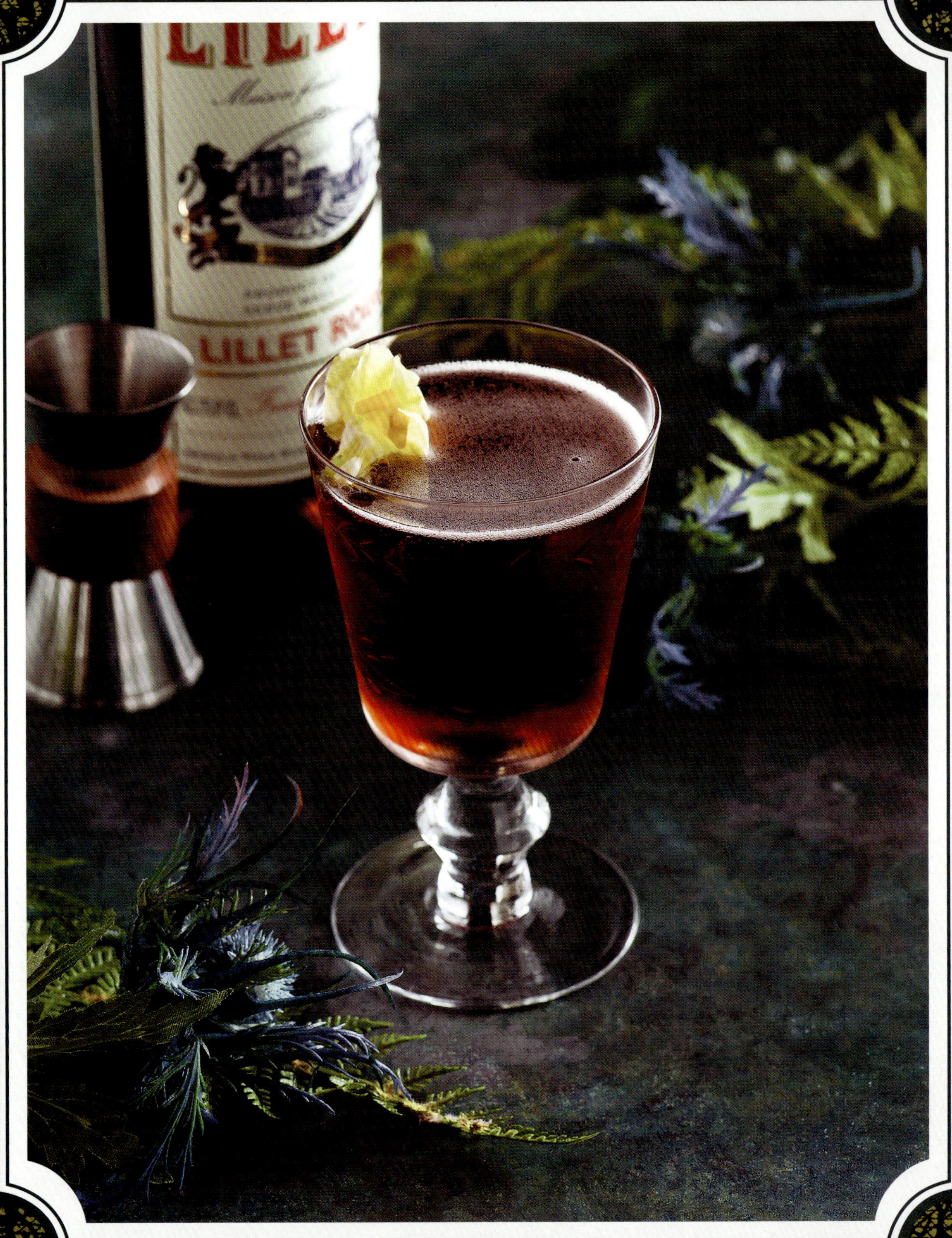
LILLET

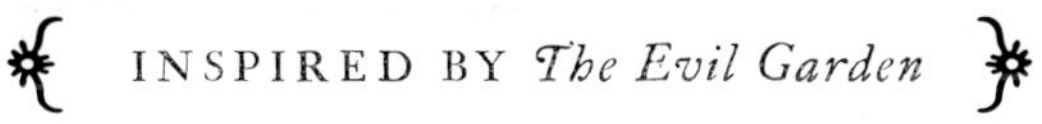

INSPIRED BY *The Evil Garden*

THE STRIPED SOCK

• **MAKES 1 COCKTAIL** • **GLASS: WINEGLASS OR GOBLET** •

Employing Gorey's whimsical rhymes, *The Evil Garden* begins with a carefree, "How elegant! how choice! how gay! To think one doesn't have to pay." But in this sinister little tale, an entire party does, in fact, pay, as the garden begins displaying its dark side when a striped-sock foot protrudes from under a rock. Chaos ensues with nibbling moths, hairy bugs, strangling snakes, and "a smell that causes one to feel unwell." This is no idyllic paradise but a garden fraught with danger.

There is nothing sinister about this refreshing spritz cocktail with a bit of mezcal adding an unexpected, smoky-earthy surprise hiding underneath light, breezy sparkling wine and floral Lillet Rosé. This spritz won't take your life and its contrasting delights are the opposite of evil. Rather, it is an ideal aperitif to sip in a non-evil garden where no bears guard the fruit and its light riches are available to all.

½ oz (15 ml) mezcal

1 oz (30 ml) Lillet Rosé

2 oz (60 ml) chilled sparkling wine (Champagne, prosecco, cava, etc.)

Garnish: Edible flower, such as a rose

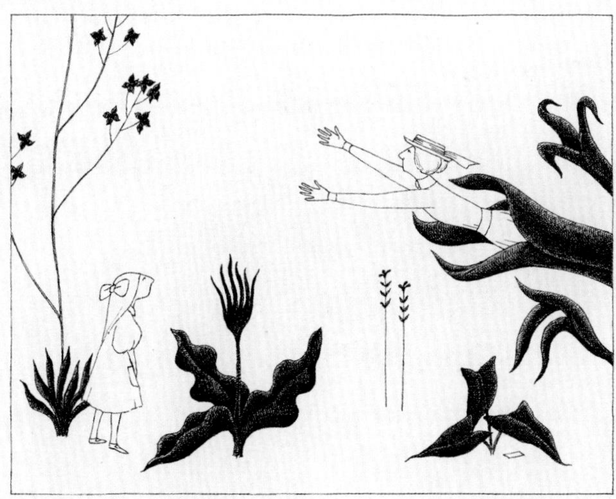

In a mixing glass with ice, stir together the mezcal and Lillet Rosé for 20–30 seconds, until well chilled. Top with the chilled sparkling wine. Strain into a wineglass or goblet. Garnish with an edible flower.

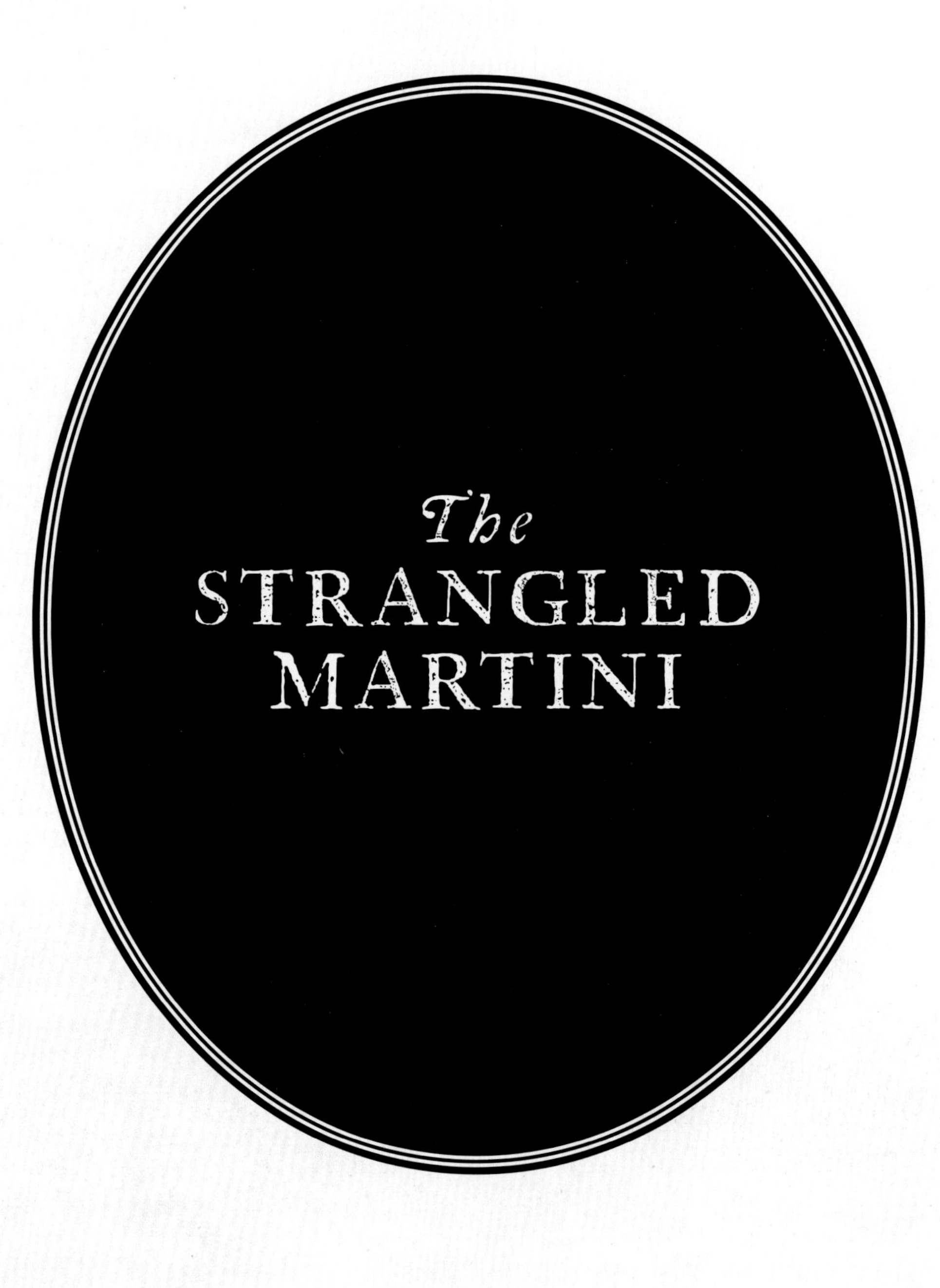

The STRANGLED MARTINI

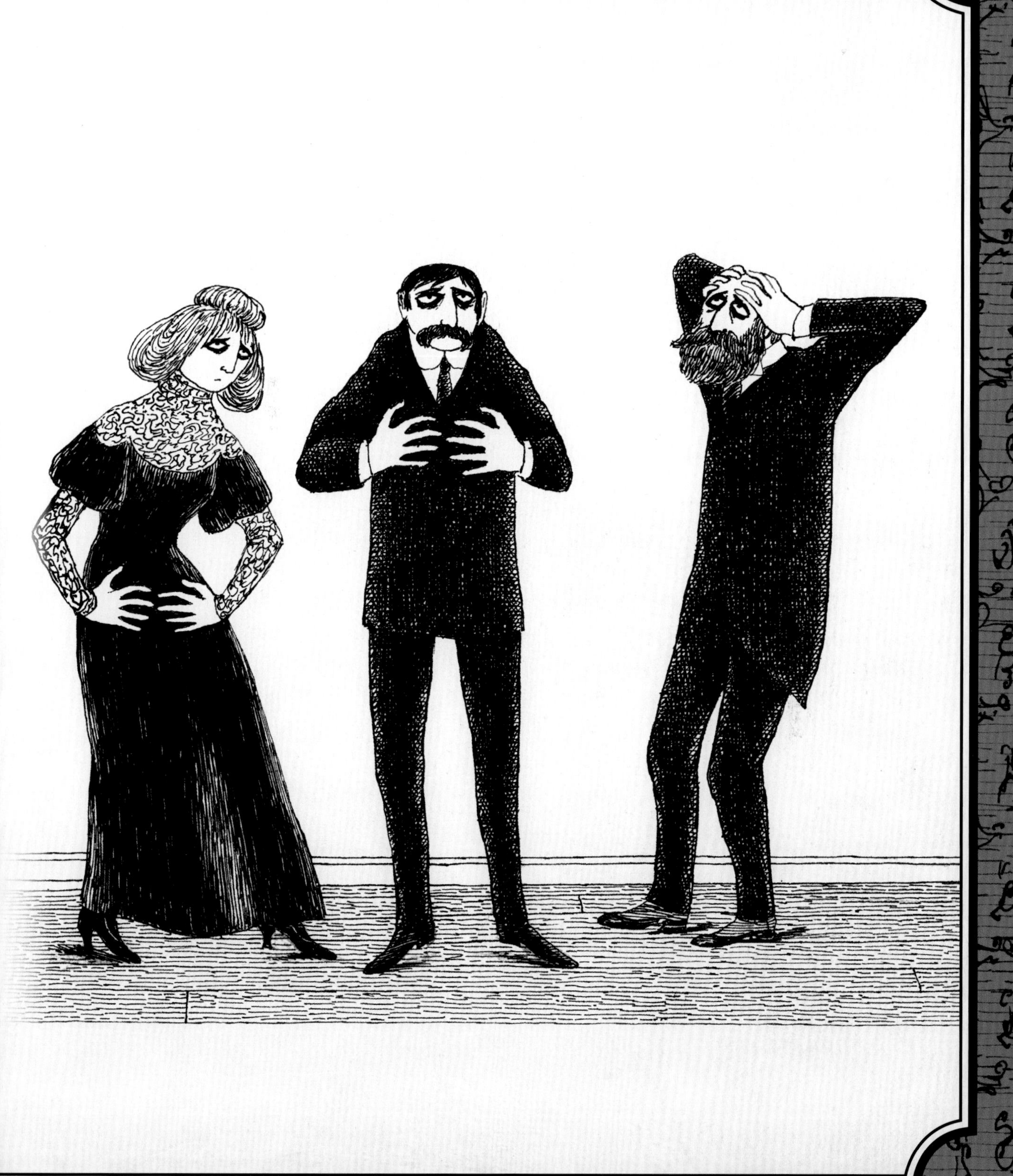

AMONG THE PICKLES AND PRESERVES

• MAKES 1 COCKTAIL • GLASS: COUPE OR MARTINI •

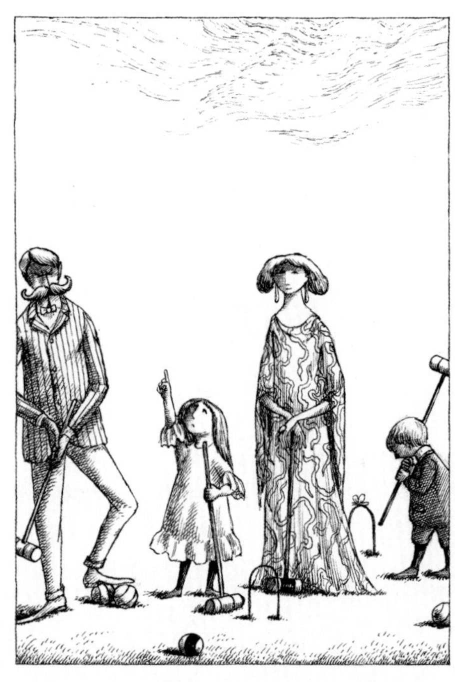

An unidentified creature "way up high . . . floating in the sky" falls through the air, hovering "morose, inflexible, aloof." It somehow morphs "right through" into the house finally going "beneath the cellar floor," never to be seen again. Like the creature, we rummage through the cellar, among the pickles and preserves, for this pickled martini. It's a drink in the spirit of a dirty martini, but instead of olive brine, it plays with pickle juice. Dill or sweet pickle juice from a jar of pickles works beautifully. The salt, vinegar, and water of the brine enliven the martini, whether with a base of vodka or gin (vodka offers a clean, bracing backdrop, while gin contributes intriguing herbaceous layers). Endless options arise if you vary the pickled ingredients and brine, whether a pickled onion in classic Gibson cocktail style, pickled radishes, or even pickled green beans. All manner of strained pickled brine can sing in a martini.

2½ oz (75 ml) vodka or gin
½ oz (15 ml) dry vermouth
½ oz (15 ml) pickle brine
Garnish: Cornichon or small pickle

Place a coupe or martini glass in the freezer to chill completely. Combine the vodka, dry vermouth, and pickle brine in a mixing glass with ice. Stir with a barspoon for 30–40 seconds, until icy cold. Strain into the chilled glass. Garnish with a cornichon.

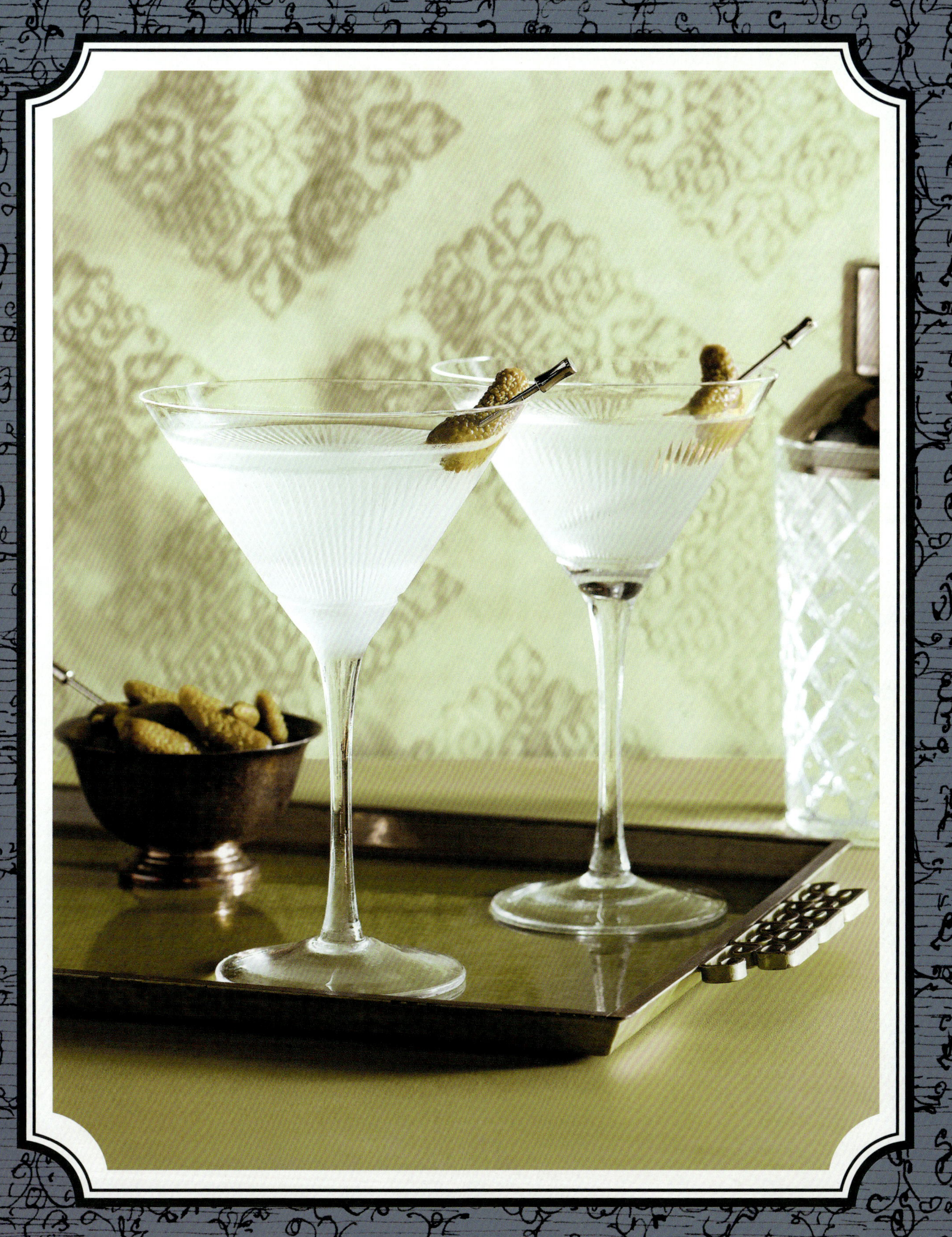

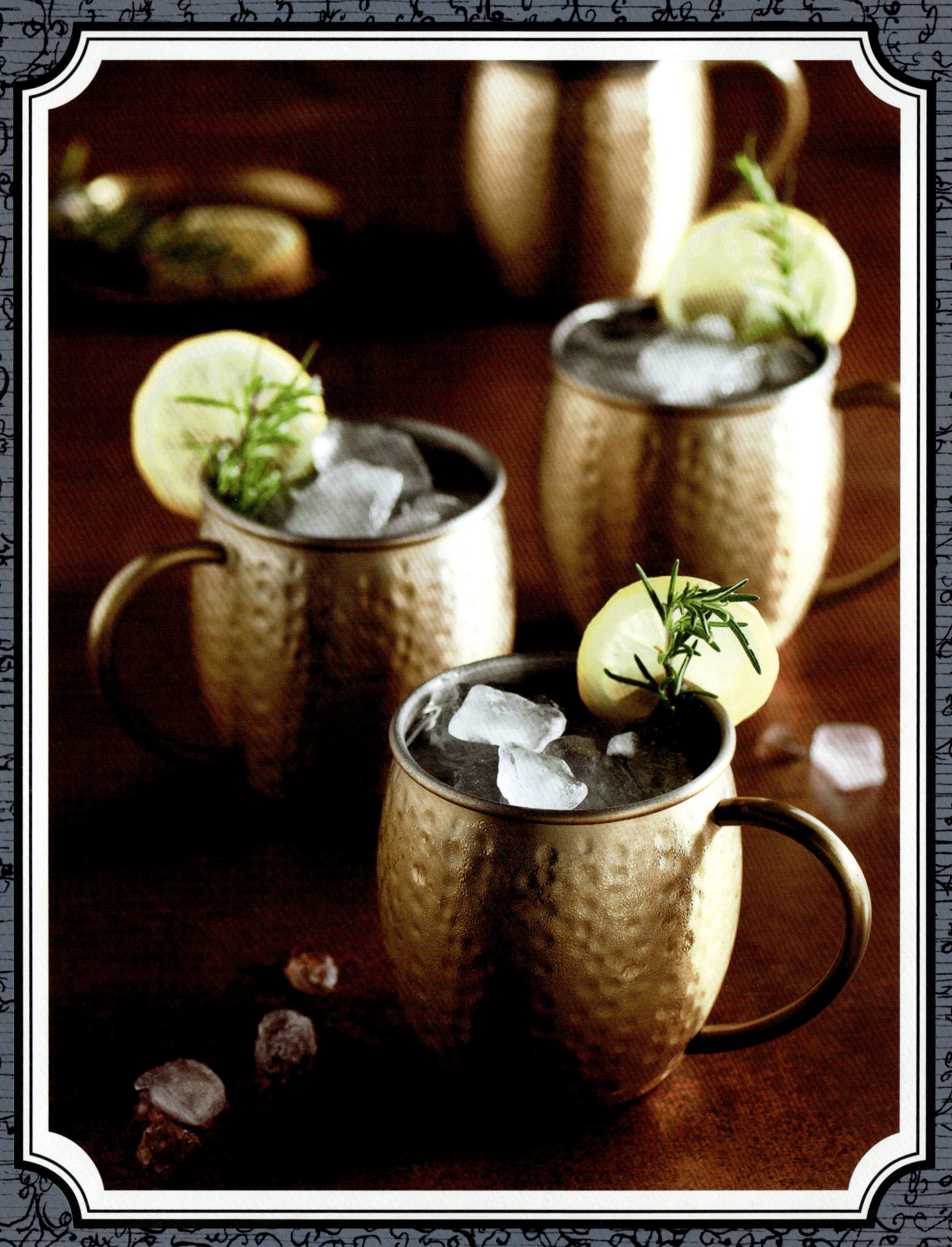

THE IZZARD MULE

• MAKES 1 COCKTAIL • GLASS: COPPER MULE MUG •

The Izzard Book is Gorey's alphabet primer using only the letter *Z*, exploring the Zephyr ("the west wind personified") on to the Zwieback ("kind of biscuit rusk"). The icy cool combination of neutral vodka with lively ginger beer breezes in like the west wind with a twist of rosemary and Meyer lemon.

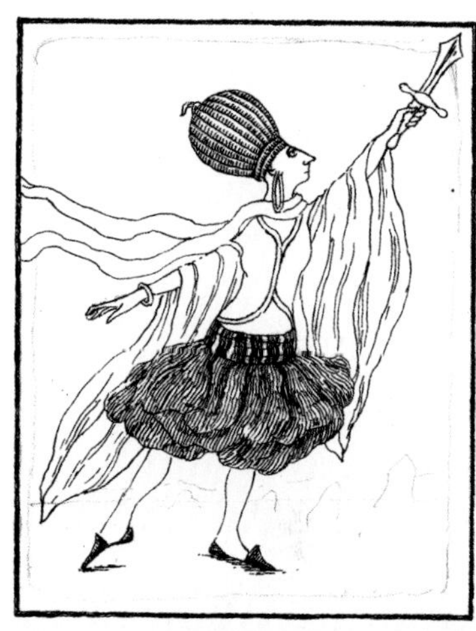

ZENOBIA
Queen of Palmyra who invaded Asia Minor and Egypt

The iconic Moscow Mule has competing origin stories. One hails from 1941, when Smirnoff owner John Martin and the owner of LA's now closed Cock 'n Bull pub, Jack Morgan, tried to get rid of excess cases of vodka and house-branded ginger beer. The other story is from Cock 'n Bull bartender Wes Price, who claimed to invent the drink to clear out the bar's basement. The Mule's iconic copper mug traces back to Sophie Berezinski, who moved to LA from Russia, where her father created the mugs. Lore goes that she walked into the Cock 'n Bull to sell mugs, met Martin, who had just recently acquired Smirnoff, and Morgan, who was crafting his ginger beer brand. Together they created the Moscow Mule.

---

2 oz (60 ml) vodka
1 oz (30 ml) fresh Meyer lemon juice
½ oz (15 ml) Rosemary Simple Syrup (page 144)
3 oz (90 ml) ginger beer
Garnish: Fresh rosemary sprig, lemon slice

In an ice-filled cocktail shaker, combine the vodka, lemon juice, and rosemary simple syrup. Cover, shake vigorously, and strain into an ice-filled copper mug. Top with the ginger beer. Garnish with a rosemary sprig and lemon slice.

THE IRON TONIC

• MAKES 1 COCKTAIL • GLASS: ROCKS OR WINEGLASS •

The Iron Tonic, subtitled *A Winter Afternoon in Lonely Valley*, is a moody, bleak tale of the "aged and unwell . . . people at the grey hotel." At this stark-looking hotel, unlucky guests are subject to toppling gas lamps, objects falling from the air, a skating pond concealing a family of eels, and a "voice both ungenteel and loud" speaking from a passing cloud. In this dark place, "the light is fading from the day. The rest is darkness and dismay."

Here, the usually refreshing and cheery gin and tonic is made Spanish style, becoming as layered and visually dramatic as that hotel. Nodding to unexpected guests but imparting beauty to a simple classic, the Spanish G&T can be served in a rocks or highball glass. But it's typically served in a copa de balon, or wide-mouthed balloon wineglass, to better show off the garnish-heavy Spanish take. It trended across Spain the past couple of decades with garnishes ranging from assorted fruits to herbs. This presents an aromatic bouquet on the nose as ingredients float in the "balloon." Take a tip from the botanicals in the gin you are using and consider garnishes to match, whether lavender, a vanilla bean pod, stone fruit, or even fennel. Also commit to a quality tonic and you'll welcome a guest more delightful than doubtful.

---

4 oz (120 ml) tonic water
2 oz (60 ml) gin
2 dashes Angostura bitters

Garnish: Juniper berries, grapefruit slice, edible flowers, fresh rosemary or thyme sprig

---

Fill a rocks or wineglass with ice. Add the tonic water, gin, and Angostura bitters. Gently stir to combine. Garnish with juniper berries, a grapefruit slice, edible flowers, and/or fresh herbs.

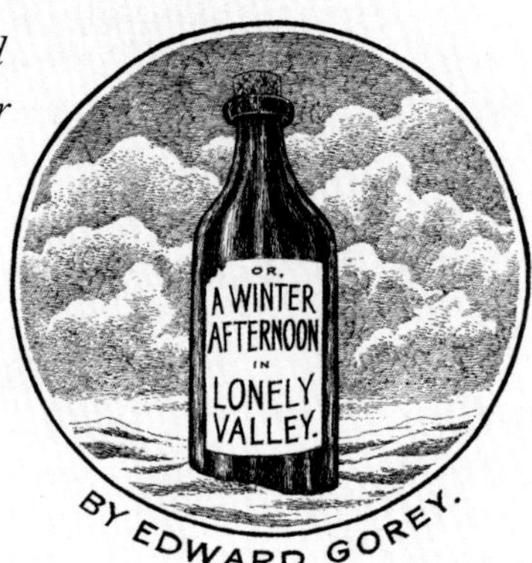

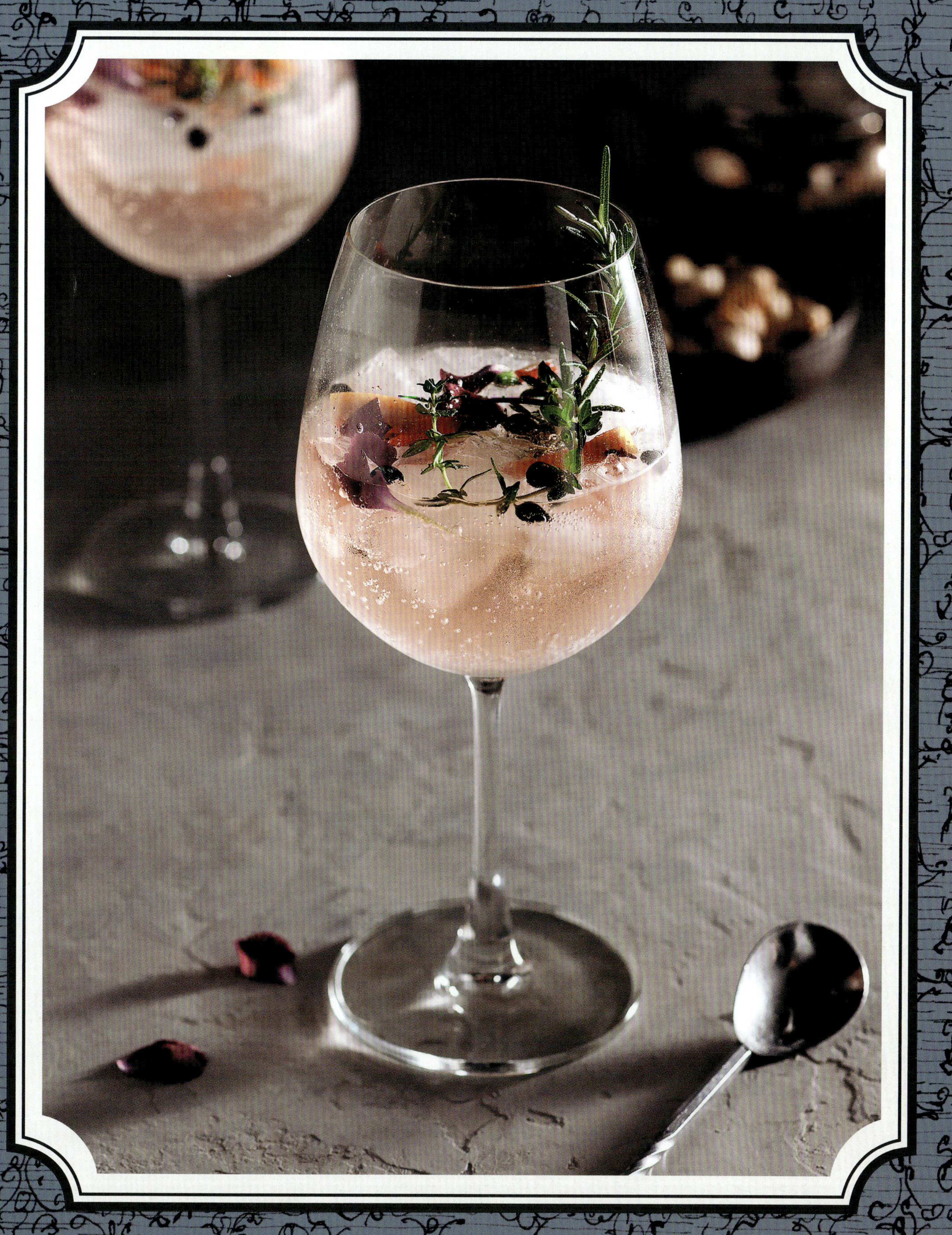

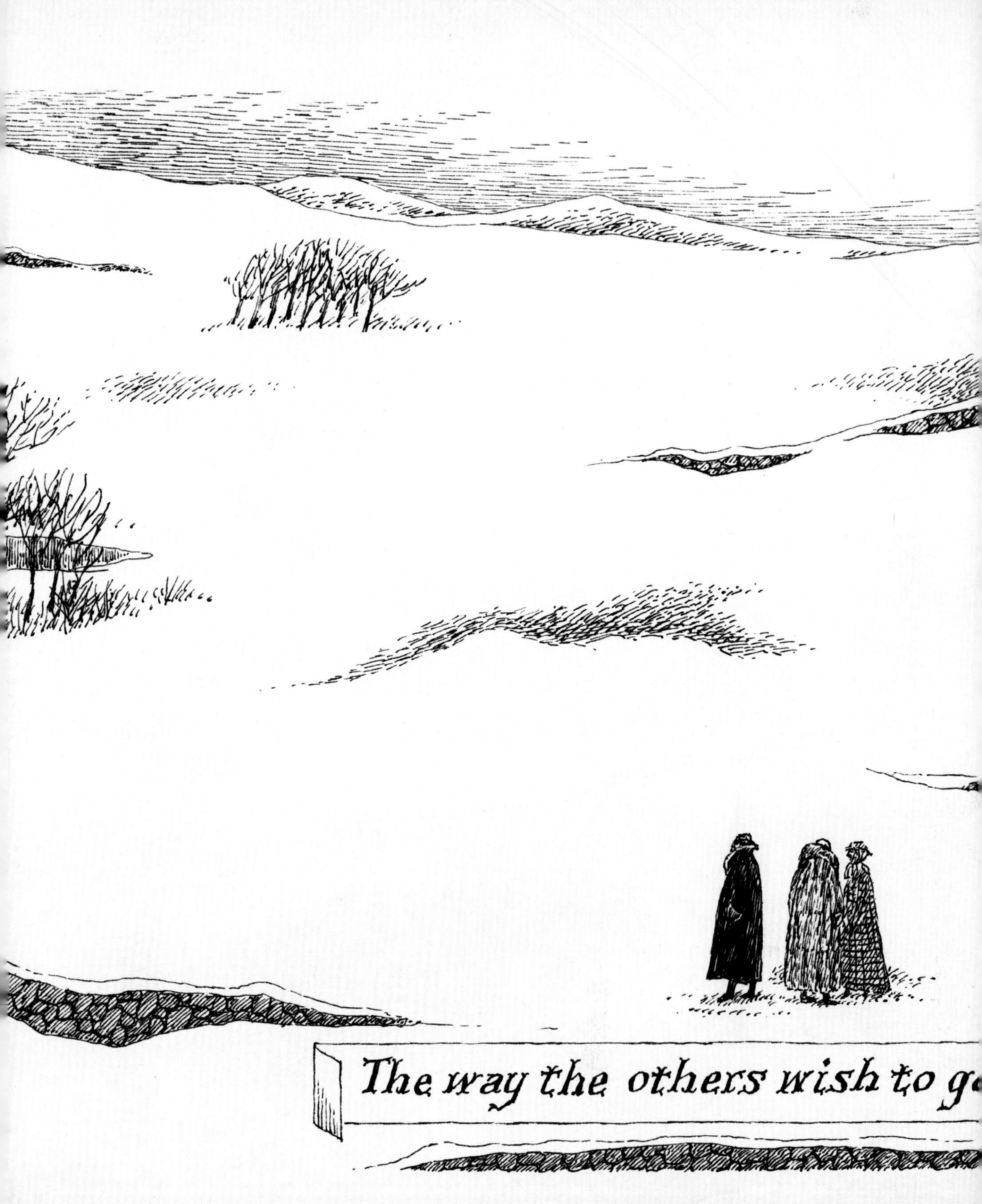
The way the others wish to g

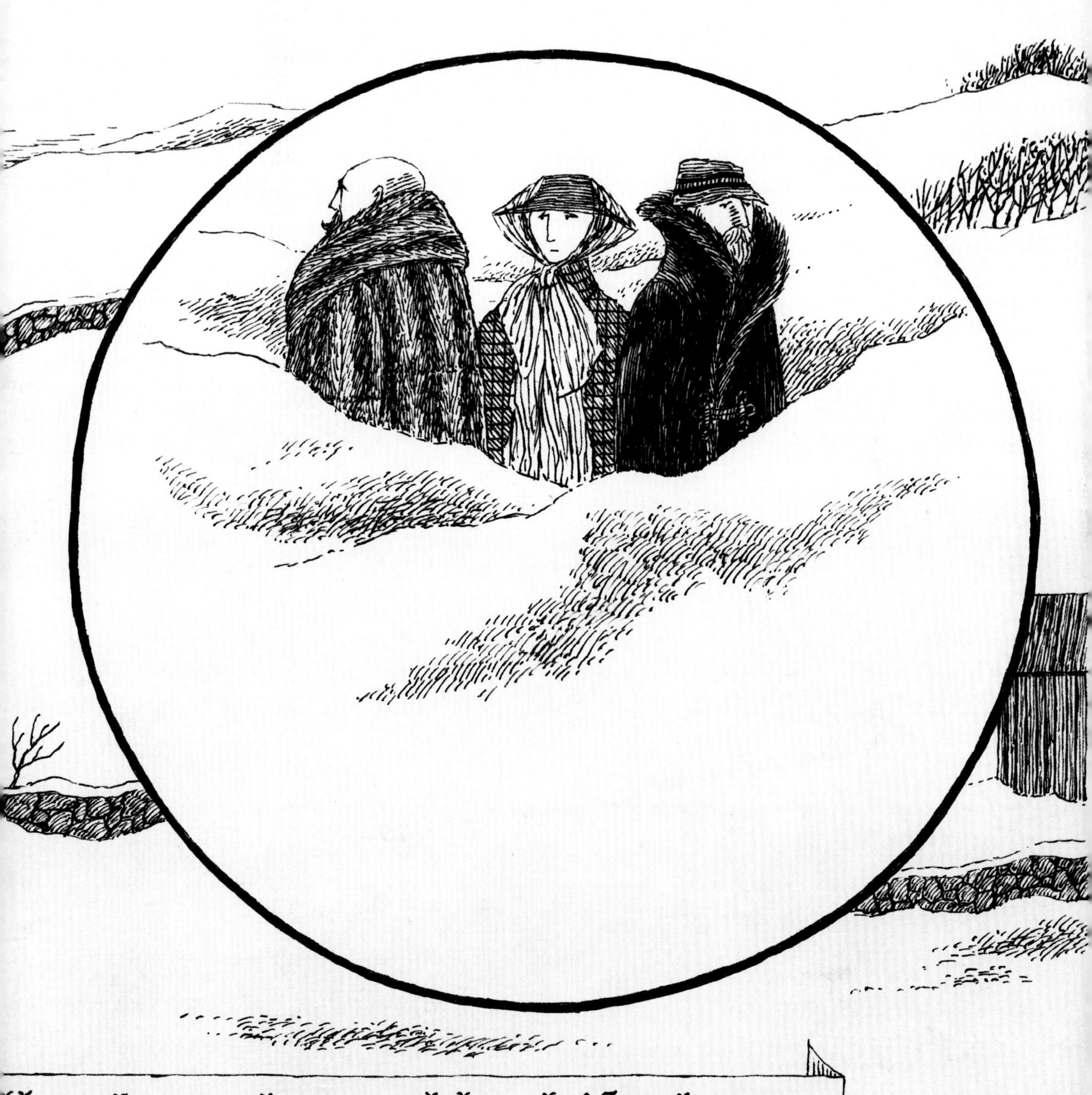

Has been obscured by drifted snow.

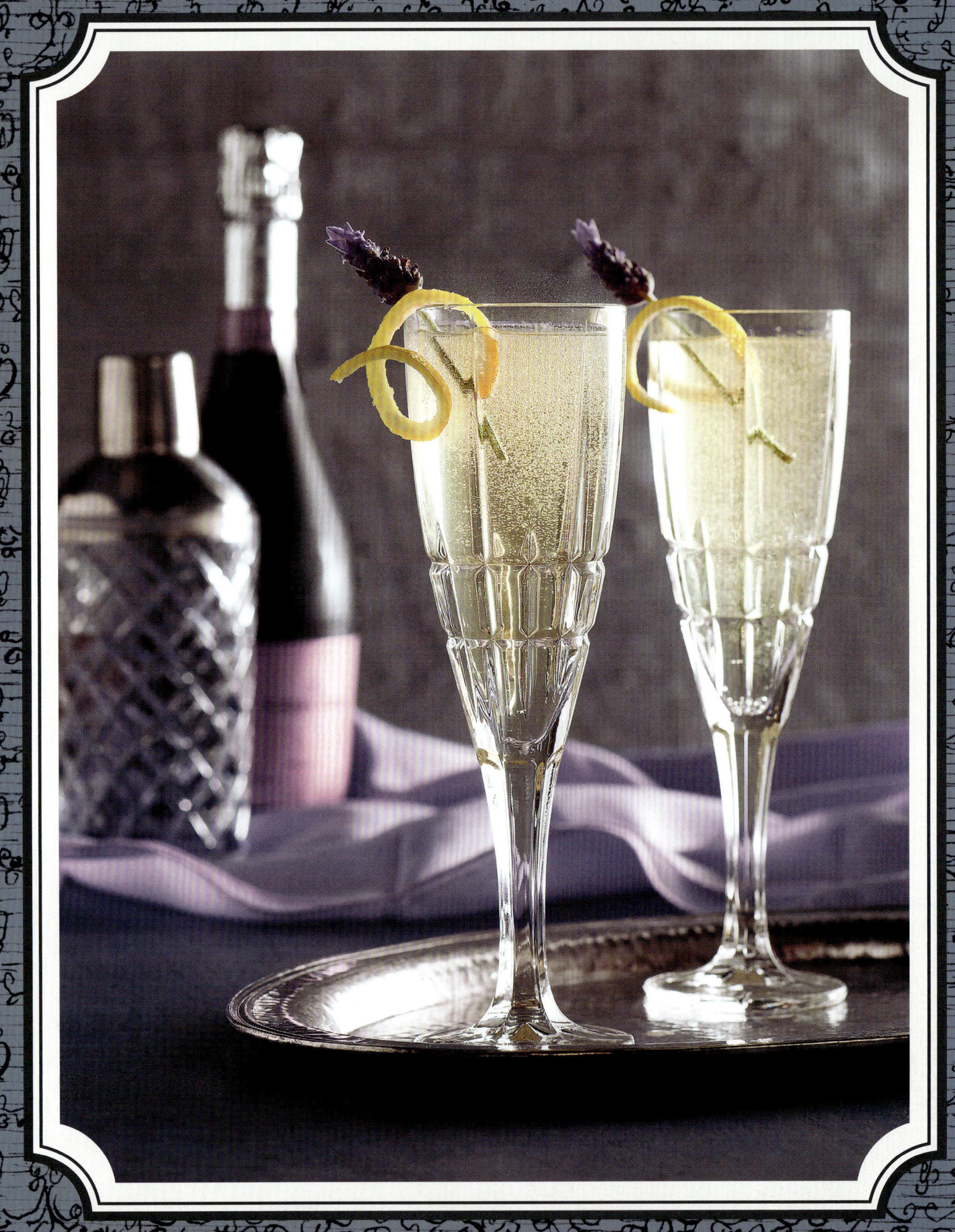

THE LAVENDER LEOTARD

• MAKES 1 COCKTAIL • GLASS: COUPE OR CHAMPAGNE FLUTE •

Ballet shows up more often than one would expect in Gorey's stories. This particular ballet adventure is centered around *The Lavender Leotard*. The story covers "two small, distant, ageless, and wholly imaginary relatives to fifty seasons of the New York City Ballet." Despite taking center stage in the name, lavender is just briefly mentioned in this story of ballet dancers, but in this drink, based on the French 75, lavender does actually take center stage, leading aromatically—even more so if you choose a gin made with lavender botanicals.

The French 75 is one of the most beloved gin cocktail classics in the world and one of the great sparkling cocktails of all time. Named for a fast-firing 75-millimeter field gun that was utilized by the French during World War I, the drink combines gin, fresh lemon juice, simple syrup, and Champagne. Here, fragrant, floral lavender is as ideal during brunch as it is in an aperitif on a warm afternoon.

---

1 oz (30 ml) gin

½ oz (15 ml) Lavender Simple Syrup (page 143)

½ oz (15 ml) fresh lemon juice

2 oz (60 ml) sparkling wine (Champagne, prosecco, cava, etc.)

Garnish: 2 fresh lavender sprigs, 1 lemon twist

In a cocktail shaker filled with ice, combine the gin, lavender simple syrup, and lemon juice. Cover and shake vigorously for 20–30 seconds, until well chilled. Strain into a coupe or champagne flute. Top with the sparkling wine. Garnish with lavender sprigs and a lemon twist.

HAMISH'S PRIDE

◆ MAKES 1 COCKTAIL ◆ GLASS: ROCKS ◆

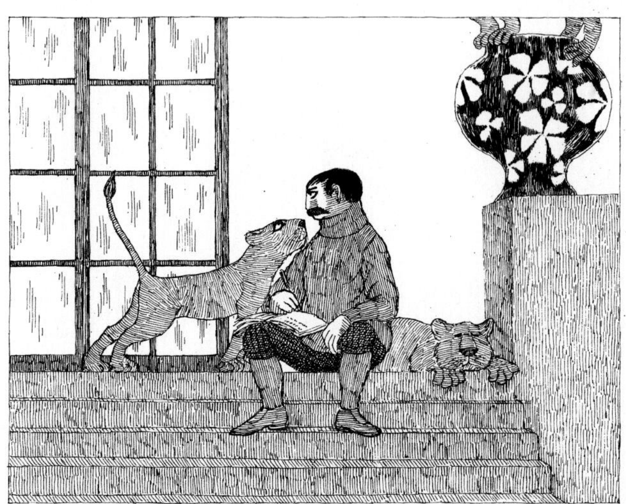

In *The Lost Lions*, a "beautiful young man" named Hamish "kept a voluminous diary" and once he "bought a stylish house in extensive grounds," he began to raise lions. After time in South America, he returns to raise even more lions. Eventually a trip to New York to meet with a publisher of his diary leads him to a farm in New Jersey, where a pair of his lions had traveled to, but "he was told they had been sent to Ohio for the winter."

We nod to the two partners, the lost lions, with a classic Old Pal, one of the best Negroni variations in existence that remains underrated today compared to ubiquitous Negroni twists like the Boulevardier. As with the Boulevardier, the Old Pal subs out whiskey for the Negroni's original gin. But smartly, the Old Pal uses dry vermouth instead of sweet.

1½ oz (45 ml) rye whiskey or a high-rye Canadian whisky

1½ oz (45 ml) dry vermouth

1½ oz (45 ml) Campari

Place a rocks glass in the freezer to chill completely. Combine all the ingredients in an ice-filled mixing glass. Stir for 20–30 seconds, until well chilled. Strain into the chilled glass.

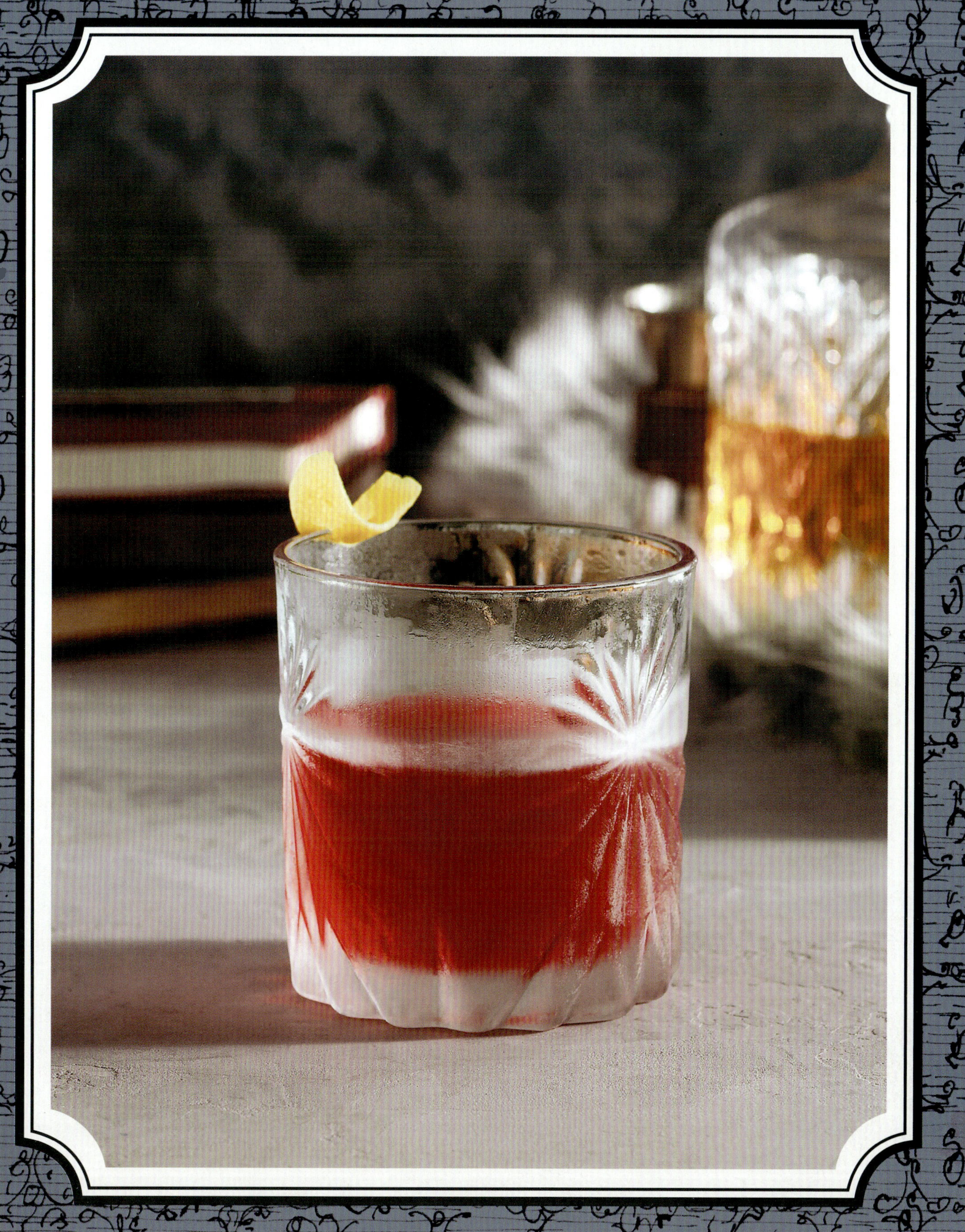

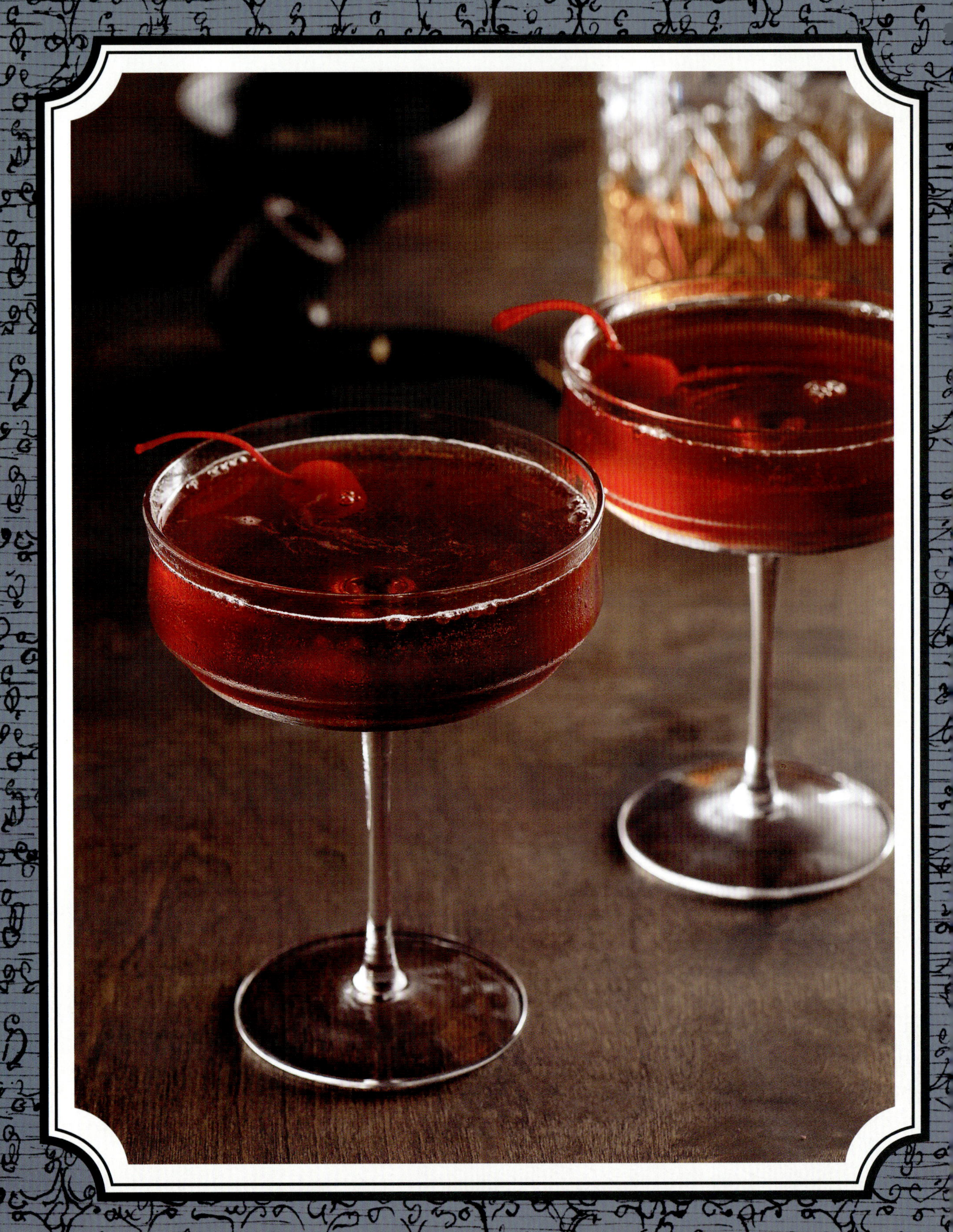

INSPIRED BY *The Deadly Blotter*

THE DEADLY BLOTTER

• MAKES 1 COCKTAIL • GLASS: COUPE •

The Deadly Blotter is another alphabet-based Gorey story cleverly detailing a murder at a mansion, complete with detective questioning and attempts to trap the murderer until "extenuation yields zero." Pre-Prohibition yielded many of the most iconic cocktails, and while everyone knows a Manhattan, the Boothby is a lesser known great with a similar body—rye whiskey, sweet vermouth, two types of bitters—and Champagne or sparkling wine making it lighter, effervescent, playful. The Boothby is believed to have been created at the Palace Hotel in San Francisco around 1910, named after its creator, William "Cocktail" Boothby, a Bay Area bartender and cocktail book writer since the late 1800s. This Boothby variation feels like the perfect imbibement for a household of elegantly dressed people exchanging "fearful glances" as the detective examines their "likely motives" and "notable emissions."

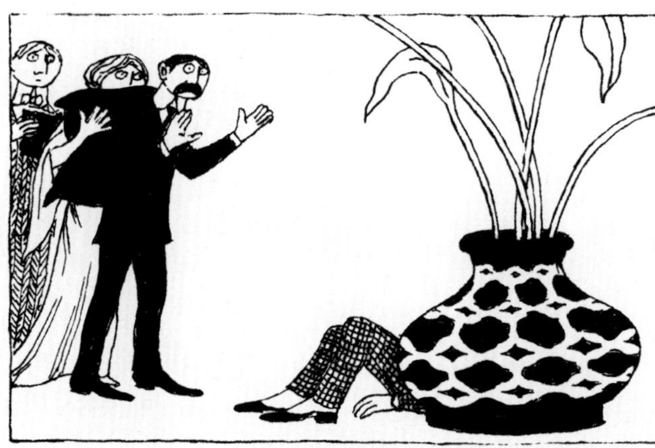

Corpse.

---

2 oz (60 ml) rye whiskey
1 oz (30 ml) sweet vermouth
3 dashes Angostura bitters
1 oz (30 ml) sparkling wine, preferably brut
Garnish: Maraschino cherry

Place a coupe glass in the freezer to chill completely. Combine the whiskey, sweet vermouth, and Angostura bitters in an ice-filled mixing glass. Stir for 20–30 seconds, until well chilled. Strain the cocktail into the chilled glass. Float the sparkling wine on top and garnish with a cherry.

INSPIRED BY *The Insect God*

THE FRASTLEY SWIZZLE

• MAKES 1 COCKTAIL • GLASS: COLLINS •

Named after Gorey's poor Millicent Frastley, rather than being stunned, stripped, and stuffed inside a pod to be sacrificed to the Insect God as she was, this lovely swizzle tributes "the dear little thing" who went missing after she was alone at the edge of the park, picked up by a black motor car. The drink mimics the layers of this story. But though *The Insect God* unfolds with horror, the Frastley Swizzle does not. These layers are crushable and delicious, a drink as ideal at a dinner party as it is poolside.

This 1800s classic is visually beautiful and refreshingly delicious, layered in vivid green and Angostura red over crushed ice. Combining mint, demerara rum, lime juice, simple syrup, and Angostura bitters in layers over a tall glass of ice, the drink's secret "sauce" is demerara rum, imparting deep, earthy, caramel flavors (use a rum like Hamilton Demerara 86 proof or easier-to-find El Dorado rum). A swizzle is a cocktail category originating from the Caribbean, centered by cracked, crushed, or pebble ice and by being swizzled with a swizzle stick.

10–12 fresh mint leaves
¾ oz (20 ml) 1:1 Simple Syrup (page 142)
2 oz (60 ml) demerara rum
1 oz (30 ml) fresh lime juice
5 dashes Angostura bitters
Garnish: fresh mint sprig

Pile the mint leaves in the bottom of a Collins glass and pour the simple syrup on top. Gently muddle (do not bruise) with a muddler or wooden pestle. Add the rum, lime juice, and 2 dashes of the Angostura bitters. Fill the glass until almost full with crushed or pebble ice, then swizzle with a swizzle stick or barspoon until the glass is frosty. Top off the glass with more crushed or pebble ice, forming a mound protruding from the top of the glass. Douse the ice mound with the remaining 3 dashes of Angostura bitters. Garnish with a mint sprig

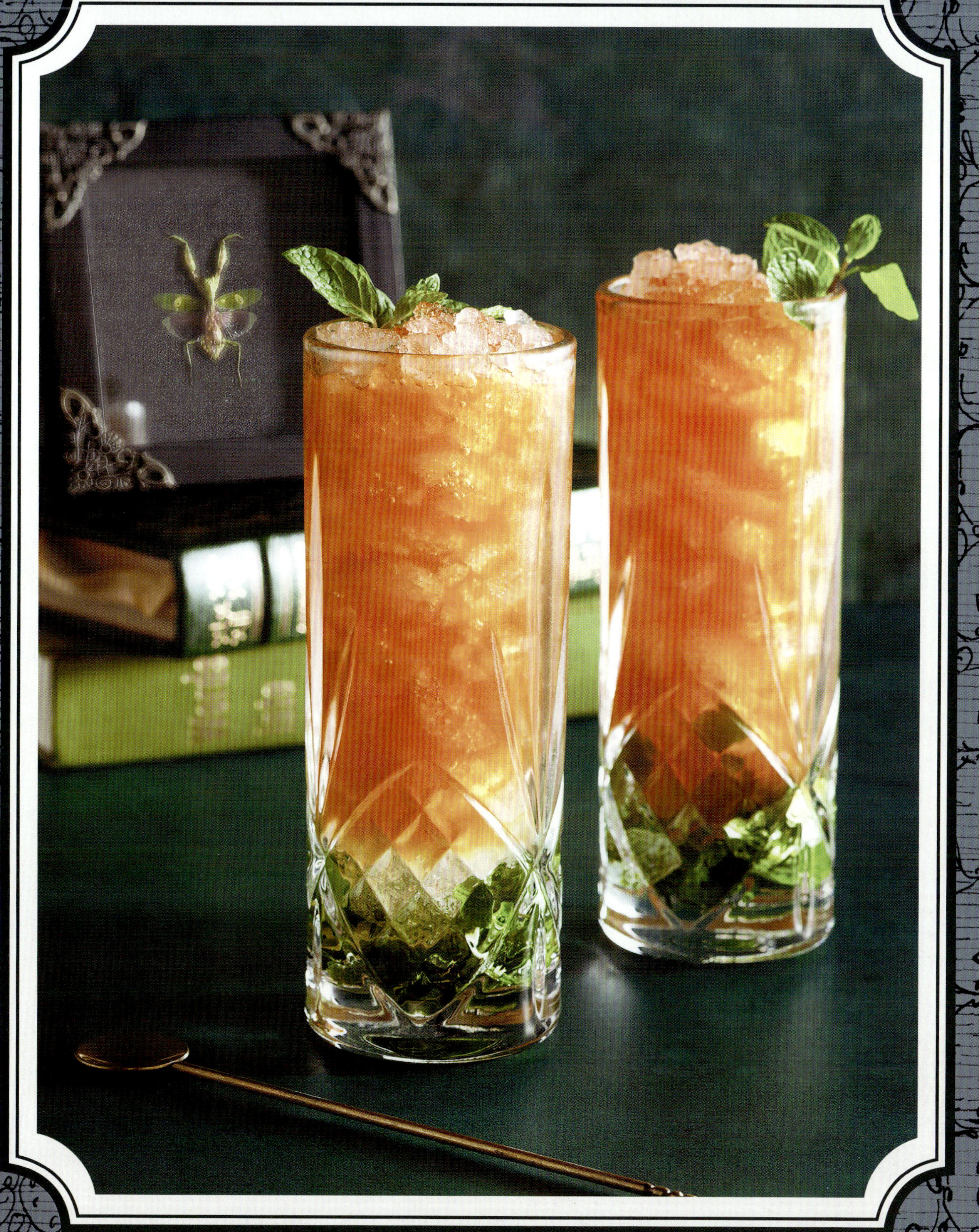

FROM *The Insect God*

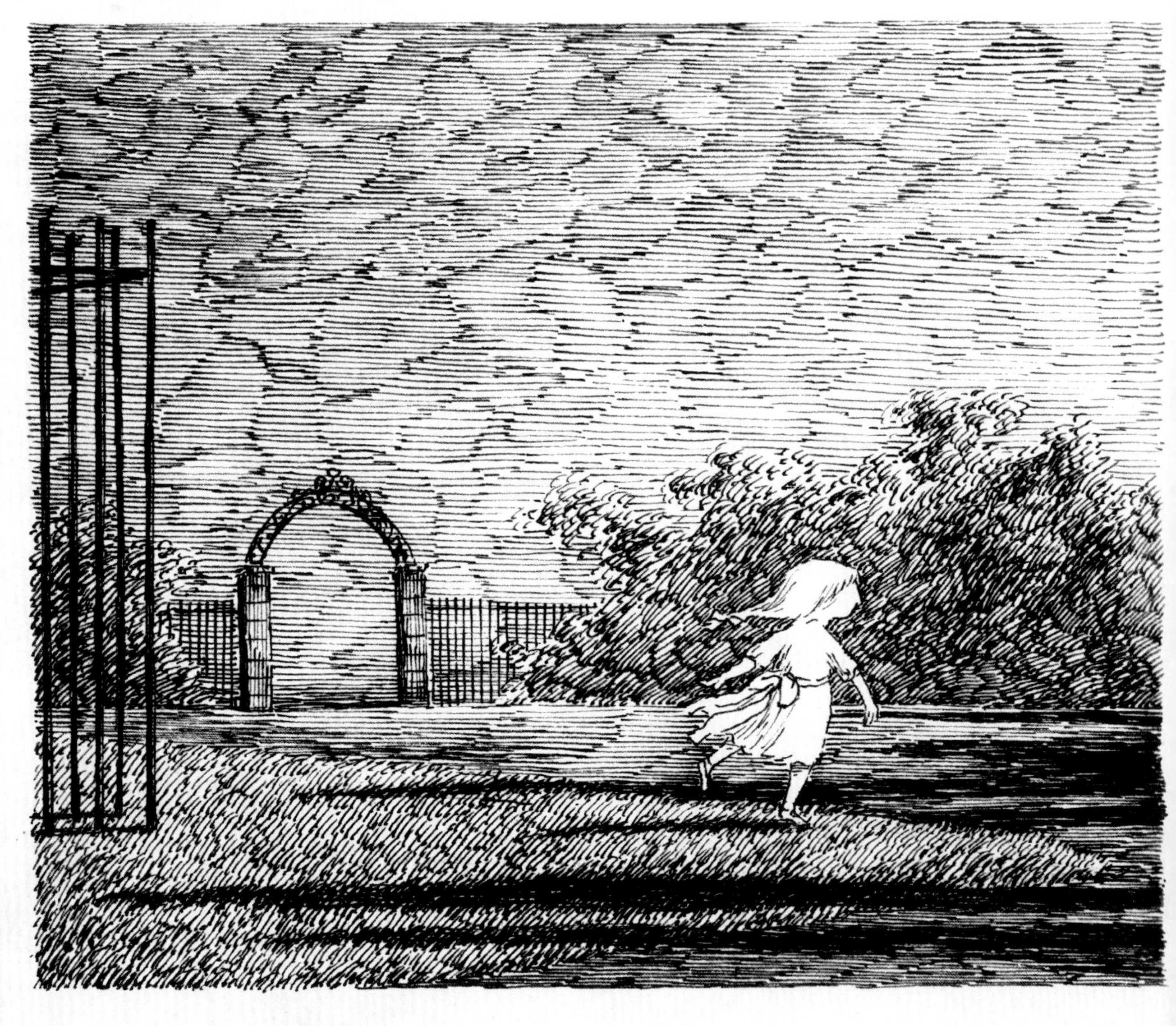

O what has become of Millicent Frastley?
Is there any hope that she's still alive?
Why haven't they found her? It's rather ghastly
To think that the child was not yet five.

The nurse was discovered collapsed in some shrubbery,
But her reappearance was not much use;
Her eyes were askew, her extremities rubbery,
Her clothing was stained with a brownish juice.

She was questioned in hopes of her answers revealing
What had happened; she merely repeatedly said
'I hear them walking about on the ceiling'.
She had gone irretrievably out of her head.

O feelings of horror, resentment, and pity
For things, which so seldom turn out for the best:
The car, unobserved, sped away from the city
As the last of the light died out in the west.

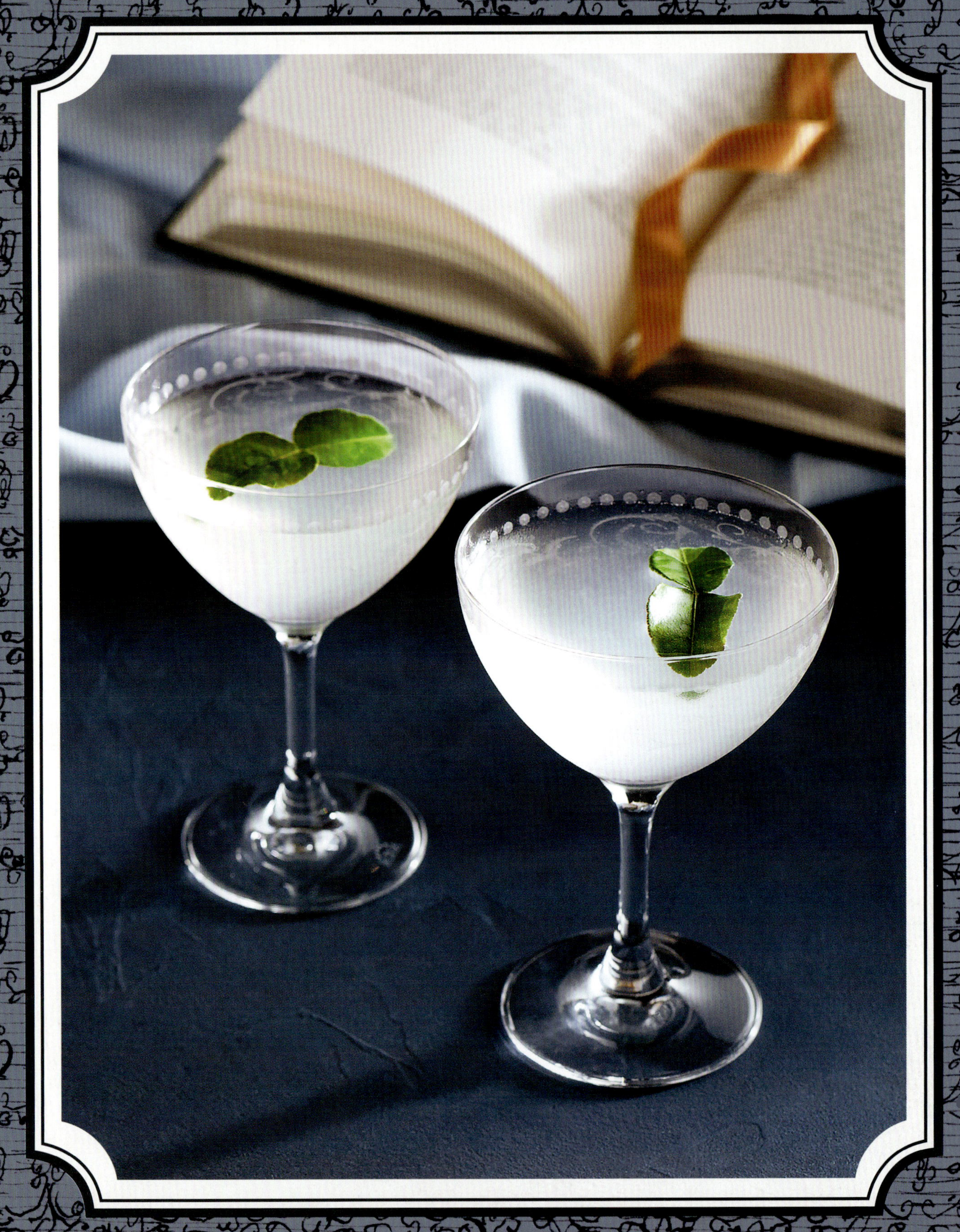

INSPIRED BY *Seasonal Confusion*

THE FLUSTERED DAQUIRI

• MAKES 1 COCKTAIL • GLASS: COUPE •

Seasonal Confusion is a brief series of four drawings brilliantly showcasing Gorey's irreverent humor told through a sleepless man trying to deal with a time change in the night. He asks, "Is it early or late? Should I hurry? Or wait?" Only to conclude, "Perhaps I shall go back to bed."

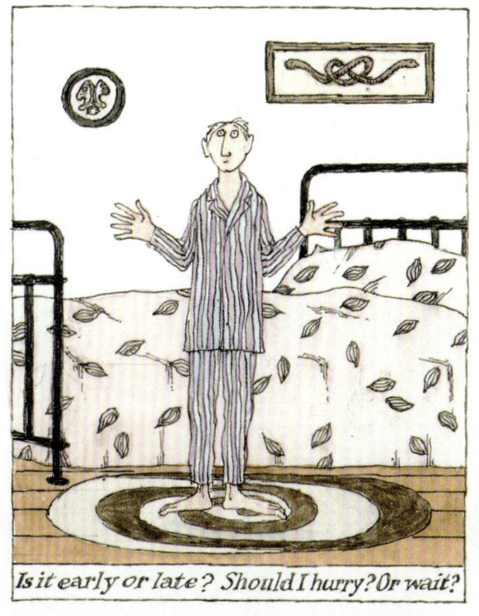
Is it early or late? Should I hurry? Or wait?

Rather than go to bed, we celebrate a fitting kind of "seasonal confusion" in the form of one of the greatest rum cocktails of all time, the daiquiri. With the simple purity of rum, lime juice, and simple syrup, a daiquiri is only as good as the rum and the bartender's skill in balancing the drink's tart, sweet, and sugarcane elements. The "confusion" in this variation is of a blissful kind: Am I in Thailand or Cuba? The answer could be both with this Thai daiquiri showcasing the aromatic beauty of makrut limes with rum. The choice of rum makes a massive difference in the drink's flavor profile, whether you go grassy-fresh with an agricole r(h)um or robust and funky with a Jamaican rum, as just a couple of possible variations.

---

2 makrut lime leaves, plus more for garnish
2 oz (60 ml) rum
1 oz (30 ml) fresh lime juice
½ oz (15 ml) Makrut Lime and Rosemary Oleo Saccharum (page 143)

In a pint glass, muddle the two makrut lime leaves. Add the remaining ingredients and ice. Gently stir together until well chilled, 20–30 seconds. Strain into a coupe glass. Garnish with a lime leaf.

Variation: Make it frozen by adding a heaping ½ cup (70 g) crushed ice and blending until the texture is creamy and the ice is uniformly crushed.

INSPIRED BY *The Willowdale Handcar: Or the Return of the Black Doll* 

MR. QUEEVIL'S DARK AND STORMY

• MAKES 1 COCKTAIL • GLASS: ROCKS •

The Willowdale Handcar: Or the Return of the Black Doll is a lesser-known Gorey tale of three figures traveling by handcar from Willowdale through a cast of characters and varied scenery, whether a burning house or a baked-bean supper at the Halfbath Methodist Church. A delectable moment comes at Bogus Corners.

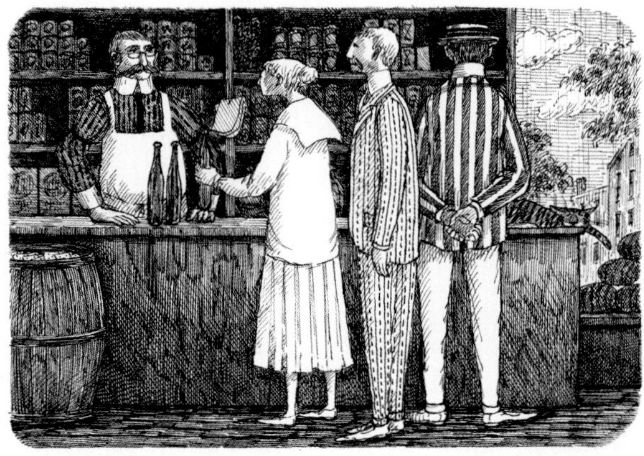

At Bogus Corners, the next town down the line, they stopped to buy soda pop and gingersnaps at Mr Queevil's store. 'How are things over in Willowdale?' he asked. 'Dull' they said.

This dark 'n' stormy is a variation on the classic and, like its cousin, the Moscow mule, is very easy to make. The sweeter vanilla, caramel, and spice notes of Goslings Black Seal rum are behind the drink, which the brand registered as a trademark in 1991, so technically, the official dark 'n' stormy can only be made with this rum. A spicy, quality ginger beer is the other key to a good dark 'n' stormy. But this variation amps up the typically straightforward, irresistible drink, nodding to the gingersnaps bought at Mr. Queevil's with a gingerbread simple syrup.

---

2 oz (60 ml) dark rum

¾ oz (20 ml) fresh lime juice

½ oz (15 ml) Gingerbread Simple Syrup (page 145)

3 oz (90 ml) ginger beer

Garnish: Cinnamon stick, crystallized ginger slice

In a chilled rocks glass, combine the rum, lime juice, and gingerbread syrup. Add ice and stir. Top with the ginger beer and more ice. Garnish with the cinnamon stick and crystallized ginger.

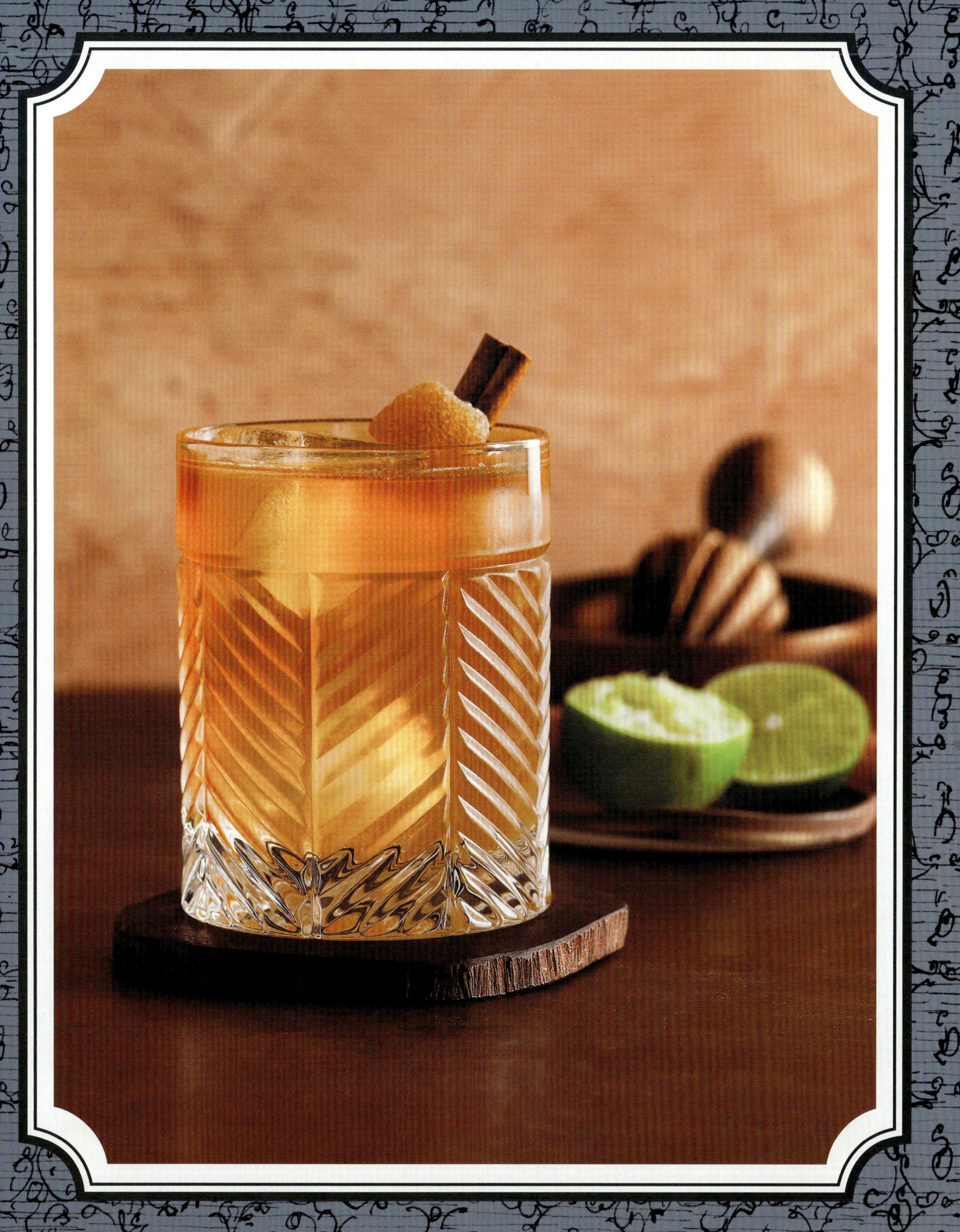

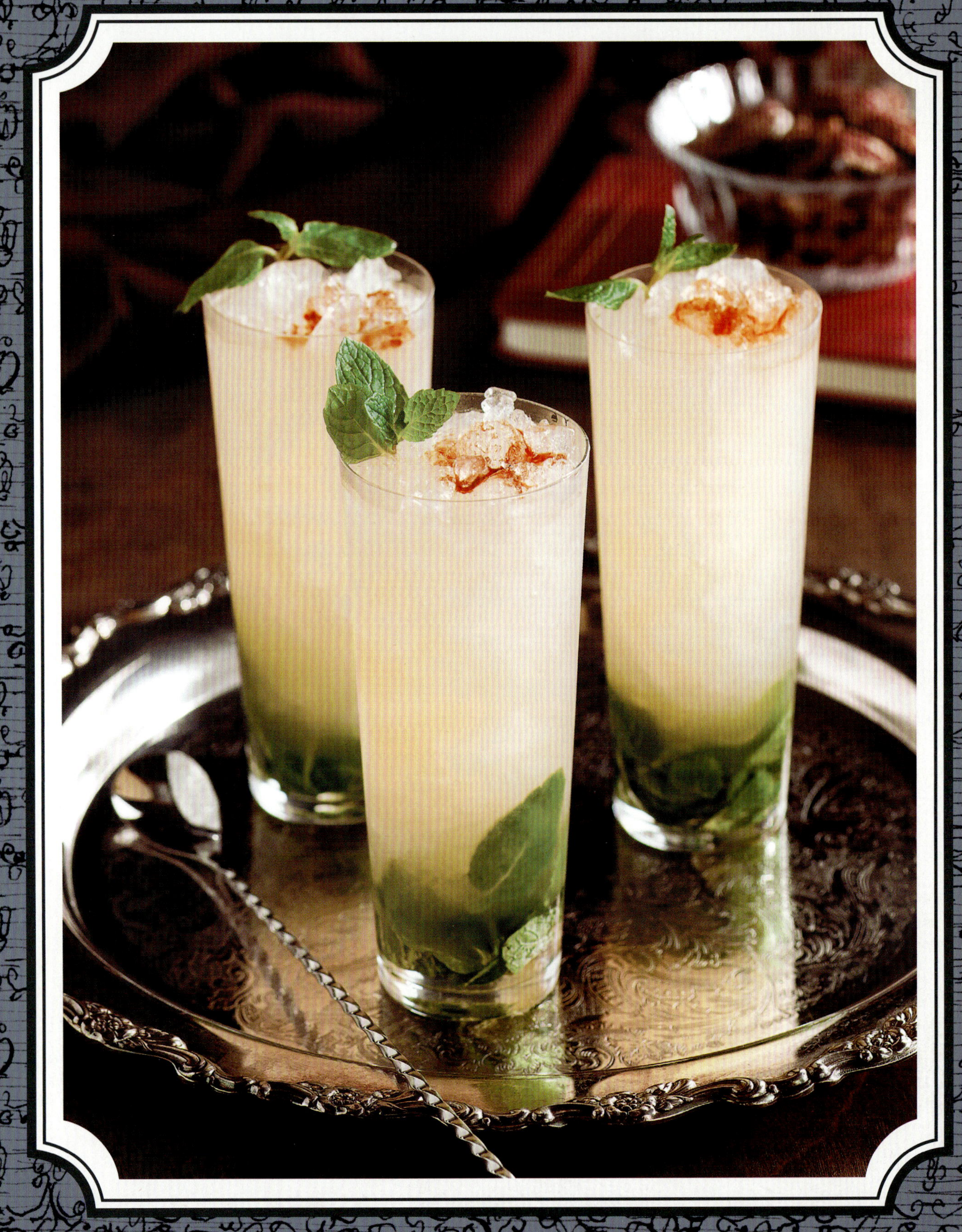

INSPIRED BY *Random Walk*

JANE'S PERAMBULATION

• MAKES 1 COCKTAIL • GLASS: COLLINS •

Random Walk is a spare, short little Gorey tale of four drawings about a "trendy young woman named Jane." Out of step with the majority of his black-and-white sketches, this tale goes brightly colorful with one key hue. Jane "spent a fortune on clothes," in particular, a wild, fire engine–red outfit. Covering her from head to toe, this memorable outfit centers the story, while Jane makes "the mistake of refusing to take / A cab when it started to rain," thus rendering her beautiful outfit soggy and drooping.

Layered in vibrant green, gold, and a float of red from Angostura bitters, this drink recalls Jane's outfit as its best in a play off a classic Queen's Park Swizzle with rosemary simple syrup to add herbaceous depth. Back in 1946, Bay Area Tiki founding father Trader Vic called this swizzle "the most delightful form of anesthesia given out today." The choice of rum greatly affects the flavor profile. French Caribbean agricole r(h)um, an unaged Mexican rum, Haitian clairin, Brazilian cachaça, or sugarcane-based agricole-style rum brings grassy, green, bright notes. All sing with the mint and bitters.

10–12 fresh mint leaves

¾ oz (20 ml) Rosemary Simple Syrup (page 144)

2 oz (60 ml) agricole r(h)um

1 oz (30 ml) fresh lime juice

6 dashes Angostura bitters

Garnish: Fresh mint sprig

Layer the mint leaves in a Collins glass, pour the rosemary simple syrup on top, and gently muddle (do not bruise) with a muddler or wooden pestle. Add the rum, lime juice, and 3 dashes of the Angostura bitters. Fill the glass nearly full with crushed ice and swizzle with a swizzle stick or barspoon until the glass is frosty. Top the glass with more crushed ice and form into a mound slightly above the top of the glass. Top with the remaining 3 dashes of Angostura bitters. Garnish with a mint sprig.

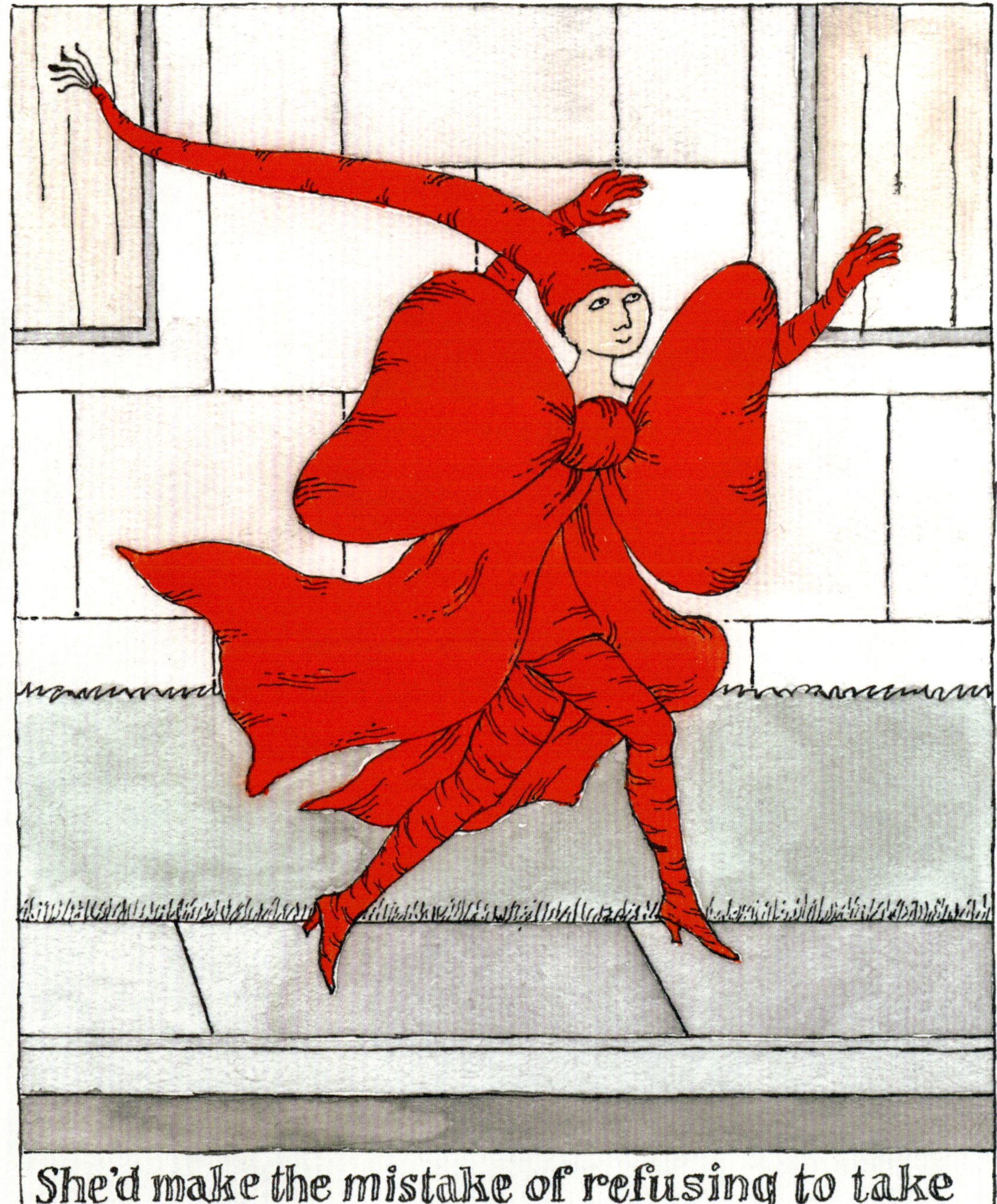
She'd make the mistake of refusing to take

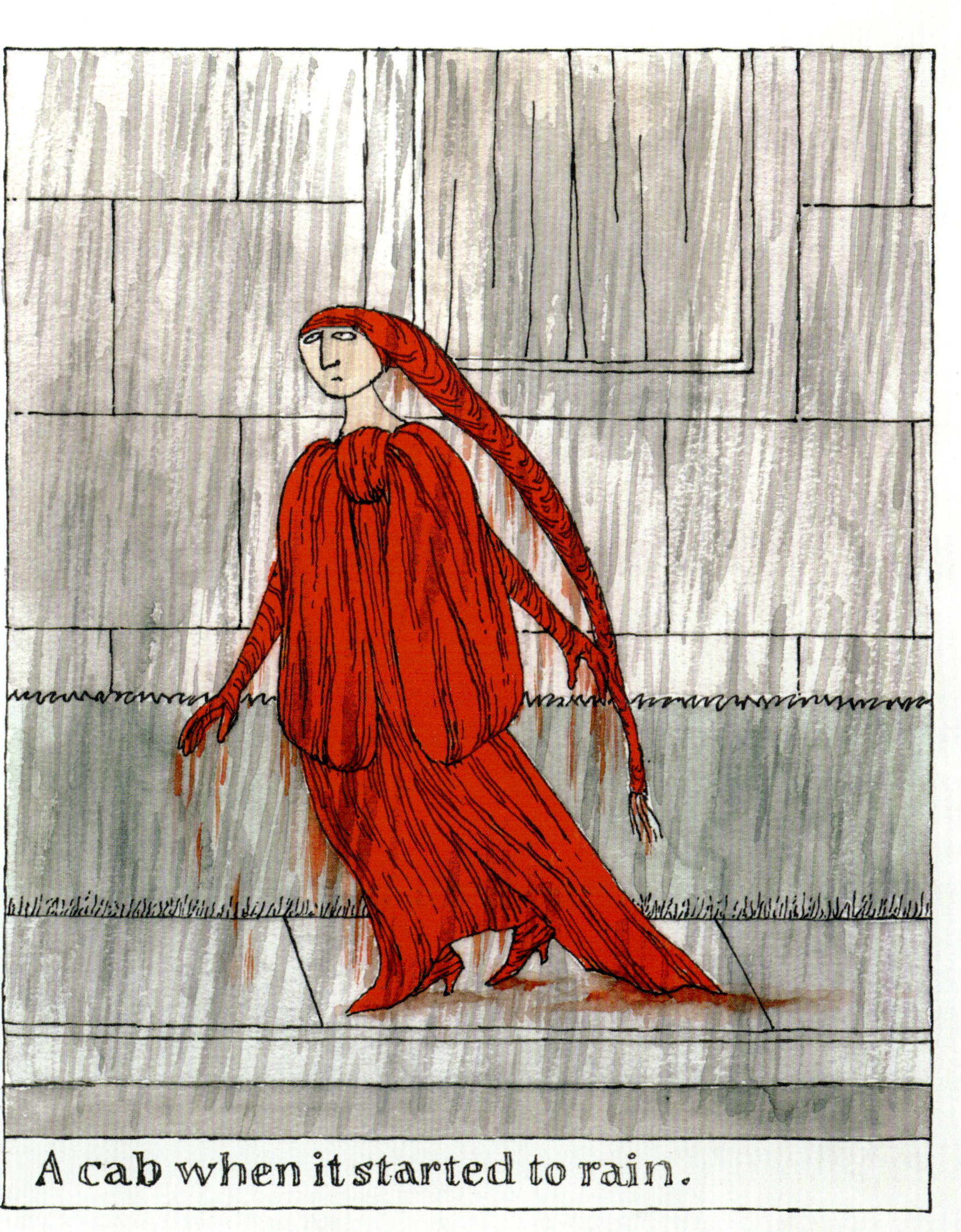

A cab when it started to rain.

INSPIRED BY *The Raging Tide: Or, the Black Doll's Imbroglio* 

SKRUMP'S OLD FASHIONED

• MAKES 1 COCKTAIL • GLASS: ROCKS •

Skrump, Naeelah, Figbash, and Hooglyboo get into a battle that unfolds over thirty drawings in Gorey's *The Raging Tide* and their ways of assaulting and attacking are creative and, at times, downright hilarious. This wild foursome even tries to make peace and pardon "over stewed prunes," eventually forgiving each other "over boiled turnips."

Thankfully, there are no turnips or prunes in this spicy ode to a Oaxaca old fashioned, this cocktail's smoky earthiness and vegetal glow from mezcal is tempered and balanced by a baseline of reposado tequila. If you use a quality reposado tequila, it can add a gentle woodiness—akin to whiskey in the original old fashioned—without masking the bright agave flavors that make tequila and mezcal true spirit treasures. We go beyond stewed prunes and boiled turnips by replacing traditional Angostura bitters with a little heat and flavor punch from firewater or jalapeño bitters.

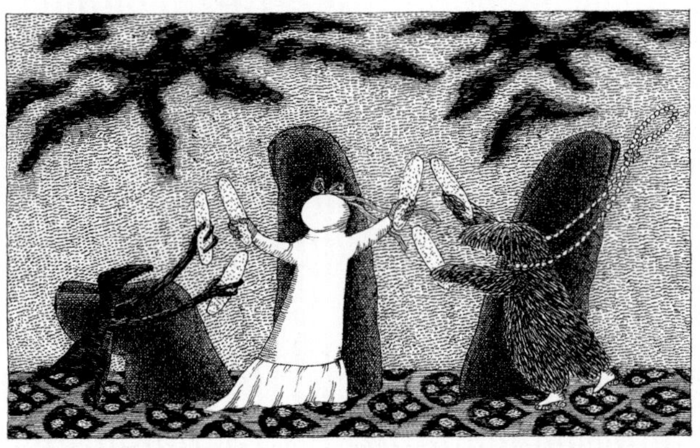

Figbash, Naeelah, and Skrump fell upon each other with loofahs.

- 1½ oz (45 ml) reposado tequila
- ½ oz (15 ml) mezcal
- 1 barspoon 1:1 Simple Syrup (page 142)
- 2 dashes firewater or jalapeño bitters
- Garnish: Flamed orange peel

Add the tequila, mezcal, simple syrup, and firewater bitters to a rocks glass with one large ice cube and stir for 30–40 seconds, until well chilled. Flame an orange peel over the top of the drink to express its oils, then garnish the cocktail with the peel.

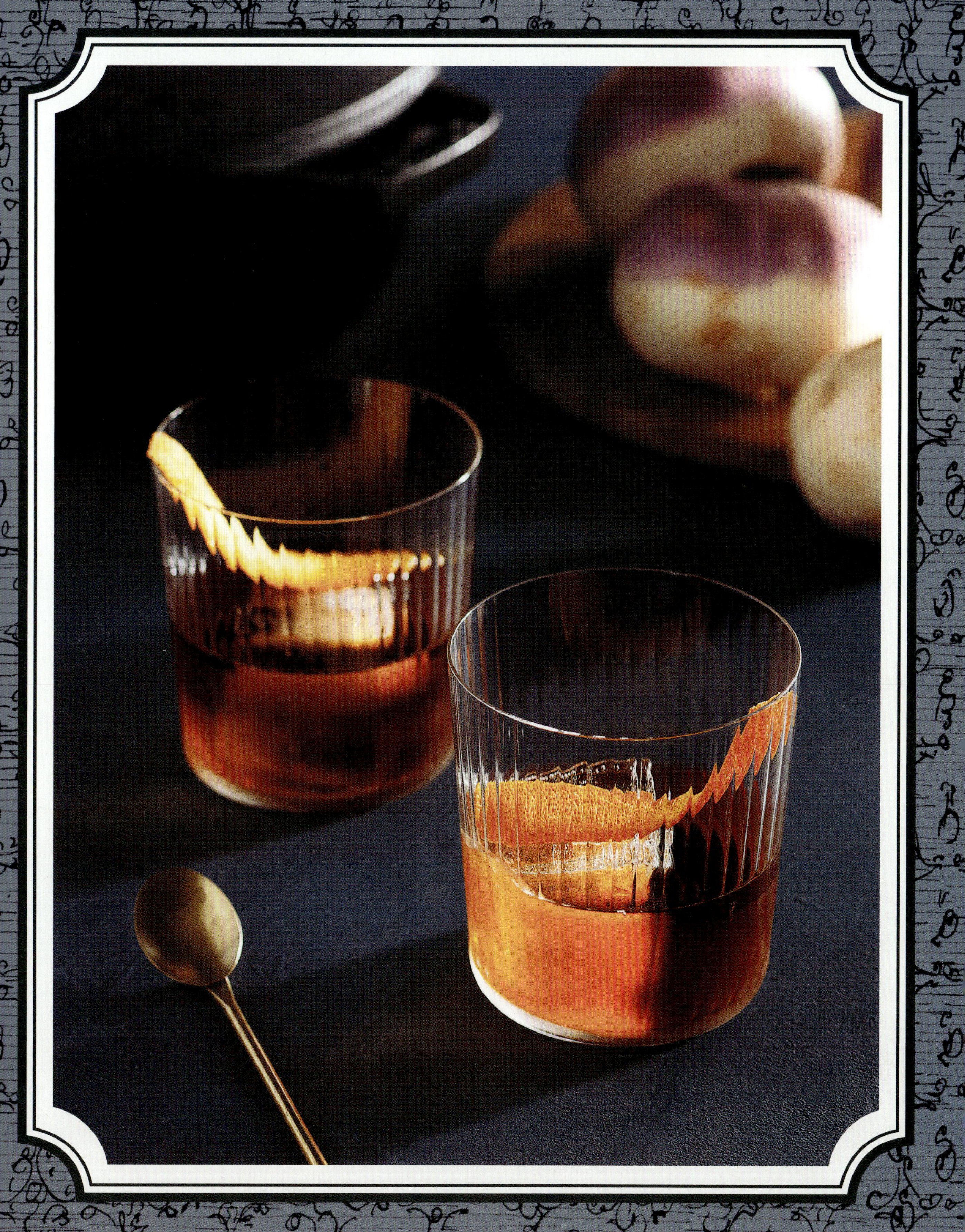

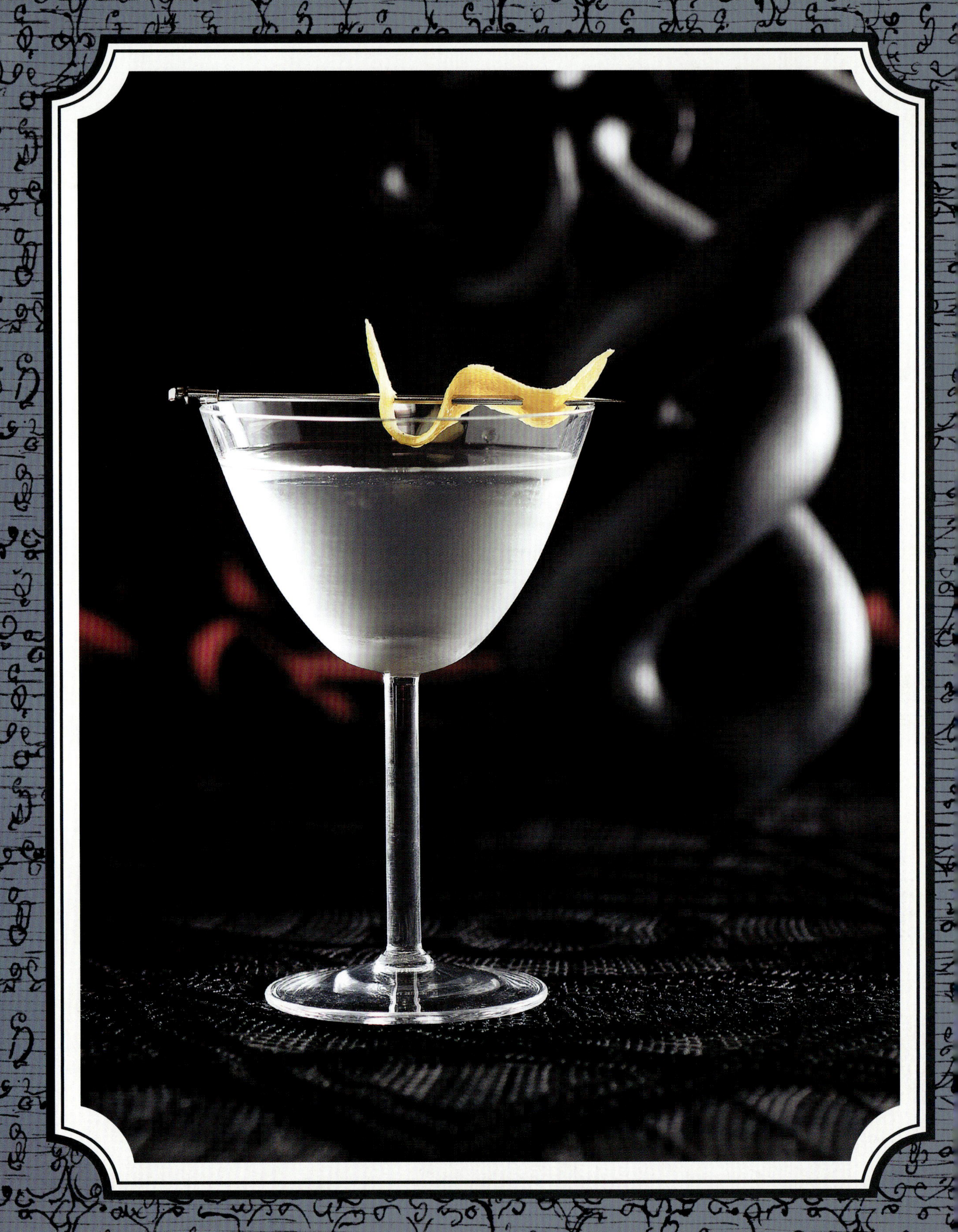

INSPIRED BY *The Disrespectful Summons*

MISS SQUILL'S 50/50

• MAKES 1 COCKTAIL • GLASS: COUPE OR NICK AND NORA •

Poor Miss Squill is attacked and marked by the Devil himself in *The Disrespectful Summons*. In this dark tale, a little flying creature named Beelphazoar eventually flies through her door, bringing "a recipe for fudge / Of pounded pencil-stubs and sludge" and dropping off a book called *Ninety-Two Entirely Evil Things to Do*. Whether using voodoo-like pins and tacks to stick into wax figures she makes of her neighbors or cindering "toast and rotted silk, / Corroded tin and curdled milk," Miss Squill carries out the Devil's work faithfully. Until one Sunday afternoon when he returns, seizes her hair, "and with his hoof / He kicked a way out through the roof," before dropping her "in the Flaming Pit."

No Devil's work here, rather an attempt to avoid that Flaming Pit with lower alcohol in the form of a vermouth-forward martini. It's a way to ward off proverbial demons with a lower-proof tipple, combining dry and white vermouth to further round out this elegant version of one of history's most iconic and beloved cocktails, the martini.

¾ oz (20 ml) London dry gin
½ oz (15 ml) dry vermouth
½ oz (15 ml) bianco (white) vermouth
1 dash orange bitters
Garnish: Lemon peel

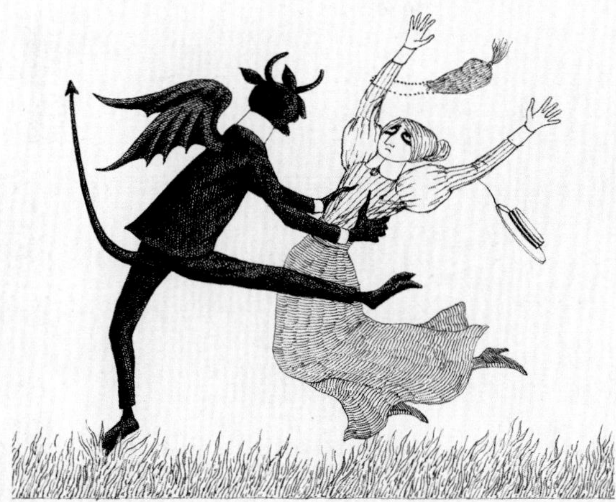

Combine the gin, dry vermouth, bianco vermouth, and orange bitters in a pint or mixing glass. Add ice and stir for 30–40 seconds, until well chilled. Strain into a coupe or Nick and Nora glass. Express the lemon peel over the drink and garnish with the peel.

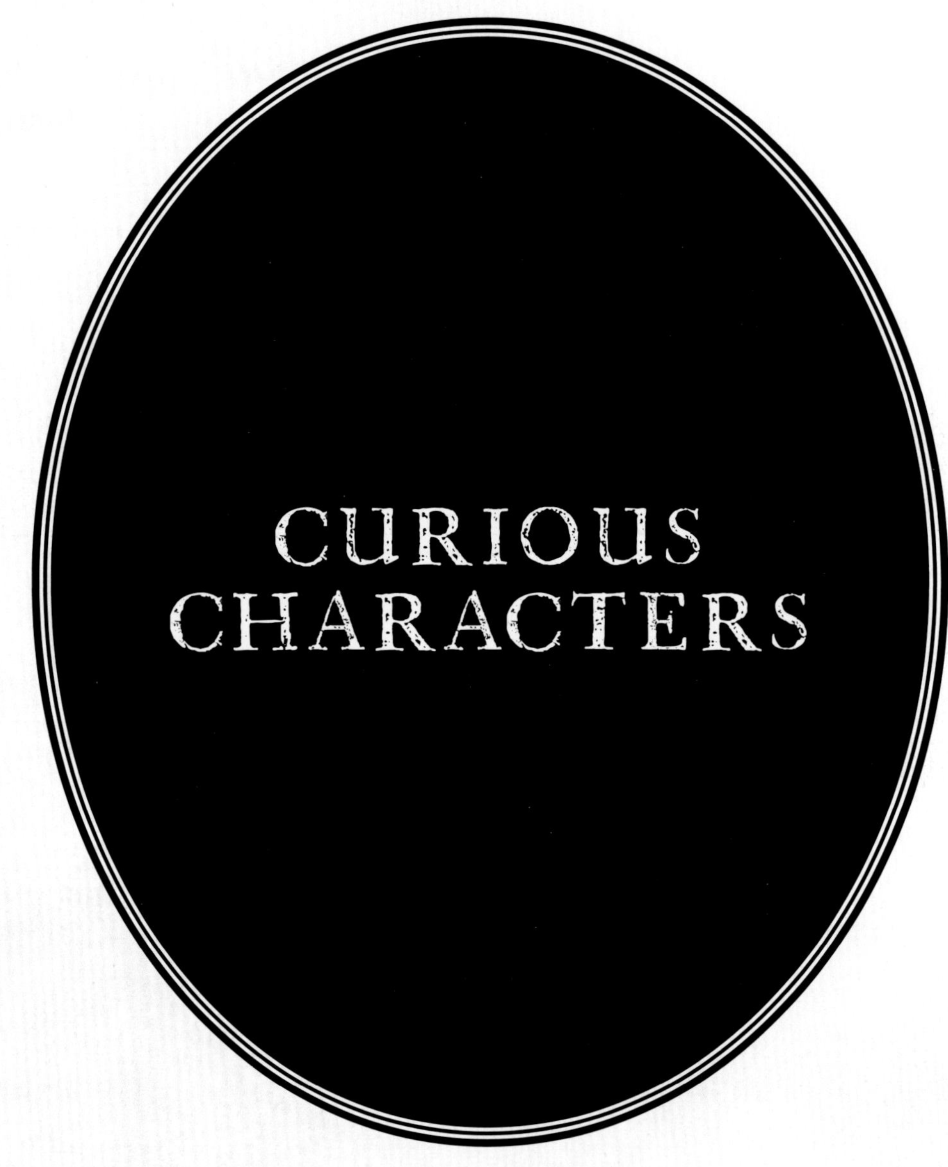

CURIOUS CHARACTERS

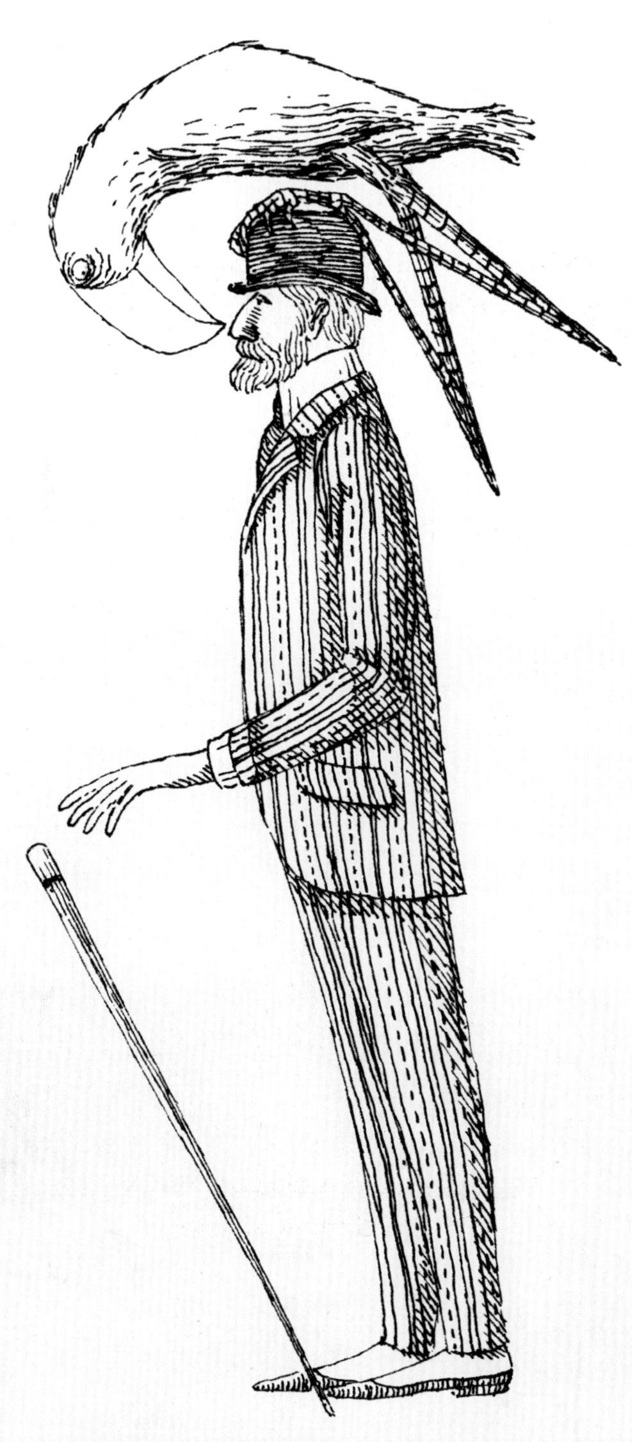

THE JOURNALIST'S GIMLET

• MAKES 1 COCKTAIL • GLASS: ROCKS •

The Fatal Lozenge is another alphabet-ordered Gorey fable of twenty-six characters with peculiar stories and often dark circumstances. Each letter's story rhymes, set to Gorey's ever-vivid drawings. One example is "The Nun is fearfully bedeviled / She runs about and moans and shrieks; / Her flesh is bruised, her clothes disheveled / She's been like this for weeks and weeks." *The Journalist* is a particularly violent sketch of two bodies strewn over chairs, bloody with slashes, while the writer gazes over them with a drink in hand.

The Journalist's Gimlet is not a gin-and-water but, instead, a refreshing play on a classic gimlet. Traditionally, this is a tart sour-style cocktail of gin, lime juice, and simple syrup. We stay tart with grapefruit juice and go aromatic with sage, best expressed by steeping in a simple syrup. Grisly murders and diluted, watery gin aside, this is the kind of cocktail that refreshes on a summer day or brightens up a meal with its food-friendly citrus herbaceousness.

2½ oz (75 ml) gin
1 oz (30 ml) fresh grapefruit juice
½ oz (15 ml) Sage Simple Syrup (page 144)
Garnish: Fresh sage leaf, grapefruit slice

In a cocktail shaker filled with ice, combine the gin, grapefruit juice, and sage simple syrup. Cover and shake vigorously for 20–30 seconds, until well chilled. Strain into an ice-filled rocks glass. Garnish with a sage leaf and the grapefruit slice.

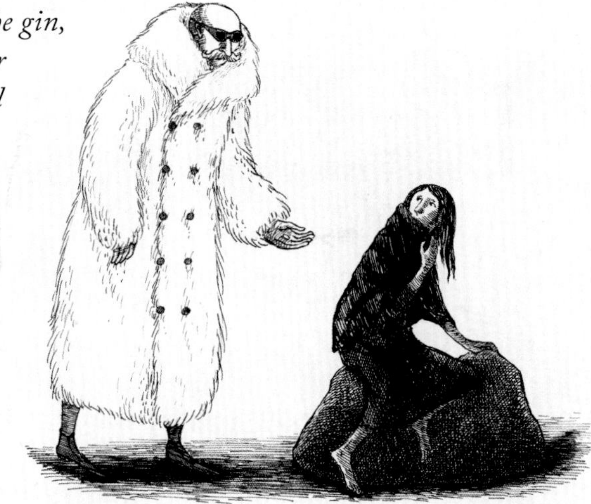

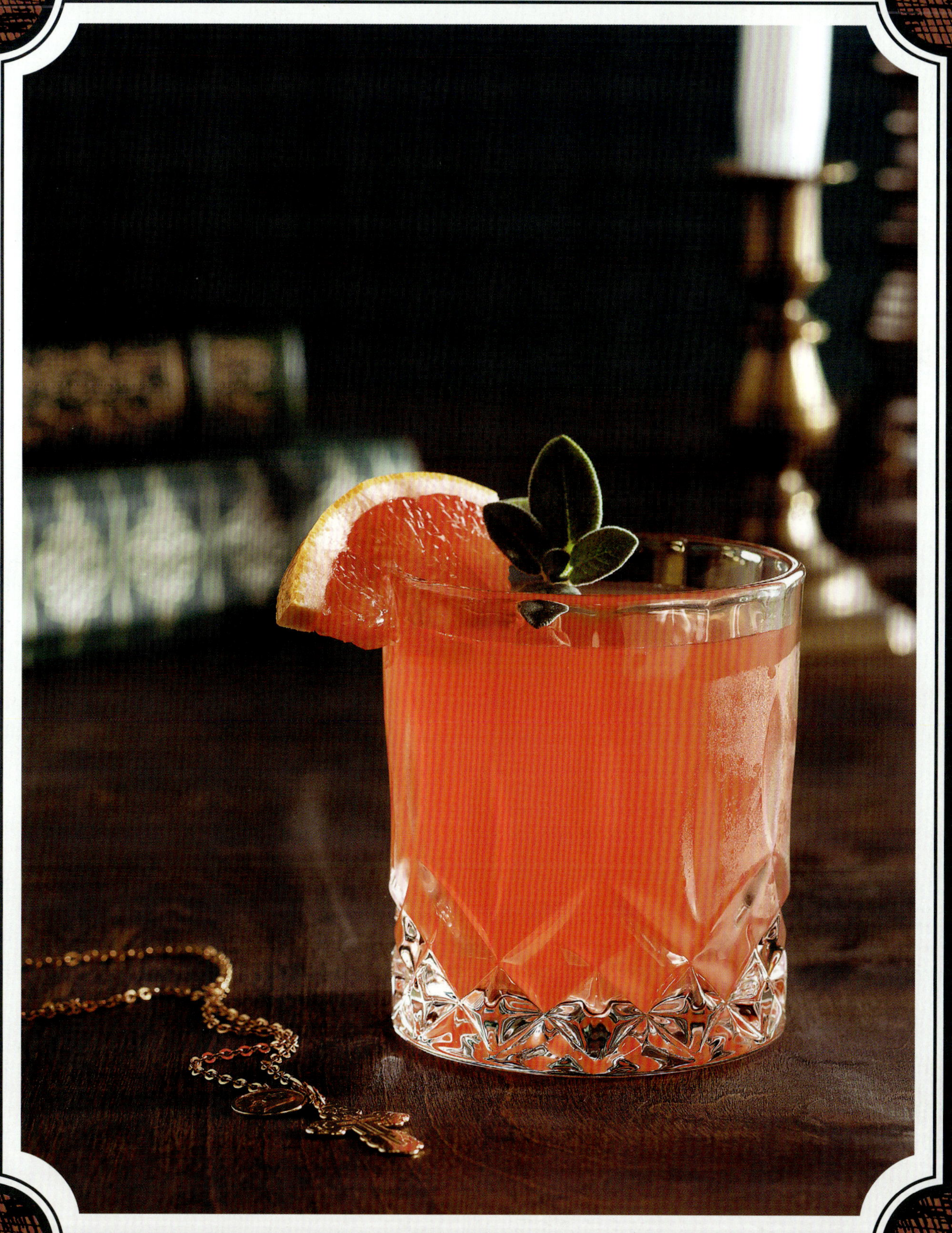

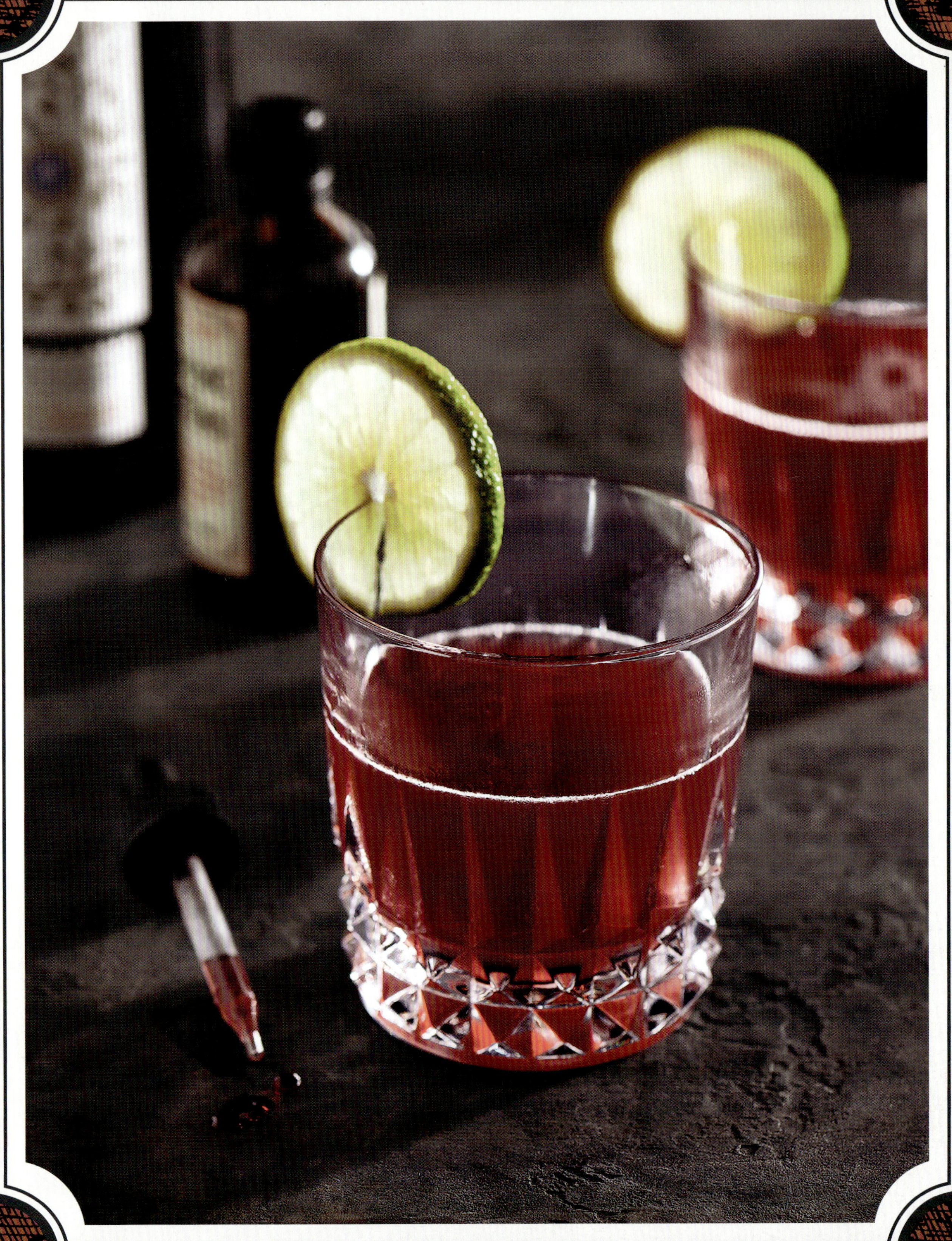

Q.R.V. NO. 222

• MAKES 1 COCKTAIL • GLASS: ROCKS •

Gorey referred to Q.R.V., or "The Universal Solvent," as a restorative tonic that's hard enough to clean toilets and soft enough to drink. What is it? It's whatever you need it to be.

In our case, it's a mysterious black currant gin sipper. Crème de cassis is French for blackcurrant liqueur, a traditional, sweet, dark red liqueur made from blackcurrants. Current greats include Giffard's Crème de Cassis Impérial, but you can find small-batch versions from across the United States and beyond. A fresh, tart-sweet version showcases the dark little berries, an elixir that could work the wonders Q.R.V. promises in taste, if nothing else. Brightened with lime and accompanied by the herbaceous and citrus qualities of gin, this refreshing drink is good for . . . whatever you need it be.

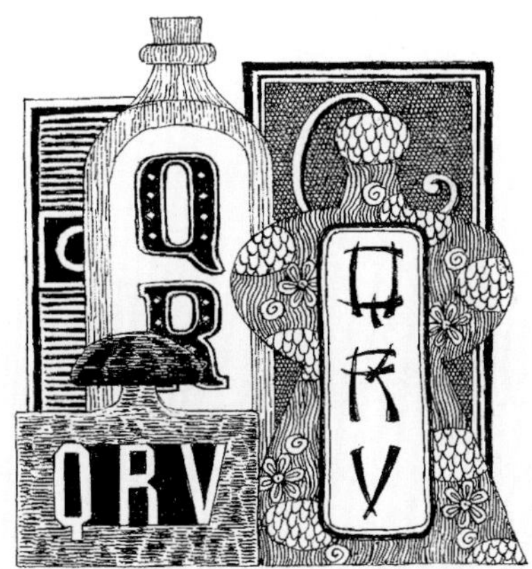

1¾ oz (50 ml) gin
¾ oz (20 ml) crème de cassis (black currant liqueur)
¾ oz (20 ml) fresh lime juice
⅓ oz (10 ml) 1:1 Simple Syrup (page 142)
1 dash Angostura bitters
Garnish: Lime wheel

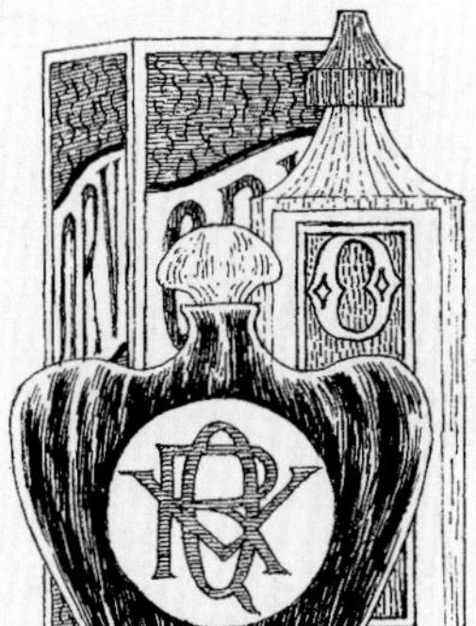

Place a rocks glass in the freezer to chill completely. In a cocktail shaker with ice, combine the gin, crème de cassis, lime juice, simple syrup, and Angostura bitters. Cover and shake vigorously for 20–30 seconds, until well chilled. Strain into the chilled rocks glass. Garnish with a lime wheel.

MISS QUARTERMOURNING'S GRIEF

• MAKES 1 COCKTAIL • GLASS: COUPE •

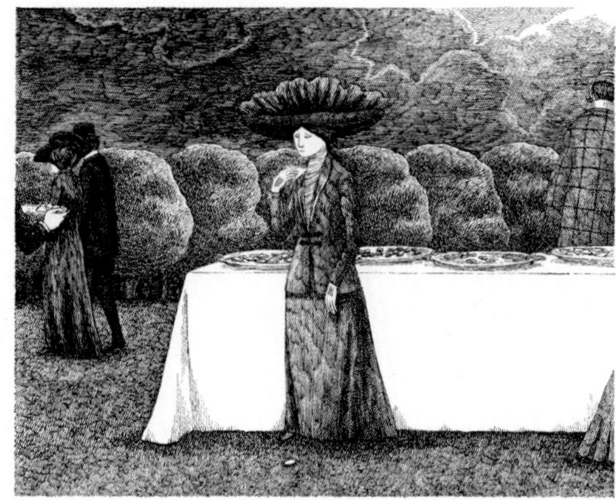

In *The Other Statue*, Gorey explores a series of whimsically, wildly named characters via vignettes at the "annual charity fête on the grounds of Backwater Hall in Mortshire." Characters like Earl of Thump and Lady Isobel Stringless, find themselves in peculiar situations, a common Gorey trope. At a buffet, Miss Quartermourning—wearing a large hat—loses a slice of cucumber from her sandwich.

No lost cucumbers here; instead, we go full cucumber in a classic gimlet cocktail. But rather than using the traditional gin, we play with aquavit. Aquavit (aka akvavit) hails from the Scandinavian countries, though there are many quality aquavits made in the United States and beyond. Just like gin, aquavit is distilled from grain or potatoes with a neutral grain base, flavored with a range of herbs and botanicals. While some botanicals overlap with gin, like anise and coriander, think of aquavit as more like a savory gin. It can lean heavy on botanicals like caraway, dill, cardamom, and cumin. Aquavit adds savory intrigue to any cocktail and can make you mouthwateringly hungry. Maybe for a cucumber sandwich?

---

3 cucumber wheels
½ oz (15 ml) 1:1 Simple Syrup (page 142)
2 oz (60 ml) aquavit
¾ oz (20 ml) fresh lime juice
Garnish: Thinly sliced cucumber wheels

Add the three cucumber wheels and simple syrup to a cocktail shaker and muddle with a muddler or wooden pestle. Add the aquavit, lime juice, and ice. Cover and shake for 20–30 seconds, until well chilled. Strain into a coupe glass. Garnish with the cucumber wheels.

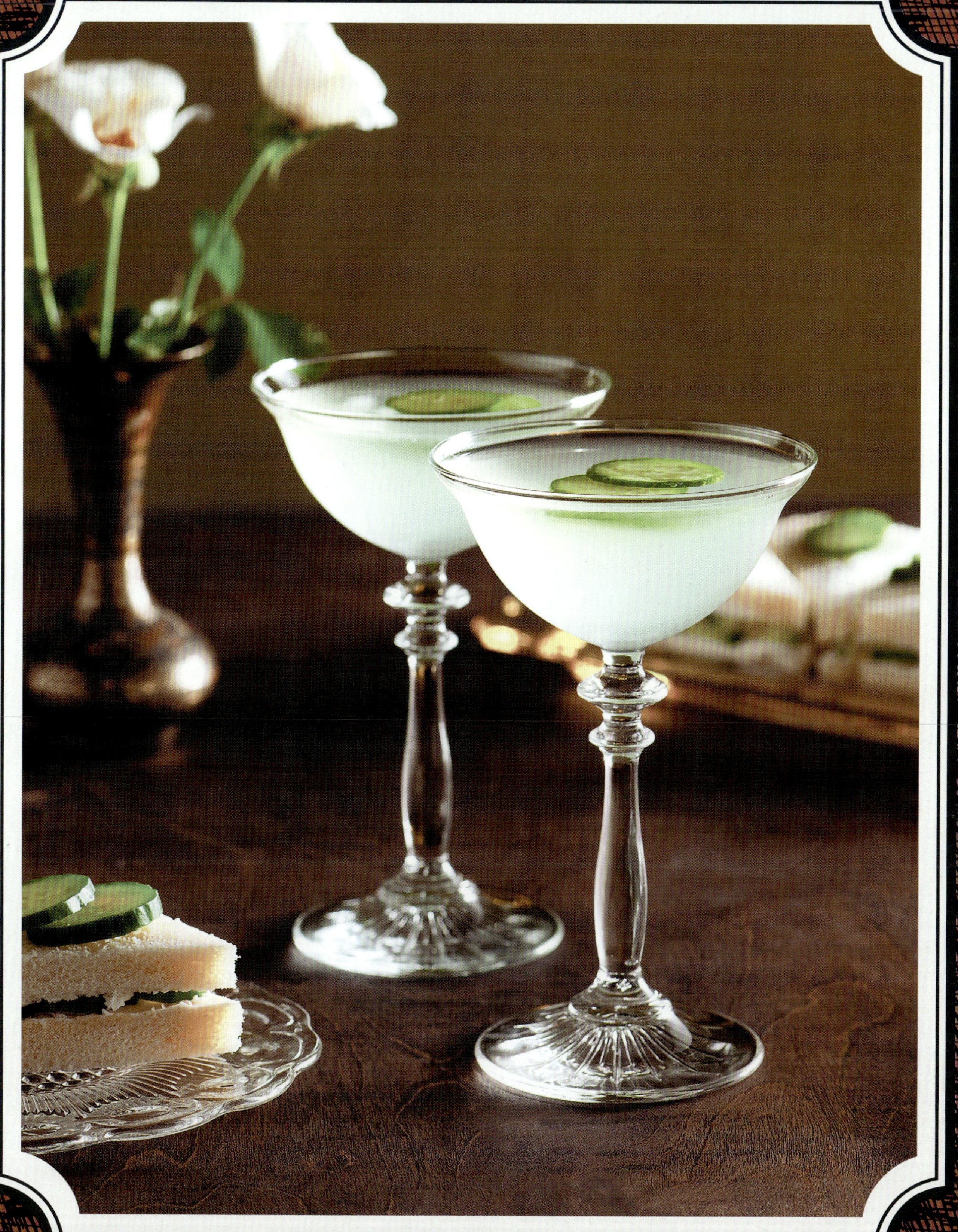

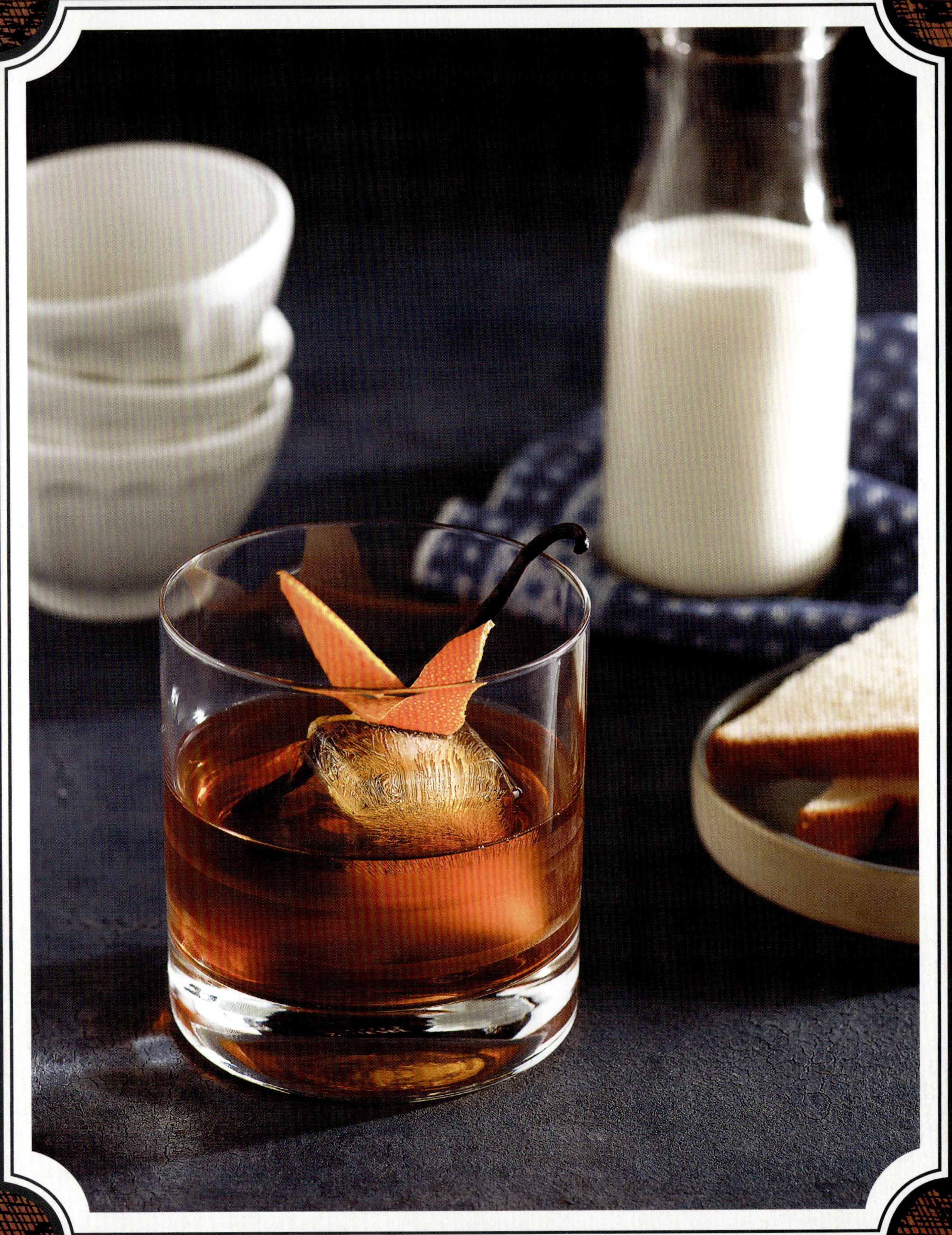

INSPIRED BY *The Wuggly Ump*

THE GLUGALUMP

• MAKES 1 COCKTAIL • GLASS: ROCKS •

As the Wuggly Ump swallows up three happily singing children, the children are fattened up on "wholesome bowls of milk and bread." Singing "tirraloo, tirralay," the unsuspecting children are sweeter than the Ump's usual diet of "umbrellas, gunny sacks, brass doorknobs, mud, and carpet tacks."

In this spirit, we sweeten up a typically gently sweet-but-robust old fashioned with, not milk and bread, but wholesome vanilla and citrus. Think of the spirit of a Creamsicle in the body of an old fashioned. Balance is everything in an old fashioned and as whiskey choices vary, so will they change the flavor profile of the drink. We recommend the often sweeter, rounder corn notes of bourbon, though rye whiskey adds bracing spice. The vanilla and citrus in this cocktail play off those same notes found in many bourbons, though less bracing, often gentler Highlands Scotches can be known for notes of vanilla and citrus.

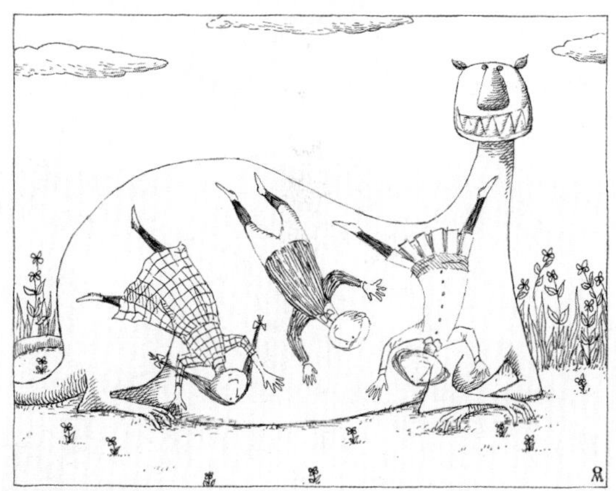

1-inch (2.5-cm) piece vanilla bean
¼ oz (7.5 ml) 1:1 Simple Syrup (page 142)
3 dashes orange bitters
2 oz (60 ml) bourbon or other whisk(e)y
Squeeze of fresh orange juice (optional)
Garnish: Orange twist, vanilla bean

In a rocks glass, muddle the vanilla bean, simple syrup, and orange bitters with a muddler or wooden pestle. Add one large ice cube, then the bourbon. Stir gently. Top with a squeeze of orange to release the juice and citrus oils, if desired. Garnish with an orange twist and a vanilla bean.

B IS FOR BASIL JULEP

• MAKES 1 COCKTAIL • GLASS: JULEP OR ROCKS •

In this imaginative rendering of the letter *B* from Gorey's twisted alphabet masterpiece *The Gashlycrumb Tinies*, Basil appears small and forlorn between two giant bears. But there is nothing forlorn about a classis julep. Especially if it's serverd in a traditional, silver-plated julep cup.

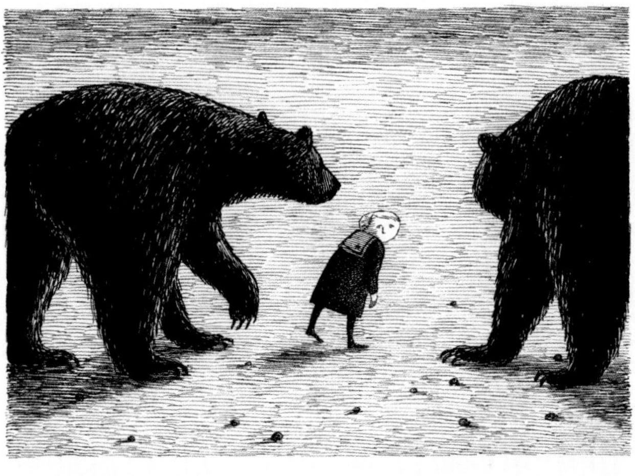

B is for BASIL assaulted by bears

Tipping our hat to poor little Basil, fresh basil stands in for mint in this Southern classic that is a staple at the Kentucky Derby. Tart lime calls out the anise green vivaciousness of basil leaves, gently muddled in the glass. The better the bourbon, the better the julep. Tightly packed crushed ice forms an almost snowcone-esque mound, keeping the whiskey from getting too quickly diluted and maintaining its cooling features on a hot day. For best effect, do not bruise the basil leaves, but muddle gently and minimally, just enough to release their aroma.

---

8 fresh basil leaves
¾ oz (20 ml) Basil Simple Syrup (page 145)
1½ oz (45 ml) bourbon
1 oz (30 ml) fresh lime juice
Garnish: Fresh basil leaf, lime wheel

Add the eight basil leaves and the basil simple syrup to a julep cup or rocks glass and gently muddle (do not bruise) with a muddler or wooden pestle. Pack the glass tightly with crushed ice. Add the bourbon and lime juice. Slightly stir until the glass is frosted on the outside and the liquids are just mixed. Top and pack with more crushed ice to form a dome. Garnish with a basil leaf and lime wheel.

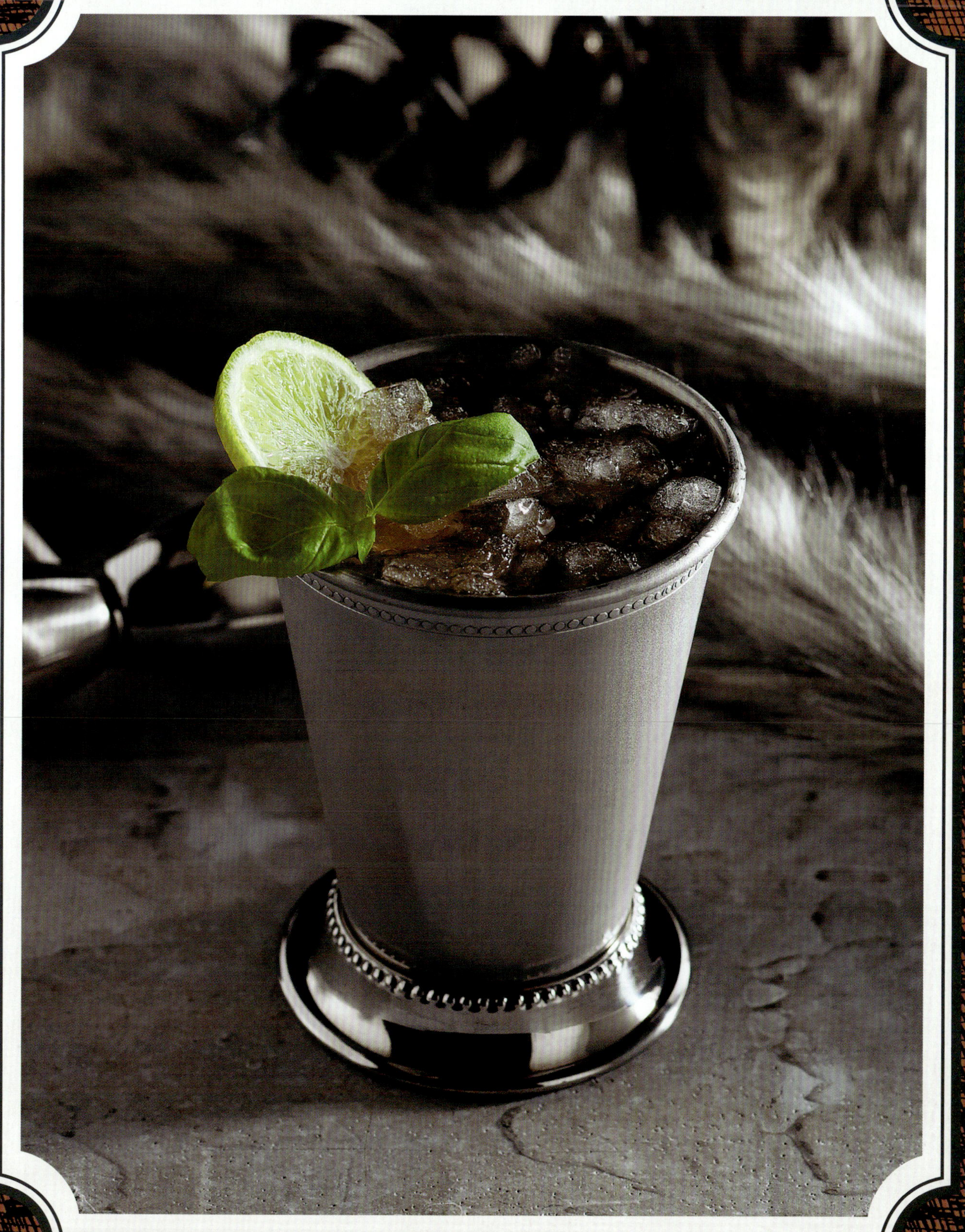

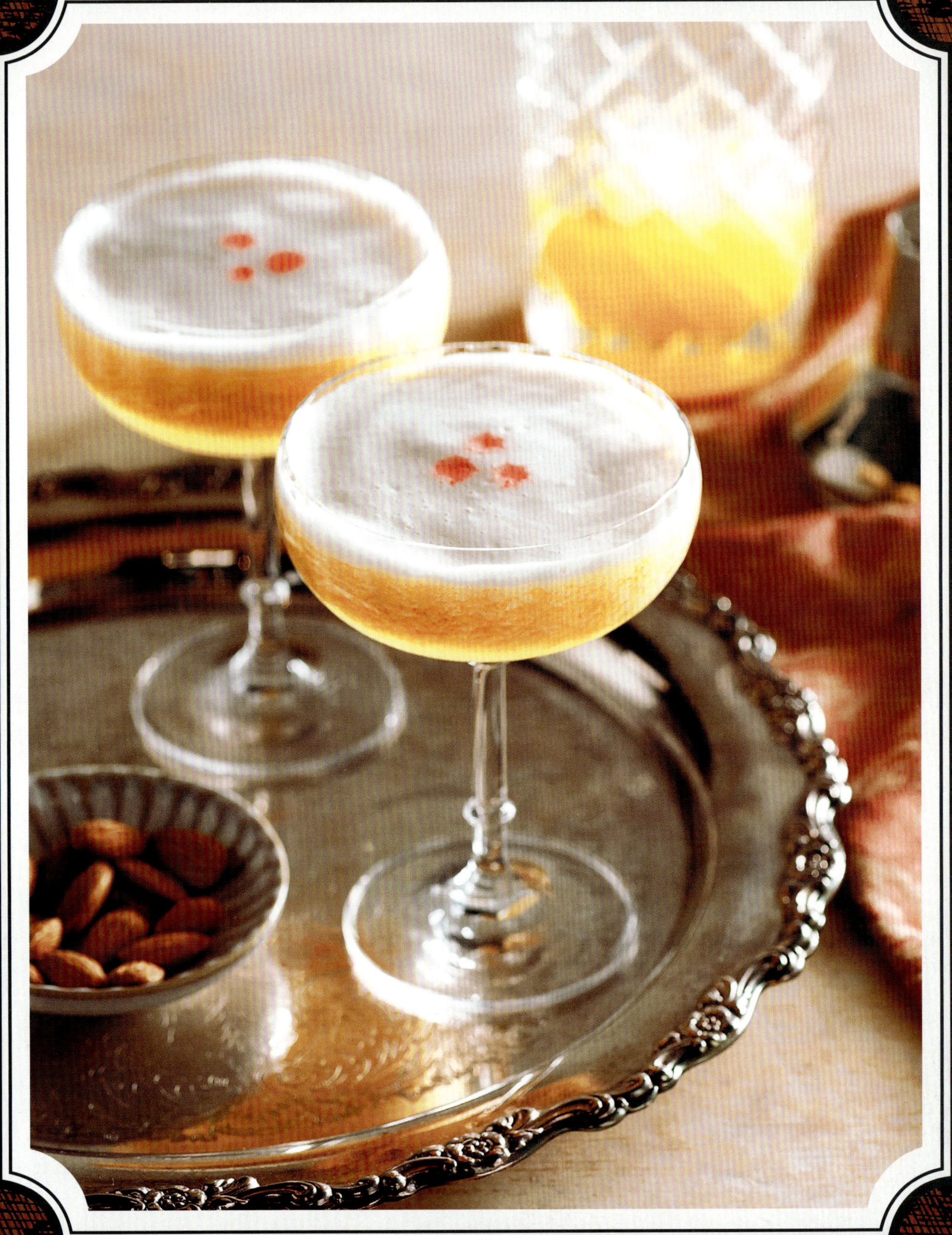

INSPIRED BY *The Admonitory Hippopotamus*

THE HIPPO'S FLIGHT

• MAKES 1 COCKTAIL • GLASS: COUPE •

In Gorey's *Admonitory Hippopotamus*, there is "bread pudding under the carpet," "forbidden jujubes," and "broiled champignons veneneux on toast." All are edible decadences as Angela spends a lifetime pursuing the intriguing "all is discovered" call of the Admonitory Hippopotamus.

A very different kind of decadence is tropical fruit. We take a jaunt to the majestic land of Peru, where the classic pisco sour is claimed to have been created. This unaged brandy cocktail is a straightforward yet magical, delicious combination of pisco, lime juice, and simple syrup, with Angostura bitters dotting the frothy egg white. Here, we toast Angela's raft adventures with this vibrant classic.

- 2½ oz (75 ml) pisco
- ¾ oz (20 ml) passion fruit purée or juice
- ½ oz (15 ml) fresh lime juice
- 1 oz (30 ml) 1:1 Simple Syrup (page 142)
- 1 egg white
- Garnish: Peychaud's bitters

In a cocktail shaker, combine the pisco, passion fruit purée, lime juice, simple syrup, and egg white and vigorously dry shake, or shake the cocktail without ice, for 30–40 seconds. Add ice and shake vigorously for another 40–50 seconds, until frothy. Strain into a coupe glass with the egg white resting on top of the drink. Dot the frothy top with Peychaud's bitters to garnish.

NOTE

For the passion fruit, use frozen The Perfect Purée passion fruit from Napa or Liquid Alchemist's passion fruit syrup. For more floral aromatics, use an Italia grape varietal pisco like Barsol. With passion fruit, use Peychaud's instead of the classic Angostura bitters typical in a pisco sour.

THE DOUBTFUL GUEST

• MAKES 1 COCKTAIL • GLASS: ROCKS •

The Doubtful Guest came and showed "no intention of going away." From eating all the syrup and toast—and part of the plate—to tearing out whole chapters from books, this curious character caused disruption and brought consternation to the entire household, "seemingly deaf to whatever they said."

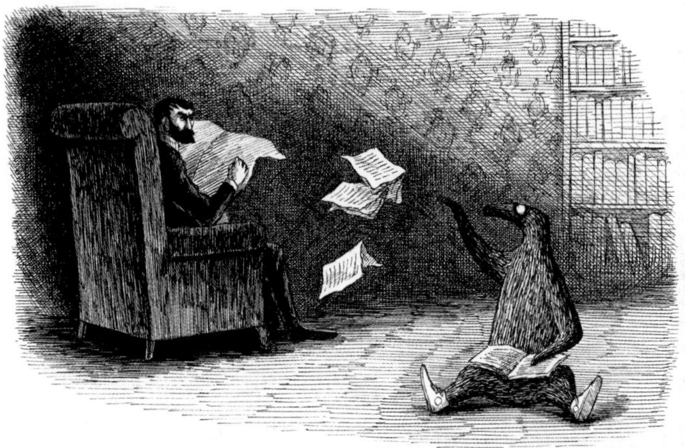

At times it would tear out whole chapters from books, Or put roomfuls of pictures askew on their hooks.

There's no consternation in a classic Sazerac, however. Sister to the old fashioned, the Sazerac combines rye whiskey or brandy, bitters, sugar, and absinthe. While brandy is reputedly the O.G. version, instead of cognac, we mix it up with one of cognac's French cousins, Calvados apple brandy. This fall-like drink with herbaceous absinthe intrigue may not help get rid of a Doubtful Guest, as any guest would like to linger over this apple orchard–evoking sipper.

---

1 demerara sugar cube
2 dashes Peychaud's bitters
2 dashes apple bitters
2 oz (60 ml) Calvados apple brandy
Absinthe to rinse glass
Garnish: Apple slice

Fill a rocks glass with ice and set aside. In a pint or mixing glass, add the sugar cube and soak it with both bitters, then muddle with a muddler or wooden pestle. Add the Calvados and stir until the sugar dissolves. Add ice, then stir for 20–30 seconds, until well chilled. Remove the ice from the rocks glass. Pour in a few drops of absinthe, then swirl to coat the glass. Strain the cocktail from the pint or mixing glass into the prepared rocks glass over one large ice cube. Garnish with an apple slice.

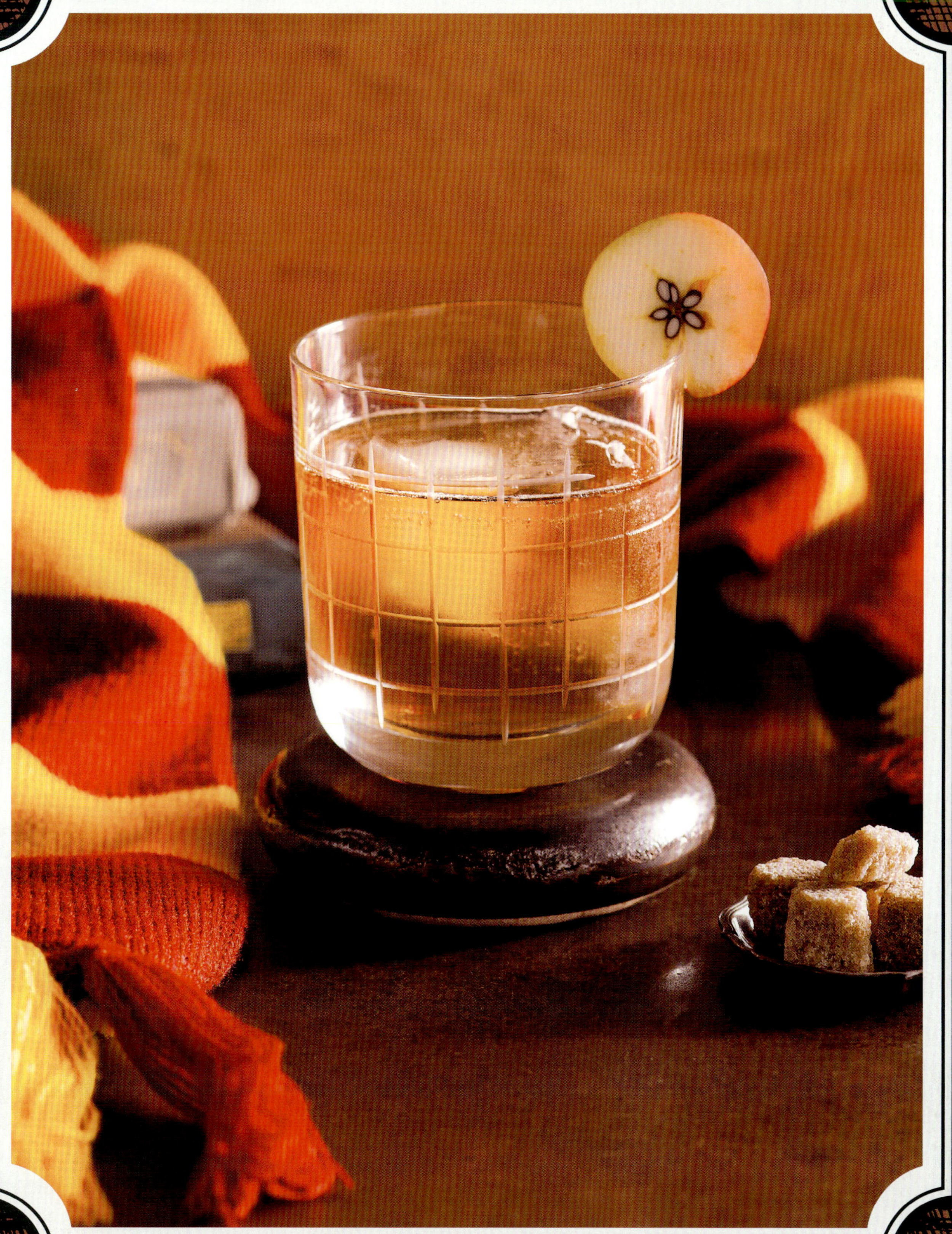

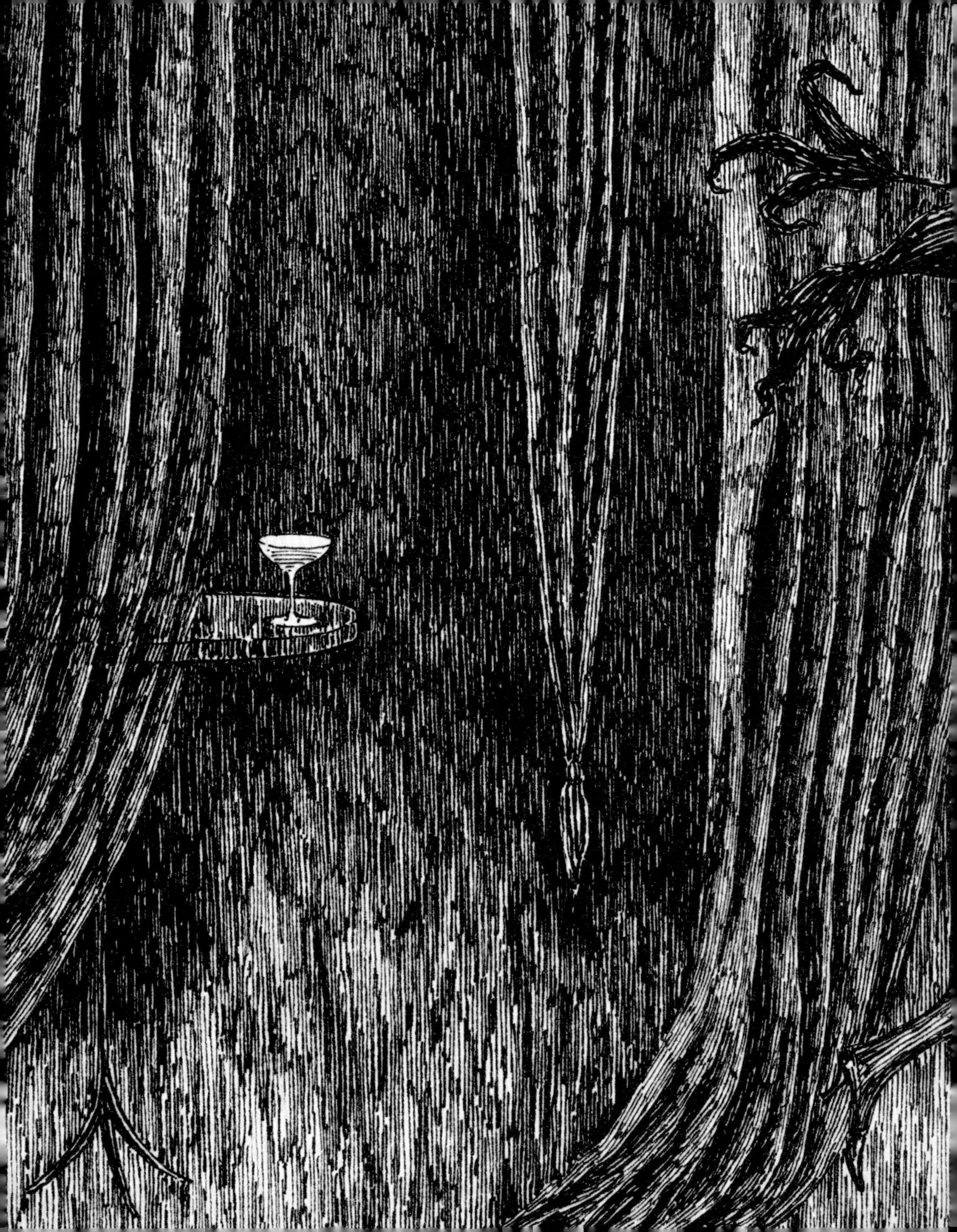

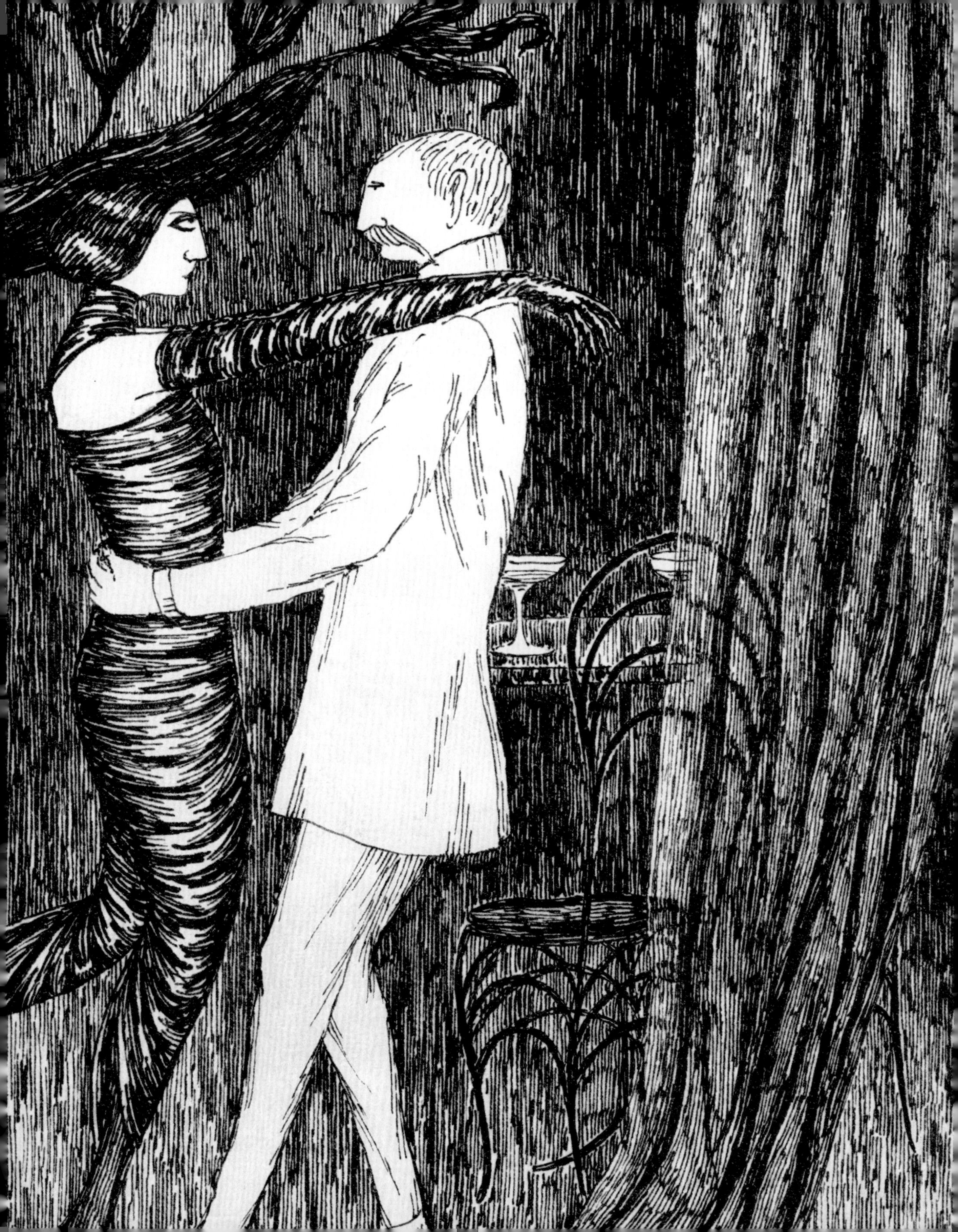

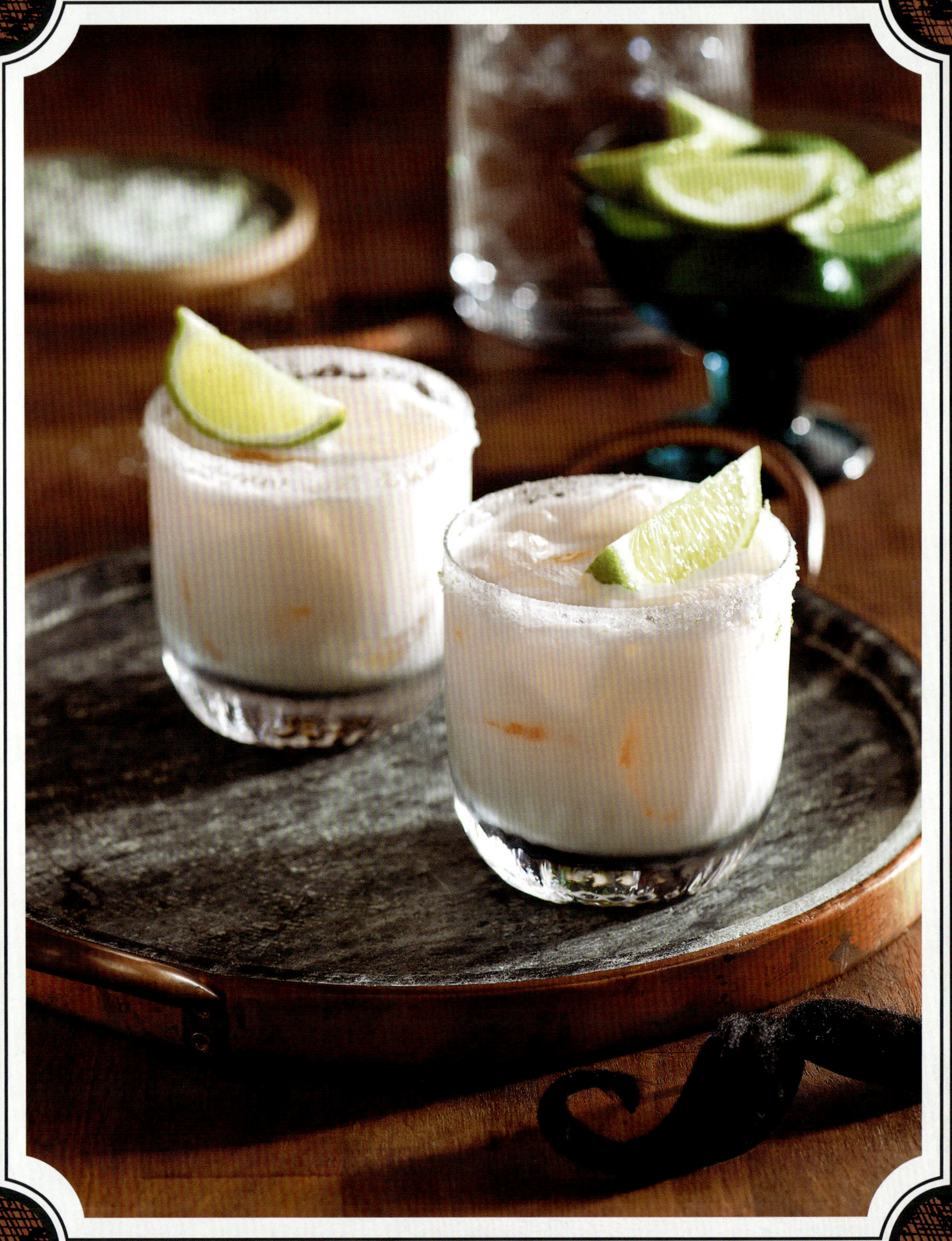

INSPIRED BY *Serious Life: A Cruise*

LETTICE AND HEREWARD

MAKES 1 COCKTAIL • GLASS: ROCKS

This colorful little tale, the lovely Lettice meets Honorable Hereward Lyke-Wake on a cruise and becomes "enraptured by the splendour of his mustache." Until all was ruined when Lettice discovered her new lover was really the pilfering thief named Harold Foop. Though Foop was "hauled below," Lettice had already given up and in the end of this sad story, she throws herself over the railing.

Yes, it's a tragic end for poor Lettice, but this creamy, bright, coconut-lime margarita is a nod to the happier days when Lettice and Hereward were first falling in love. This sunny drink goes down all too easy, never over the edge, as our heroine Lettice was.

Rim: Sea salt, grated lime zest, sugar, lime wedge

2 oz (60 ml) coconut cream or cream of coconut

1½ oz (45 ml) blanco tequila

1 oz (30 ml) fresh lime juice

½ oz (15 ml) Cointreau or orange curaçao

¼ oz (7.5 ml) 1:1 Simple Syrup (page 142)

Garnish: Lime wedge

On a small plate, combine equal parts salt, lime zest, and sugar and spread in an even layer. Gently rub the lime wedge around the rim of a rocks glass. Holding the base of the glass, dip the rim into the salt mixture. Place in the refrigerator until ready to use. Just before serving, fill the glass with ice.

In a cocktail shaker filled with ice, combine the coconut cream, tequila, lime juice, Cointreau, and simple syrup. Cover and shake vigorously for 30–40 seconds, or until well chilled. Strain into the ice-filled glass. Garnish with a lime wedge.

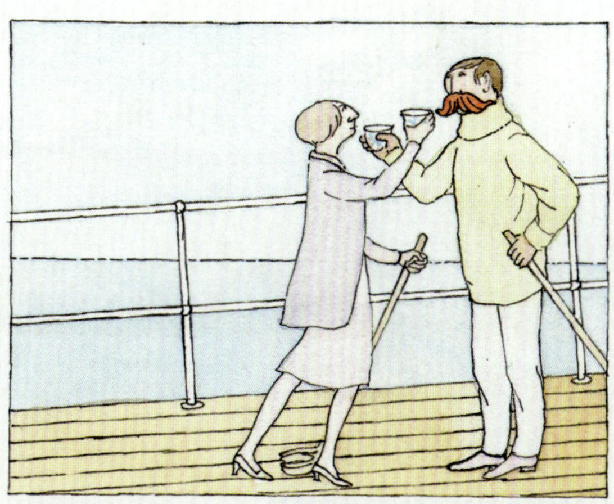

They played shuffleboard and drank cups of bouillon by day.

INSPIRED BY *The Chinese Obelisk*

J WAS THE JAM

• MAKES 1 COCKTAIL • GLASS: JULEP OR ROCKS •

Yet again, the ever-complex alphabet informs Gorey's work, here in *The Chinese Obelisk*, a series of twenty-six letter-driven drawings as "an Author went for a walk." We jump to "J was the Jam that he gave it to leave," as the Author under A gives a jar of jam to I's "Infant who clung to his sleeve."

Jam cocktails are a winning style of drink where a barspoon of jam adds sweet intrigue when properly shaken in a cocktail. Fine straining is crucial to keep the jam from clumping in this nonalcoholic drink, a riff on a classic bramble cocktail, created in 1984 by famed London bartender Dick Bradsell. Served over crushed ice, often in a julep cup, the bramble was inspired by berries that Bradsell picked growing up on England's Isle of Wight. His original cocktail features gin, fresh lemon juice, simple syrup, and crème de mure (blackberry liqueur), while yogurt imparts creaminess, lightened by the citrus and a happy partner to many a jam.

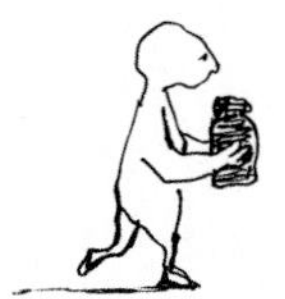

- 2 barspoons blackberry (or other fruit) jam
- 2 barspoons Greek/plain yogurt
- 1 oz (30 ml) fresh lemon juice
- 2 oz (60 ml) water (or gin for alcoholic version)
- Garnish: Fresh blackberries or other fruit, fresh mint sprig

In a cocktail shaker, combine the jam, yogurt, lemon juice, and water. Add ice. Cover and shake vigorously for 40–50 seconds, until well chilled and the yogurt and jam are thoroughly mixed. Fine strain into a julep cup or rocks glass filled with crushed ice. Garnish with blackberries and mint. Add a straw.

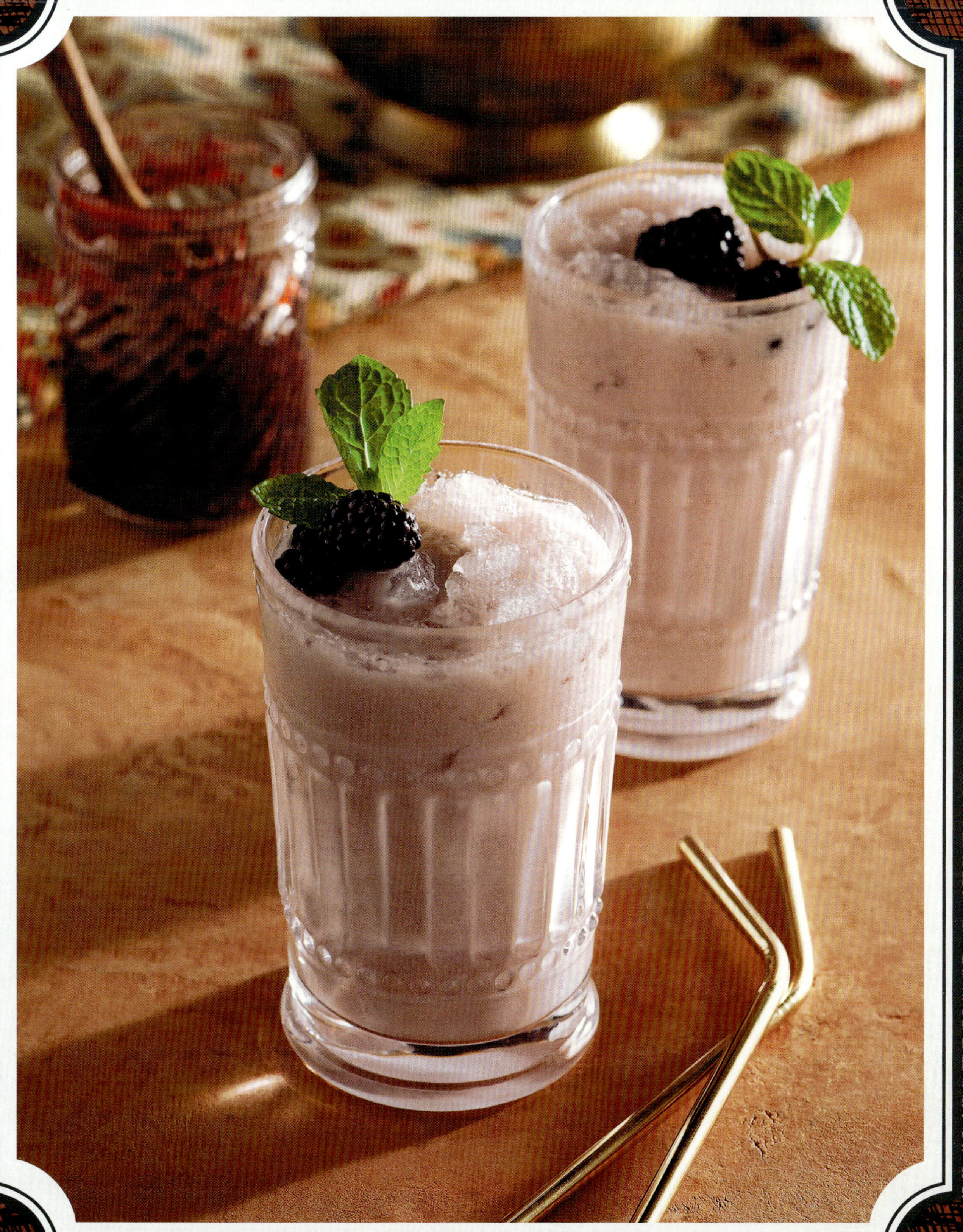

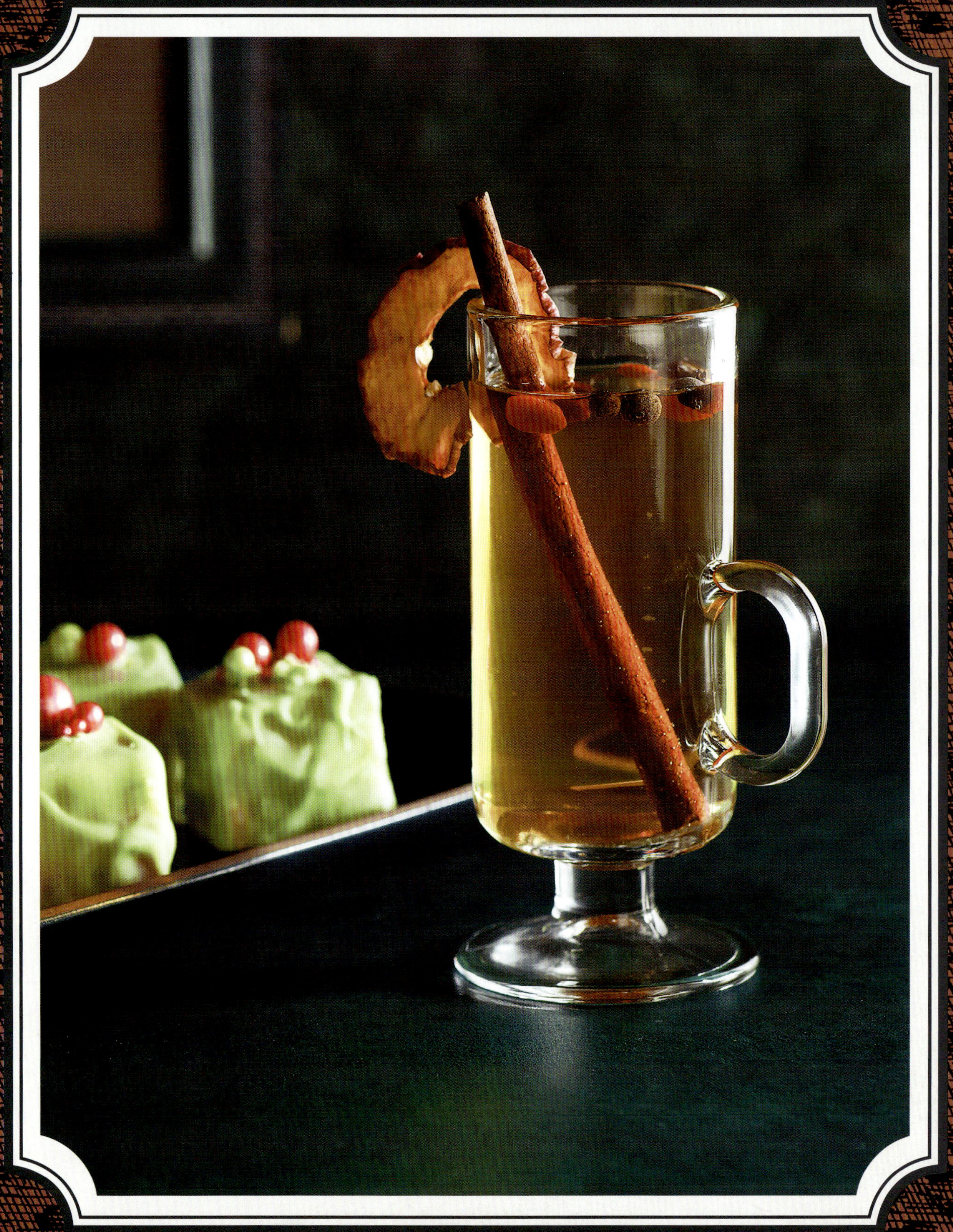

INSPIRED BY *The Object-Lesson*

THE THROBBLEFOOT SPECTRE

• MAKES 1 COCKTAIL • GLASS: MUG OR HEATPROOF GLASS •

The Throbblefoot Spectre haunts Gorey's *The Object-Lesson* in a tale where "his lordship" goes out to await the arrival of autumn. After presenting a "length of string" to the Spectre, who passes it "on to the statue of Corrupted Endeavour," his lordship meets a cast of characters, including Madame O——, who "flung herself over the parapet." In the end, they all retired for a teatime where they are served cakes "iced a peculiar shade of green."

We welcome the spirit of autumn with a nonalcoholic cardamom apple pie cider sipper. Dried apple, orange, goji berries, and cardamom pods impart a spiced apple pie vibe to cider or apple juice. The drink is best with a high-quality, fresh apple cider, ideally sourced locally from an orchard in season. Any of the garnishes can be added to the pot to steep and intensify the flavors.

¾ cup (180 ml) nonalcoholic apple cider or apple juice/cider

1½ teaspoons dried goji berries

2 oz (38.75 g) maple syrup

½ oz (15 g) dried apple slices

¼ oz (7.5 g) dried orange slices

4 whole cloves

2 cardamom pods

Garnish: Cinnamon stick, whole nutmeg, whole allspice, or dried apple or orange slices

---

In a small pan over medium-low heat, combine the apple cider, goji berries, maple syrup, apple slices, orange slices, cloves, and cardamom and simmer for 10 minutes, until heated through. Once the flavors have infused to your liking, strain into a mug or heatproof glass. Garnish with a cinnamon stick, whole nutmeg, whole allspice, or dried apple or orange slices.

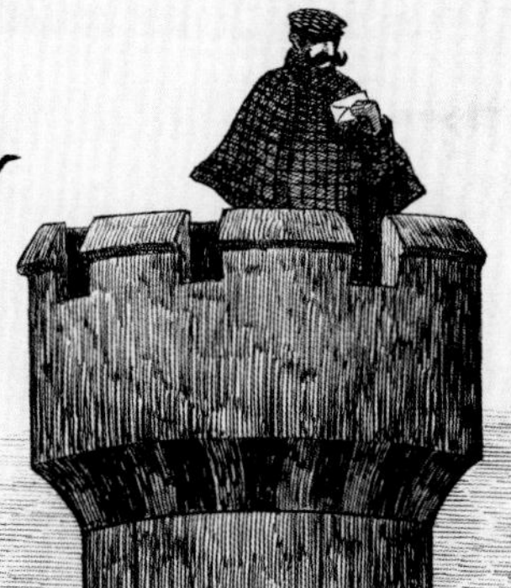

THE FRIVOLOUS BUG

• MAKES 1 COCKTAIL • GLASS: COLLINS OR WINEGLASS •

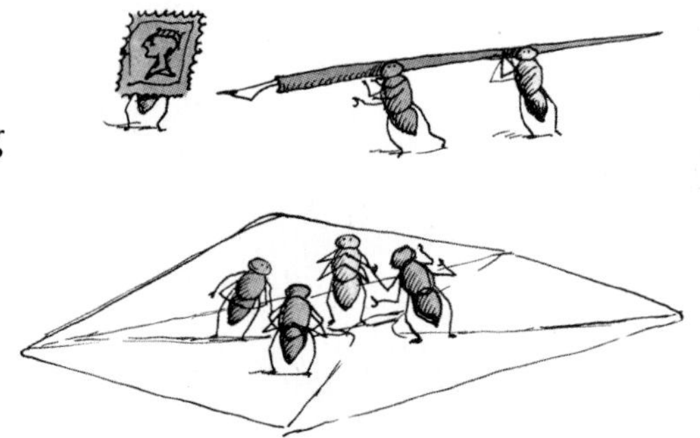

In Gorey's *The Bug Book*, we meet a group of colorful bugs being frivolous, pensive, and busy. All "were on the friendliest possible terms," reveling and embarking on excursions together until a giant black bug "broke up their parties." Together in a secret meeting they took care of the black bug as a community, then resumed their party, "complete with cake crumbs and raspberry punch."

To celebrate with our crew of blue, red, and yellow bugs, we present a nonalcoholic, effervescent rosé spritzer that looks not unlike raspberry punch. Try a quality dry nonalcoholic rosé wine like Sovi, Joyus Non-Alcoholic Rosé, Proxies Pink Salt, or Noughty Non-Alcoholic Sparkling Rosé. Bubbly and refreshing, the spritzer can also be made with a regular rosé wine if you desire alcohol. Either way, take a cue from the bugs and enjoy yourself "immensely."

---

4 oz (120 ml) nonalcoholic dry rosé wine, chilled

2 oz (60 ml) fresh pink grapefruit juice

Club soda, chilled, to top

Garnish: Fresh thyme sprig, fresh raspberries

Combine the rosé and grapefruit juice in a Collins glass or wineglass over ice. Top off with the desired amount of club soda. Rub a thyme sprig between your fingers to release its oils. Add to the drink and use as a swizzle stick to stir. Garnish with fresh raspberries.

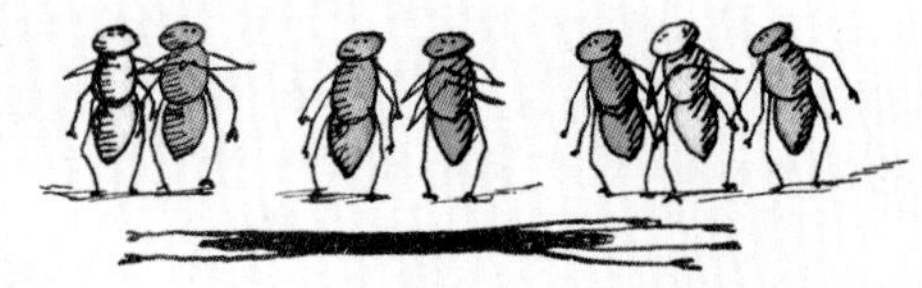

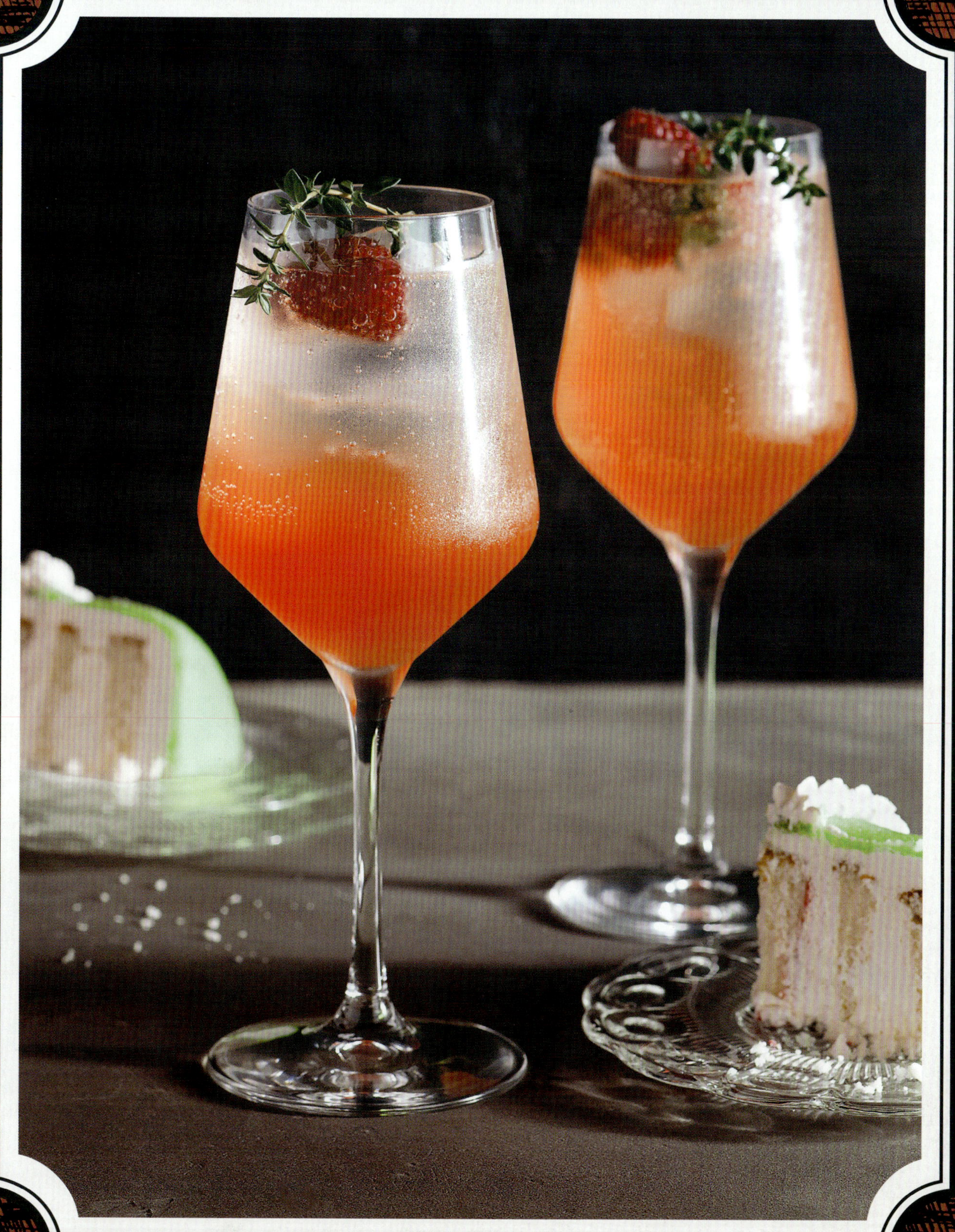

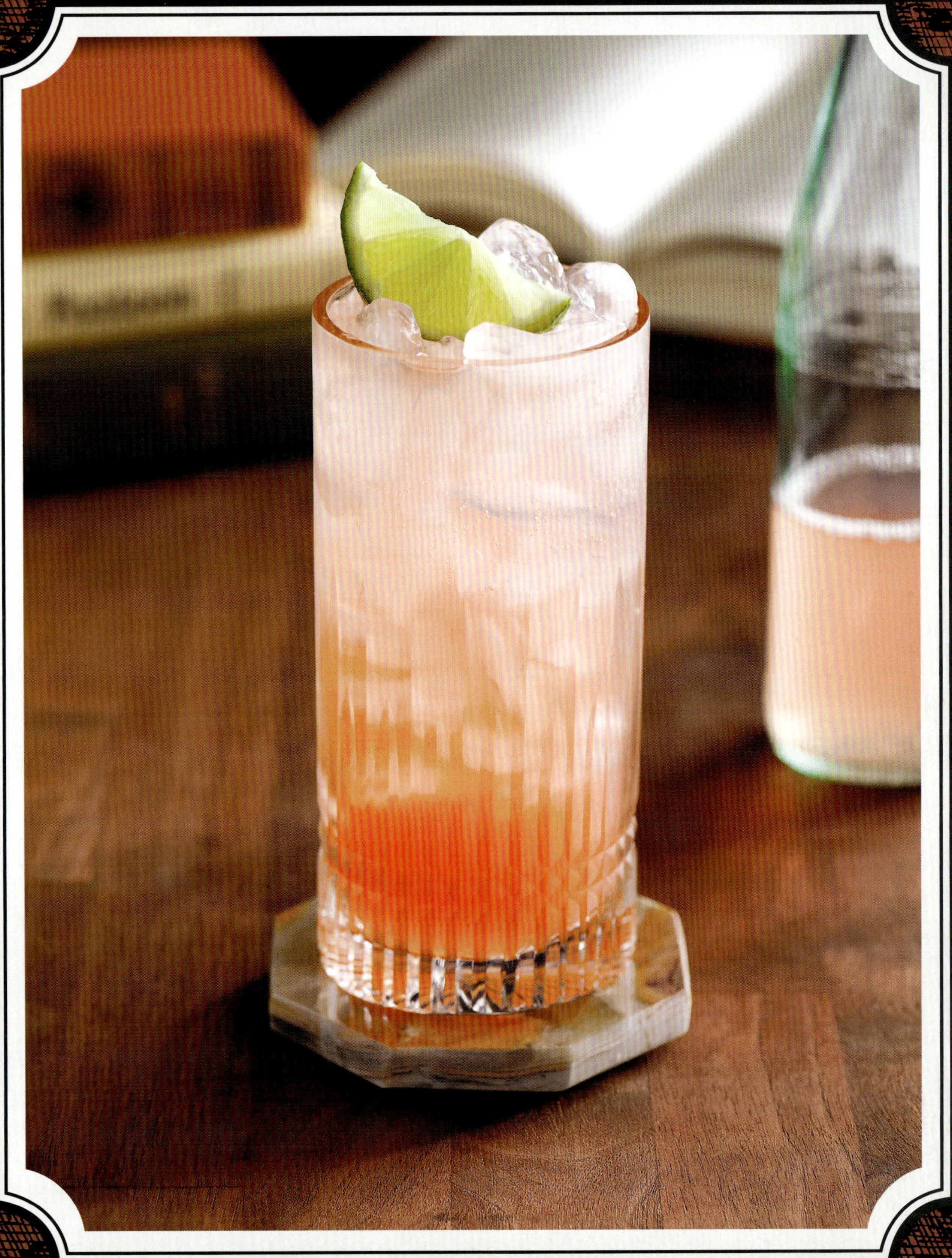

MR. EARBRASS'S FAUX-LOMA

• MAKES 1 COCKTAIL • GLASS: COLLINS OR HIGHBALL •

In Gorey's *The Unstrung Harp*, Mr. C(lavius) F(rederick) Earbrass's Faux-Loma is a well-dressed character who toils on his book, from translation to galleys that he reviews "with mingled excitement and disgust." Though legendary novelists like Hemingway are infamous for drinking to excess as they wrote, this alcohol-free twist on a classic Paloma just might help you get through writer's block or deadlines with a clear head.

One of Mexico's most beloved cocktails, the Paloma is a tequila and grapefruit crusher that is typically made with Squirt grapefruit soda. Especially sans tequila, it helps to use a quality grapefruit soda. Try grapefruit-flavored Jarritos Mexican soda or Fever-Tree or London Essence's grapefruit sodas. Either way, a little sea salt sharpens the flavor profile and imparts savory backbone to the bitter grapefruit and tart lime.

---

2 oz (60 ml) fresh grapefruit juice
1 oz (30 ml) fresh lime juice
1 oz (30 ml) 1:1 Simple Syrup (page 142)
Sea salt
3–4 oz (90–120 ml) grapefruit soda
Garnish: Lime wedge

In a cocktail shaker, combine the grapefruit juice, lime juice, simple syrup, and a pinch of sea salt. Add ice, cover, and shake vigorously for 8–10 seconds. Strain into a Collins or highball glass with ice. Top with the desired amount of grapefruit soda and garnish with the lime wedge.

FROM *The Unstrung Harp*

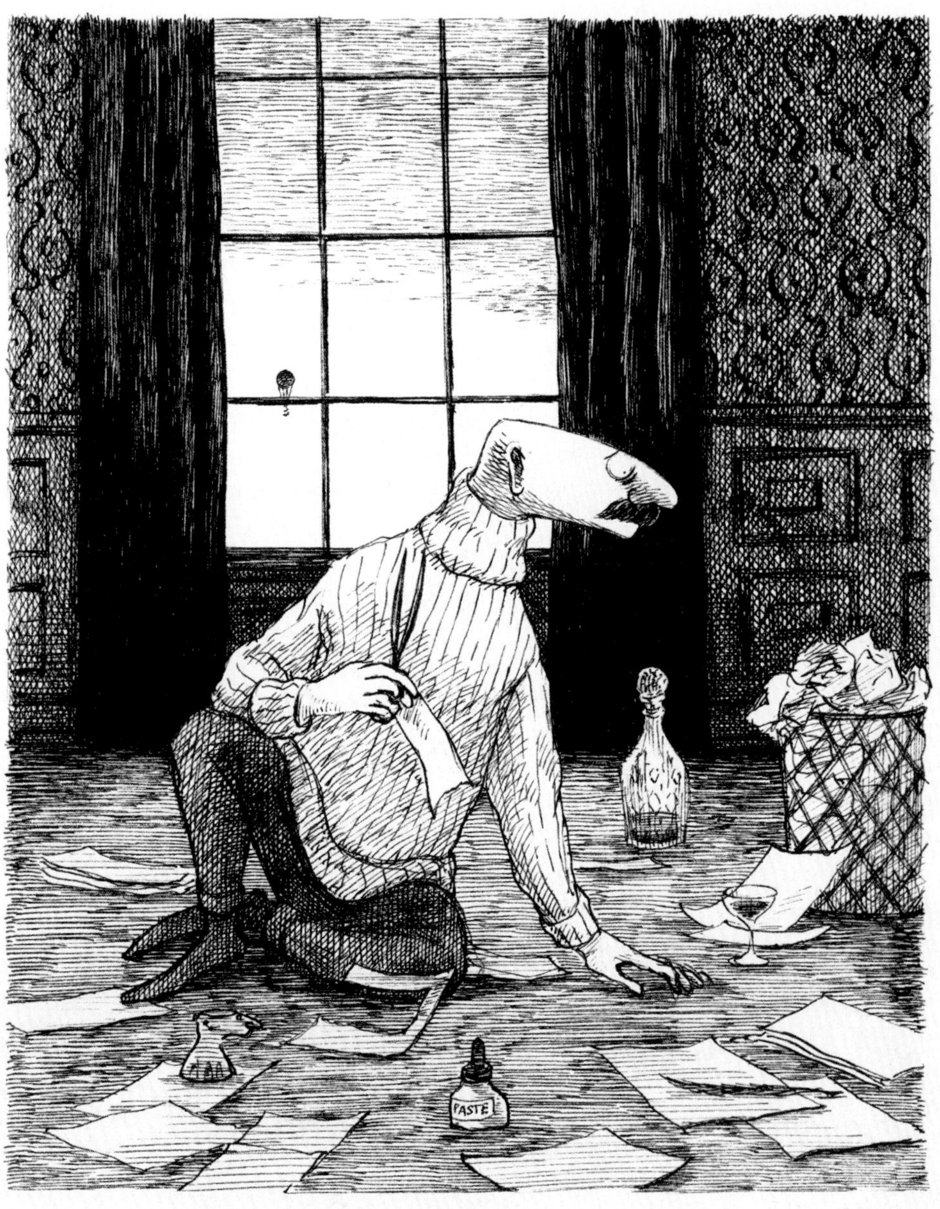

FROM *The Unstrung Harp*

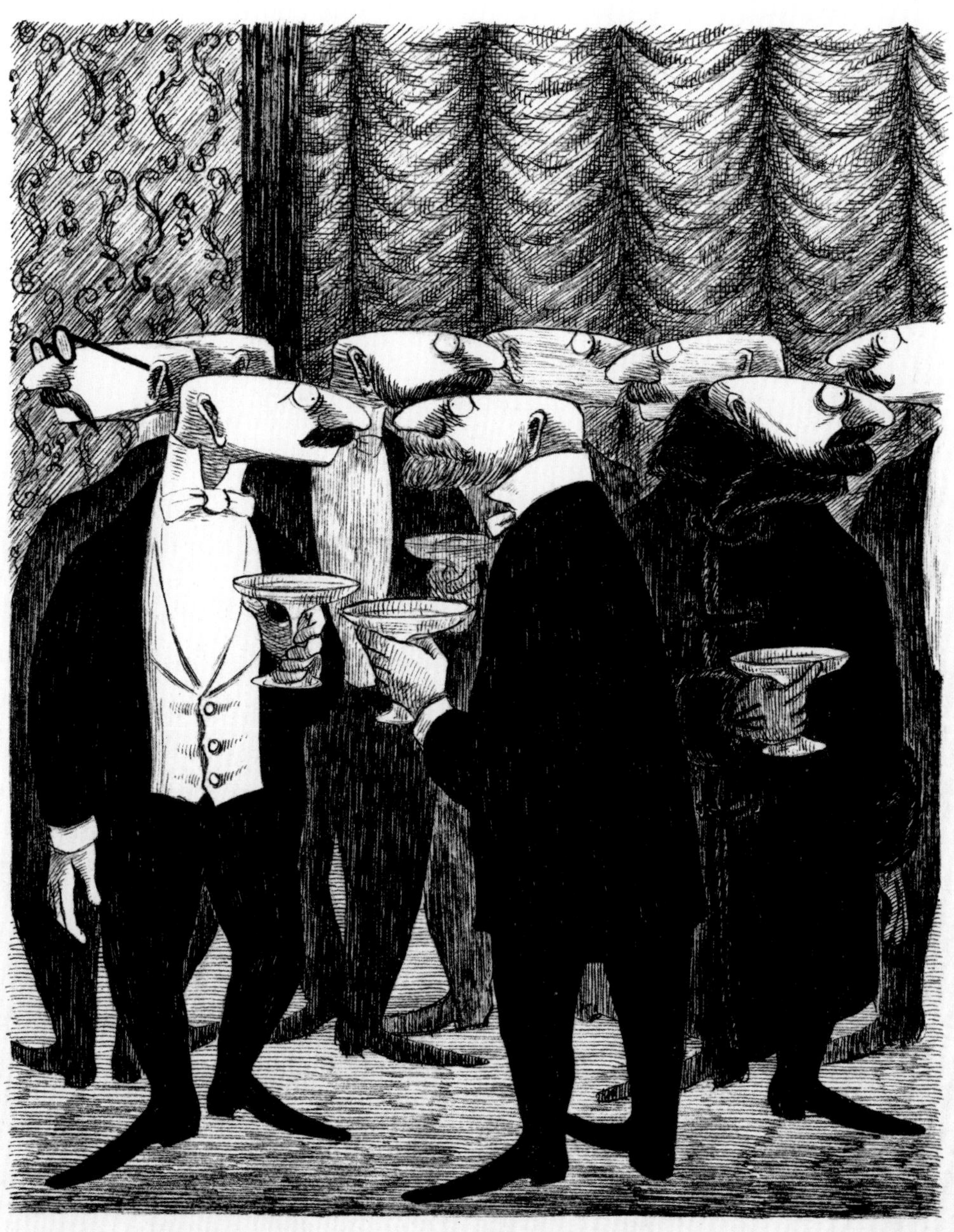

THE OSBICK

• MAKES 1 COCKTAIL • GLASS: COLLINS •

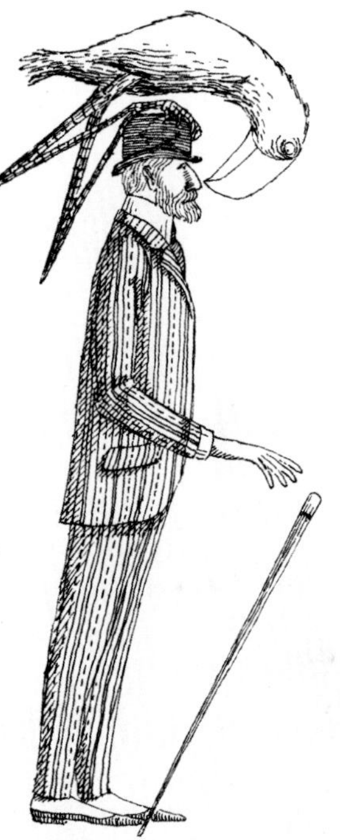

Gorey's osbick bird lands one day on Emblus Fingby's bowler hat: "It had not done so for a whim, / But meant to come and live with him." The two become fast friends, doing everything together: playing flute and lute, having tea atop a fictional zagava tree. They are partners for life, until "poor Emblus died / The obsick bird was by his side."

Tributing Emblus and the obsick bird's teatime in the treetops, this nonalcoholic cocktail is a bright, citrus-forward tipple showcasing yuzu, an Asian citrus with delicate, floral, softer lemon notes. Yuzu tea, also called yuja-cha or yuja tea, is made by mixing hot water and yuja-cheong, a yuzu marmalade. At your local Asian food market, look for yuzu tea or dehydrated yuzu peels blended with other flavors. Elderflower syrup imparts sweet, floral balance to sour, soft yuzu, while sea salt and togarashi contribute savory backbone and umami complexity to this refreshing drink.

Rim: 2 tablespoons togarashi, ⅓ cup (80 g) sea salt, lemon wedge

2 oz (60 ml) yuzu juice

4 oz (120 ml) yuzu tea, at room temperature

1 oz (30 ml) elderflower syrup

Soda water to top

Garnish: 2–3 jalapeño chile slices

On a small plate, mix together the togarashi and salt and spread in an even layer. Gently rub the lemon wedge around the rim of a Collins glass. Holding the base of the glass, dip the rim into the togarashi and salt mixture. Set the glass aside (leftover togarashi and salt mixture can be stored in an airtight jar).

In a cocktail shaker, combine the yuzu juice, yuzu tea, and elderflower syrup. Add ice, cover, and shake for 20–30 seconds, until well chilled. Strain the drink into the Collins glass filled with ice. Top with soda water. Garnish with jalapeño slices.

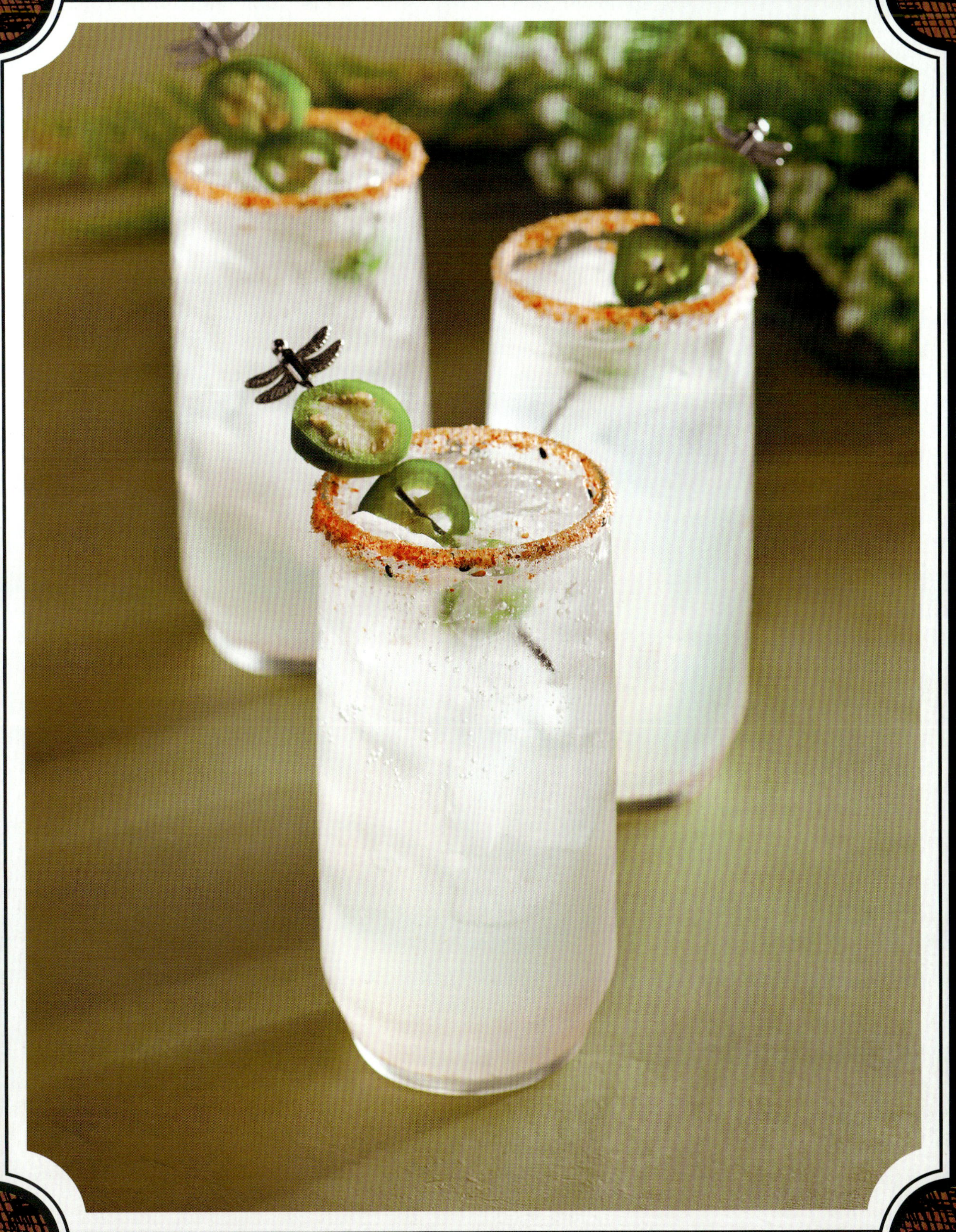

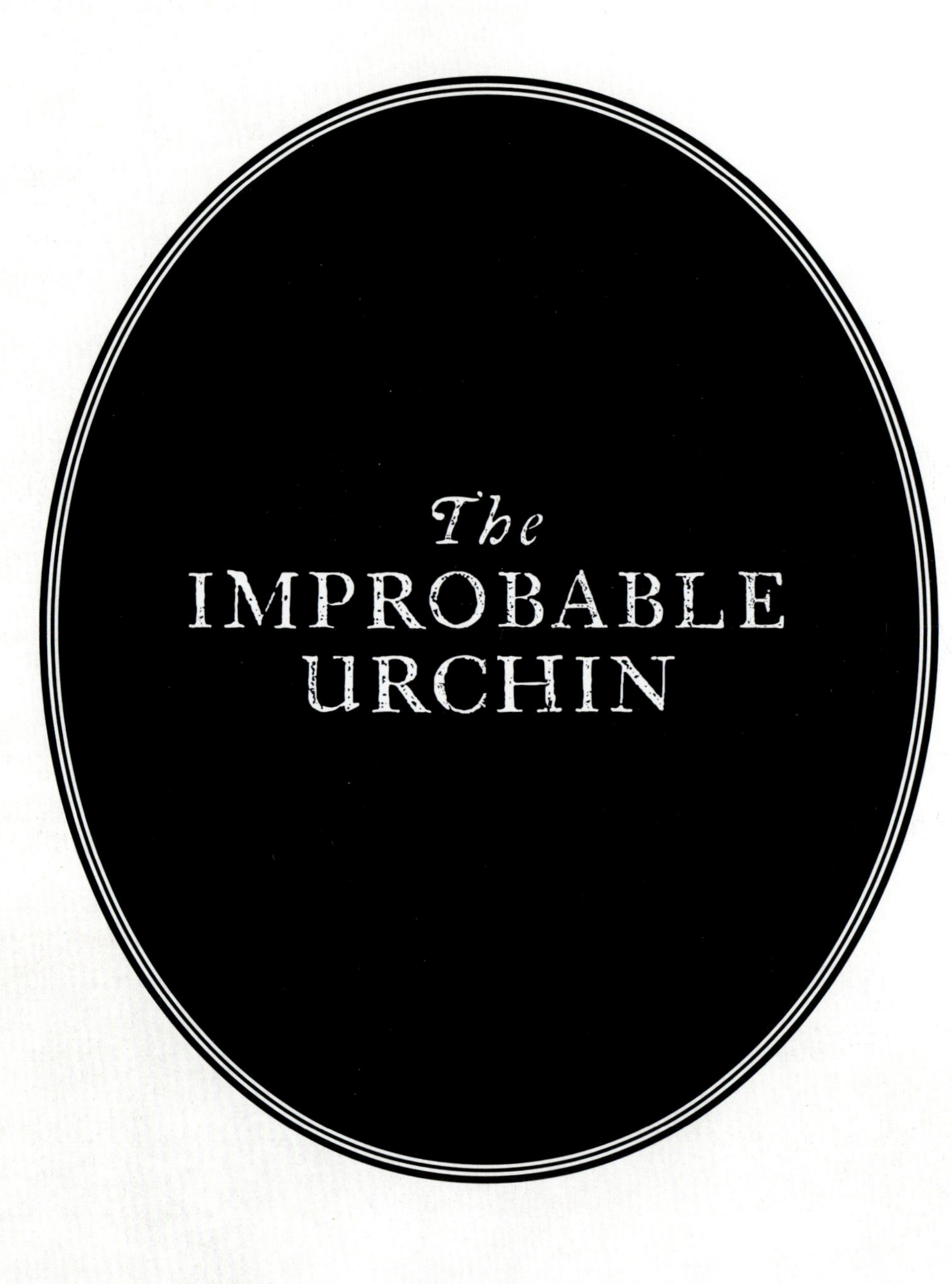

The IMPROBABLE URCHIN

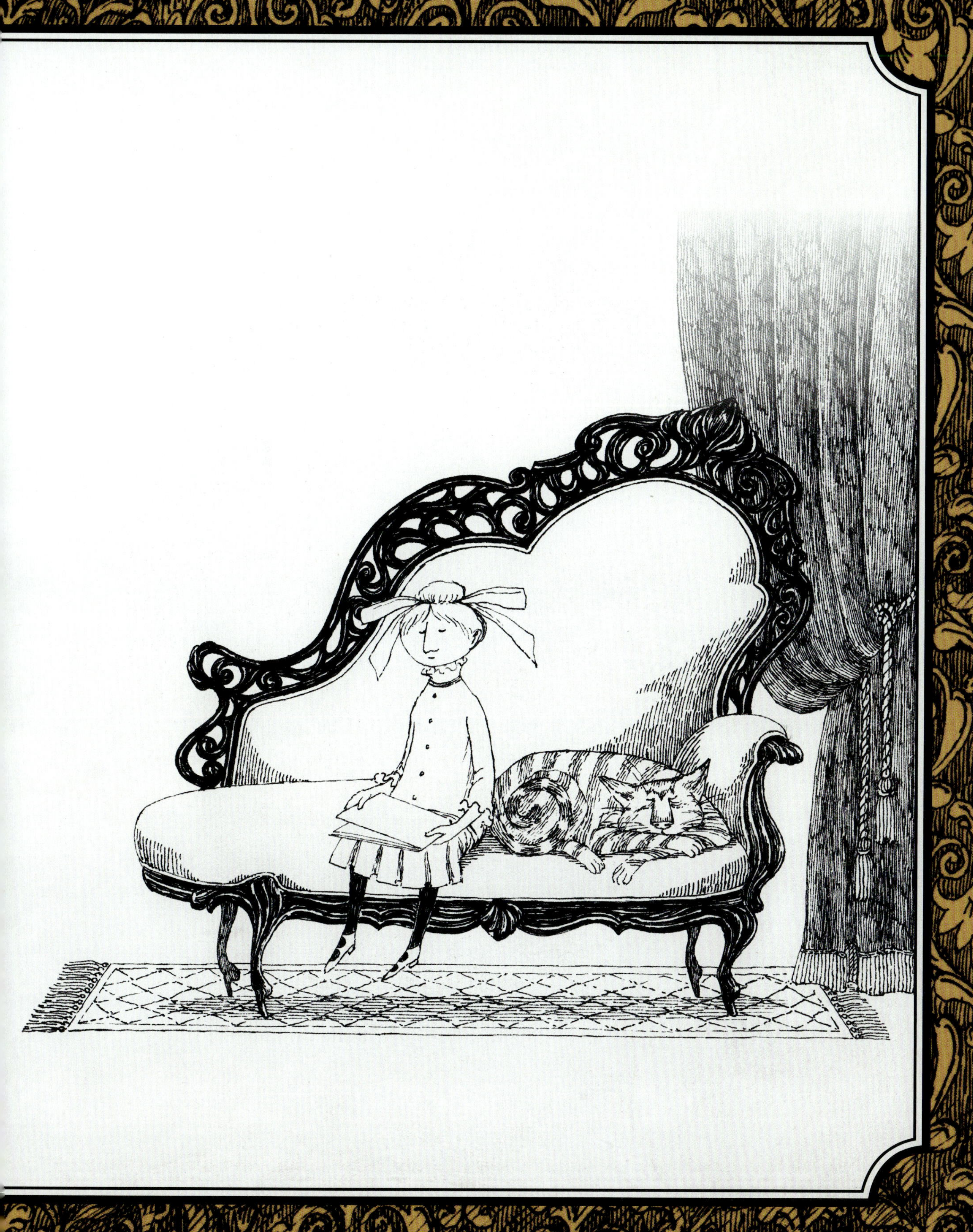

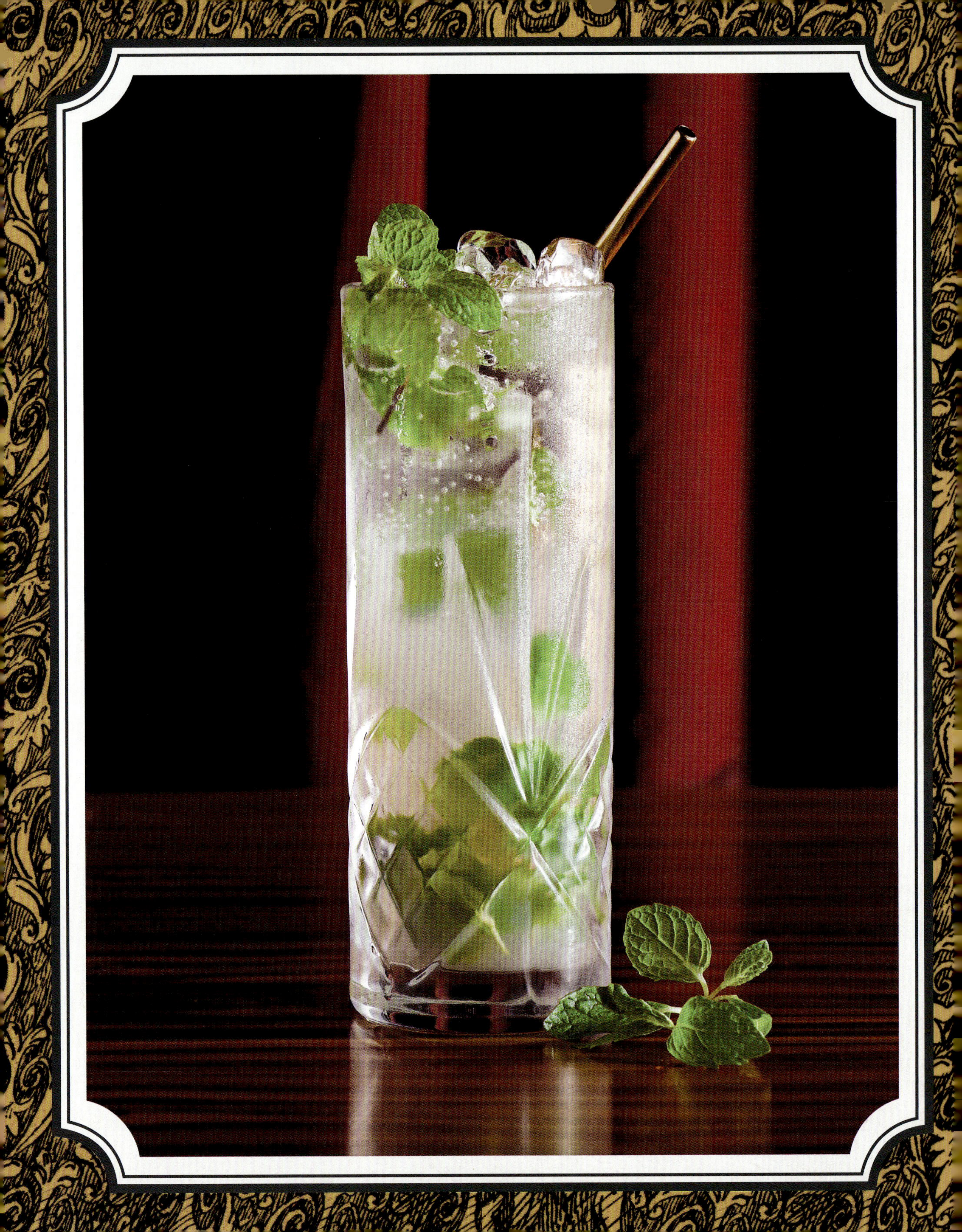

INSPIRED BY *The Gilded Bat*

MAUDIE'S MOJITO

MAKES 1 COCKTAIL • GLASS: COLLINS OR HIGHBALL •

Little Maudie grows from a five-year-old ballerina discovered by Madame Trepidovska to the adult Maud, an acclaimed ballet star. Baron de Zabrus "invited her to join his company, the most renowned in Europe," changing her name "to something more exotic:" Mirella Splatova. She became "the reigning ballerina of the age, and one of its symbols."

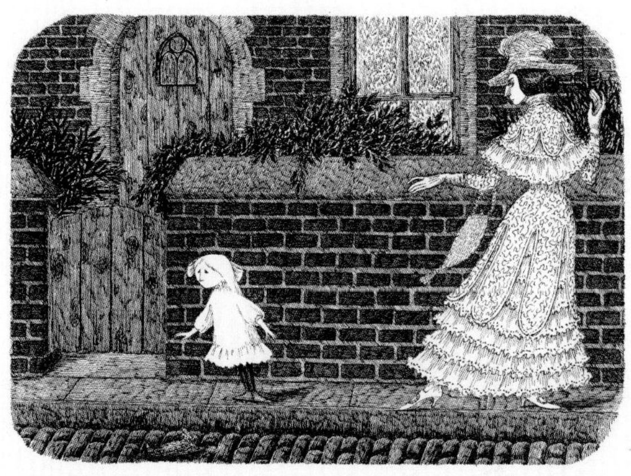

Ensuring Mirella Splatova is performance-ready, we pay tribute to her original, childhood name of Maudie in this zero-proof Mojito variation. The Mojito is one of the world's most beloved rum drinks, a Cuban-born combination of aguardiente (a pre-rum cane spirit), lime, mint, and sugar. Eventually, it morphed into using rum and was named the Mojito, first appearing in print in the 1932 edition of *Sloppy Joe's Bar Cocktail Manual.*

---

3 oz (90 ml) fresh lime juice
1 oz (30 ml) 1:1 Simple Syrup (page 142)
12 fresh mint leaves
3 oz (90 ml) club soda
Garnish: Fresh mint spring

In a Collins or highball glass, combine the lime juice, simple syrup, and mint leaves. Adjust the simple syrup up for greater sweetness, down for a more sour, dry tipple.

Muddle the mint leaves gently (do not bruise) with a muddler or wooden pestle. Fill the glass with ice, then slowly top with the club soda. Gently stir to blend. Garnish with a mint sprig.

NOTE

Add 1½ ounces (45 ml) of white rum if alcohol is preferred and reduce the club soda.

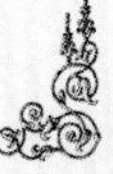

INSPIRED BY *The Hapless Child*

CHARLOTTE SOPHIA'S PALOMA

• MAKES 1 COCKTAIL • GLASS: COLLINS •

The Hapless Child tells the truly sad tale of Charlotte Sophia, who lived a life of hardship and horror that echoes the tones of *Jane Eyre*. Her long-lost, believed-dead father finally finds his daughter in the end, but it is too late. "She was so changed, he did not recognize her." Though a tragic story, this breezy, herbaceous drink honors the early days of joy when Charlotte Sophia lived with her "kind and well-to-do" parents and her beloved doll Hortense.

For this spin on the Paloma, blanco tequila is the most refreshing option, but try a reposado tequila if you prefer a richer, slightly woody flavor note. A quality grapefruit soda makes all the difference. The Paloma also works beautifully with rosemary or thyme instead of tarragon. If you prefer it to veer toward the spicy, add a dash of firewater or chili bitters.

Rim: Sea salt, grapefruit wedge

2 fresh tarragon sprigs

2 oz (60 ml) blanco tequila

2 oz (60 ml) fresh grapefruit juice

1 oz (30 ml) fresh lime juice

½ oz (15 ml) Tarragon Simple Syrup (page 145)

1 oz (30 ml) club soda

Garnish: Fresh tarragon sprig, grapefruit wedge

On a small plate, spread the salt in an even layer. Gently rub a grapefruit wedge around the rim of a Collins glass. Holding the base of the glass, dip the rim into the salt. Fill the glass with ice.

In a cocktail shaker, muddle the two tarragon sprigs with a muddler or wooden pestle. Add the tequila, grapefruit juice, lime juice, tarragon simple syrup, and ice. Cover and shake vigorously for 20–30 seconds, until well chilled. Strain into the rimmed glass over ice. Top with the desired amount of club soda. Garnish with a tarragon sprig and grapefruit wedge.

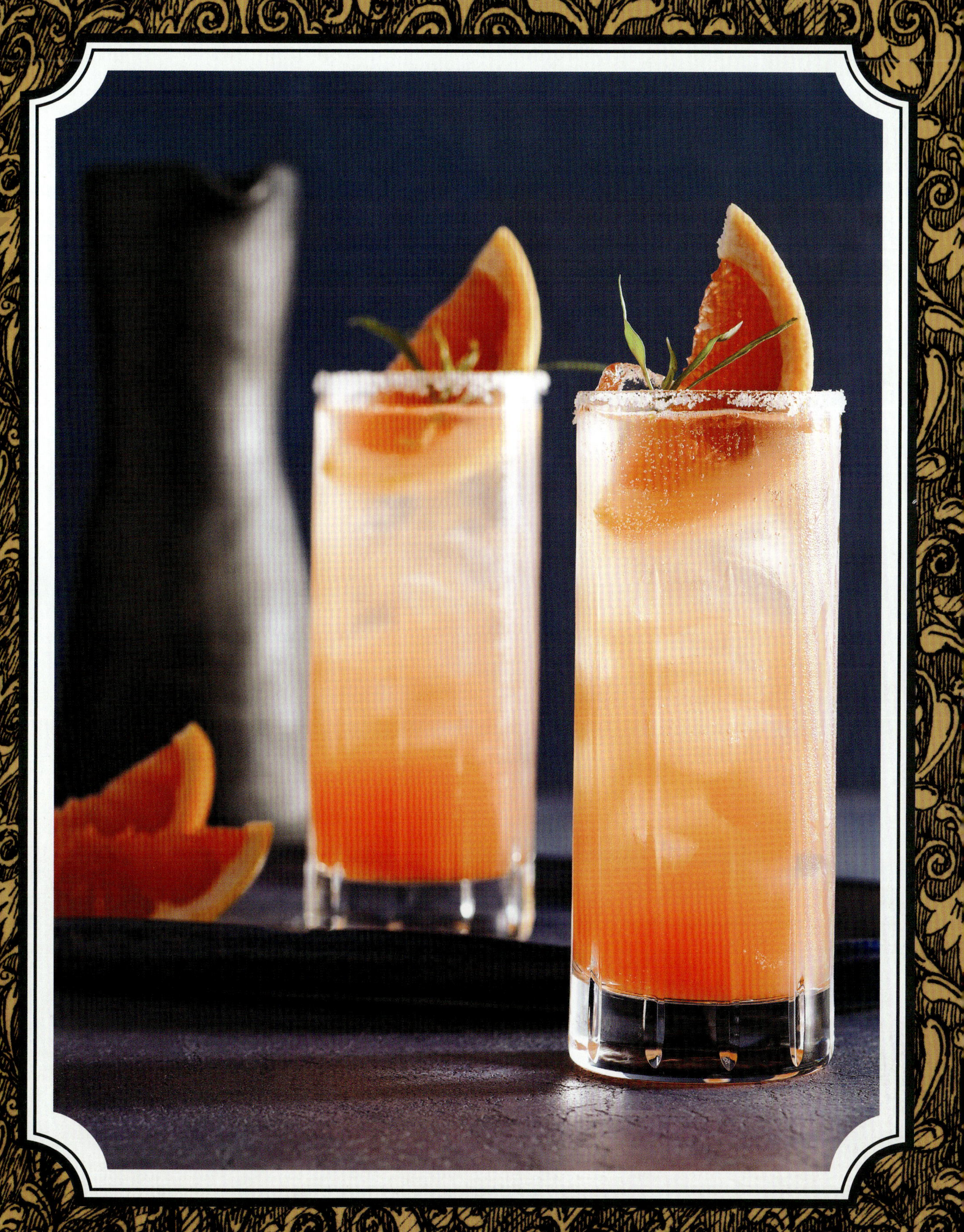

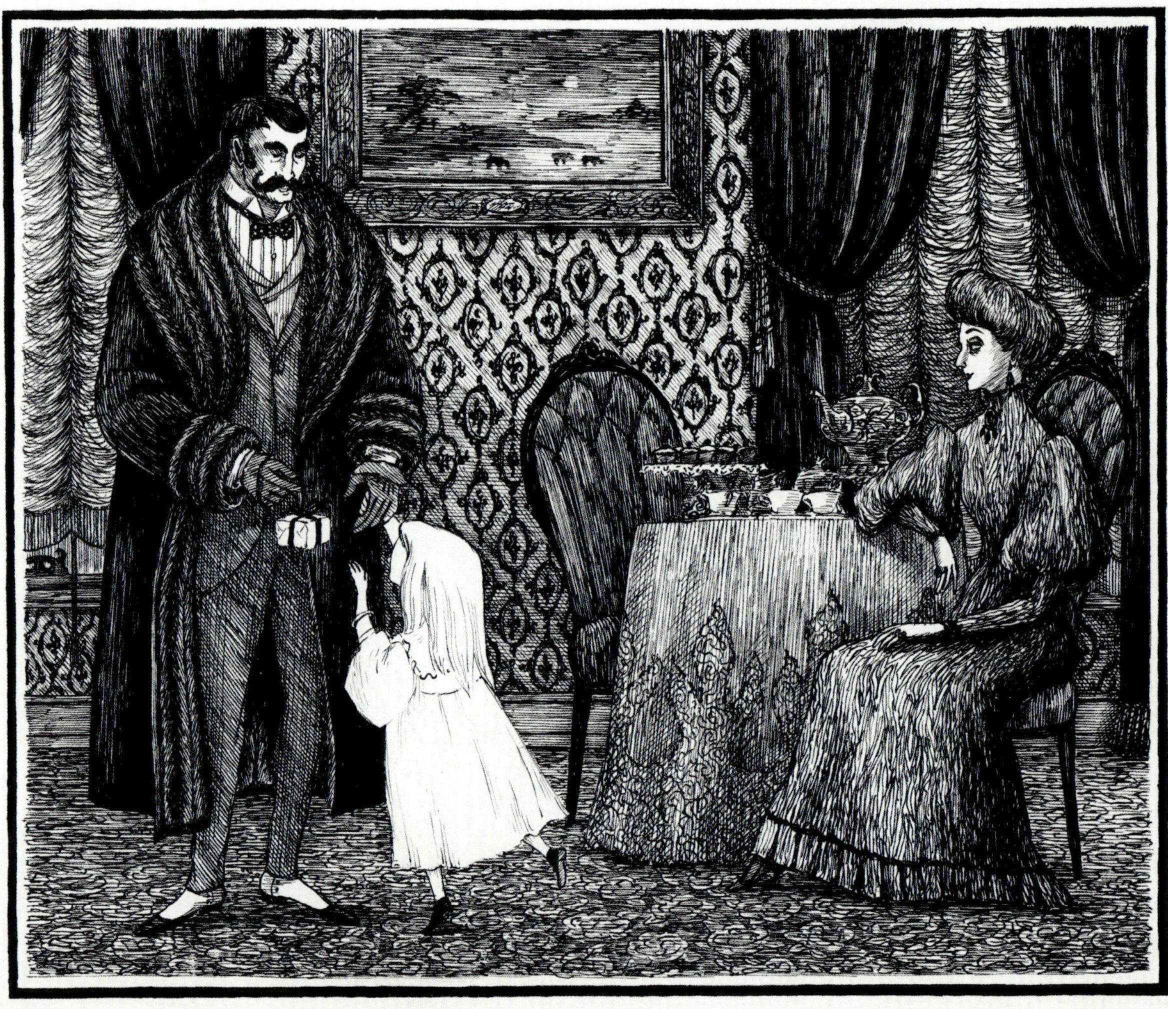

Her parents were kind and well-to-do.

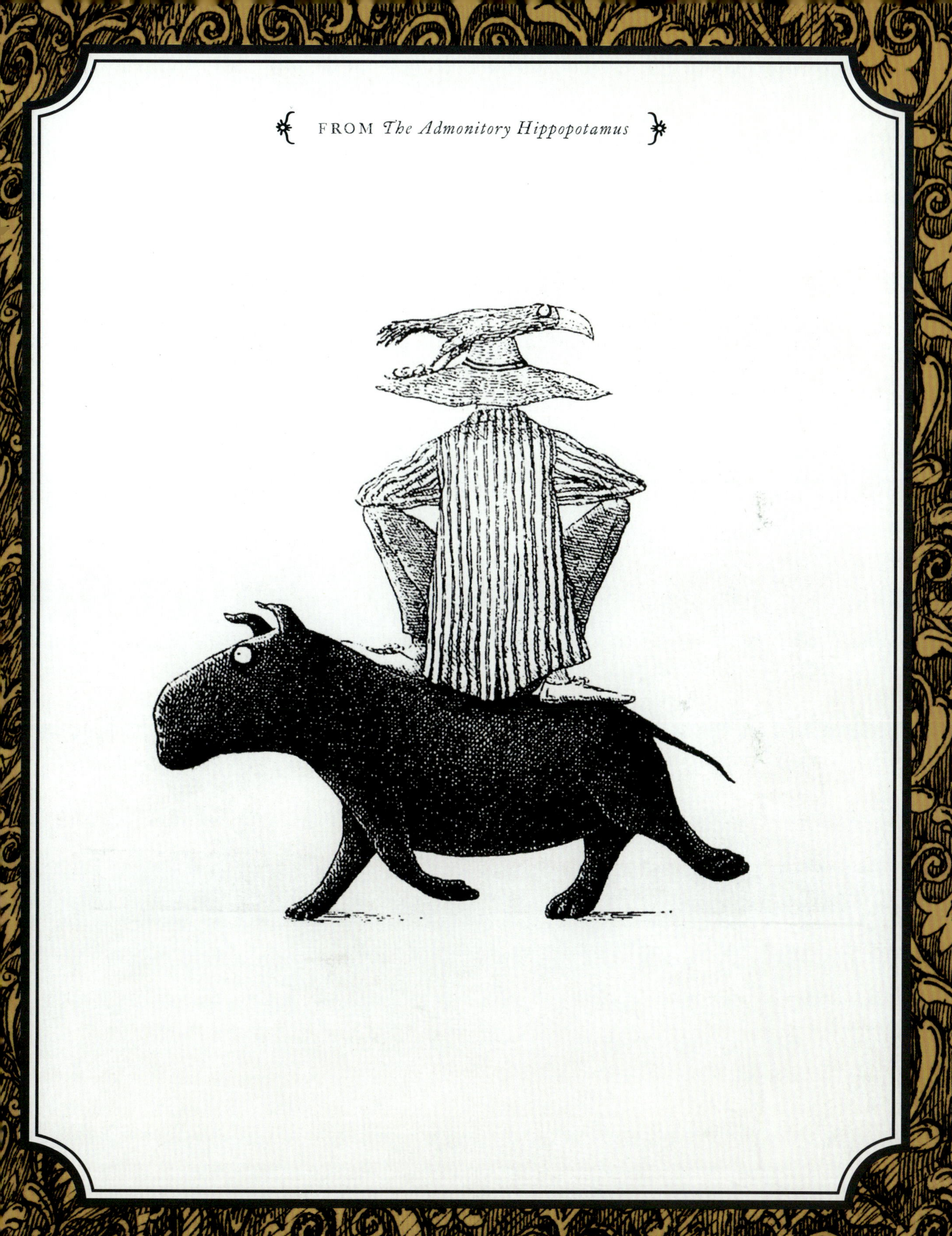
FROM *The Admonitory Hippopotamus*

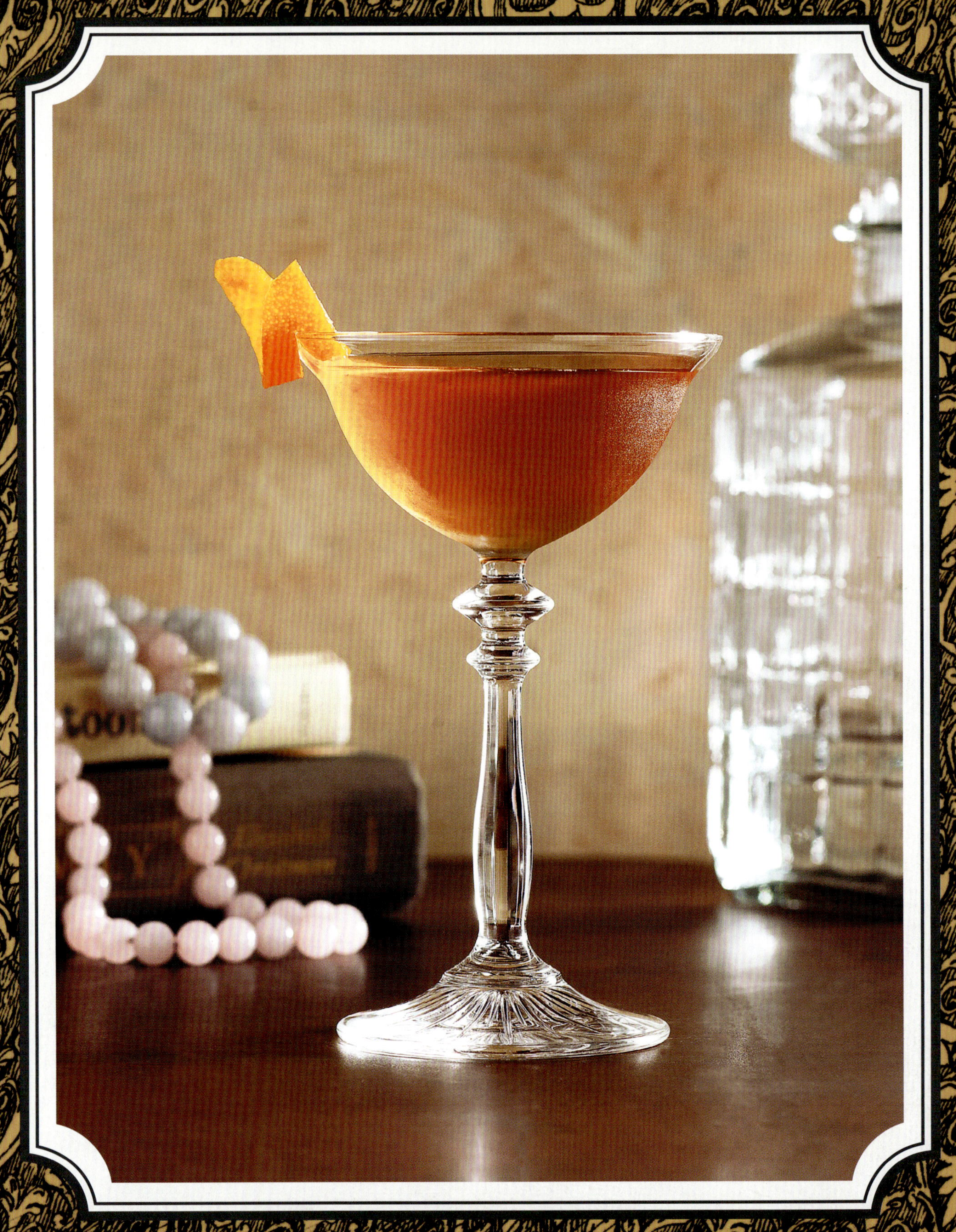

ANGELICA AND SNEEZBY

MAKES 1 COCKTAIL • GLASS: COUPE OR NICK AND NORA

Little five-year-old Angelica caught sight of a "spectral hippopotamus" who gave her the inspiring command, "Fly at once! All is discovered." Angelica ran into the woods, and was not found by the servants until the sun was going down. "Seven years later she sneaked away . . . to buy forbidden jujubes." From marriage, to "the height of her notoriety," on to her eighty-sixth year, the Admonitory Hippo continued to bring her the same message. In death as "her body fell lifeless on the bed," she could not remember what the hippo's words meant, but "Angelica rode away on the back of the hippopotamus."

We nod to this eclectic duo with a variation on the Martinez cocktail. Historically made with equal parts gin and sweet vermouth, plus bitters and a touch of maraschino liqueur, the power of this drink is its balance of Old Tom and sweet vermouth, tributing Angelica and Sneezby.

Our twist changes the equal parts proportions, omits the maraschino liqueur, and subs out classic orange or aromatic bitters with chocolate bitters. With an orange peel, the drink exudes intriguing chocolate-orange whispers that Angelia certainly would have adored.

---

2 oz (60 ml) Old Tom gin
1 oz (30 ml) sweet vermouth
2 dashes chocolate bitters
Garnish: Orange twist

Combine the gin, sweet vermouth, and chocolate bitters in a cocktail mixing glass. Add ice and stir for 20–30 seconds, until well chilled. Strain the cocktail into a coupe or Nick and Nora glass. Express the orange peel over the drink and garnish with the peel.

AMELIA EMILY'S SECRET

• MAKES 1 COCKTAIL • GLASS: COLLINS •

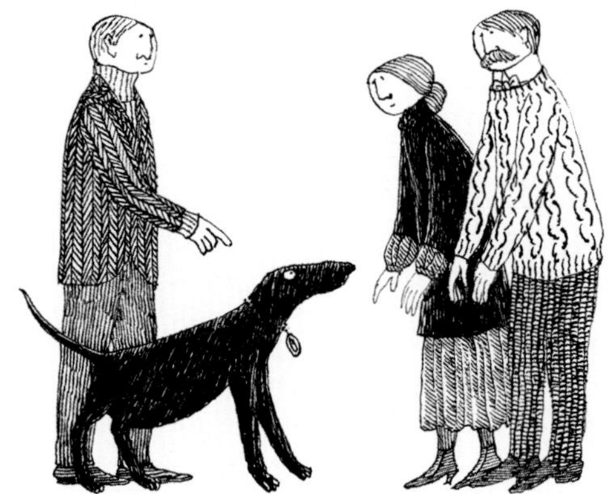

The Retrieved Locket tells the strange little tale of baby Amelia Emily, who is given a locket and then vanishes from her cradle. A neighbor brings the Fibleys a dog wearing the locket, and when it has puppies, the Fibleys name one after Amelia Emily. The Fibleys spend their final years with this pup, whom they deemed a "great-great-granddaughter" of their daughter Amelia.

As the Fibleys cozy up with puppy Amelia Emily by a fireplace centered by their daughter's baptismal photograph, we offer a cozy, after-dinner, fireside sort of sipper. With French brandy as the base, the cocktail unfolds with layers of bitter, minty, herbaceousness and the nutty, rose water whispers of orgeat. Heavy cream makes it a dessert or post-dinner sipper, while seltzer dries it all out, keeping the drink from being cloying or heavy.

1½ oz (45 ml) cognac or Armagnac

½ oz (15 ml) orgeat

½ oz (15 ml) Fernet Branca or bitter Italian-style amari

½ oz (15 ml) heavy cream

Seltzer to top

Place a Collins glass in the freezer to chill completely. In a cocktail shaker with ice, combine the cognac, orgeat, Fernet Branca, and heavy cream. Cover and shake vigorously for 10–20 seconds, until well chilled. Strain into the chilled Collins glass with fresh ice. Use a barspoon to paddle the drink furiously back and forth while adding seltzer to the rim of the glass. Let sit for a minute or two to firm up the head, then slowly drizzle in more seltzer to lift the head above the rim of the glass. Serve with a straw.

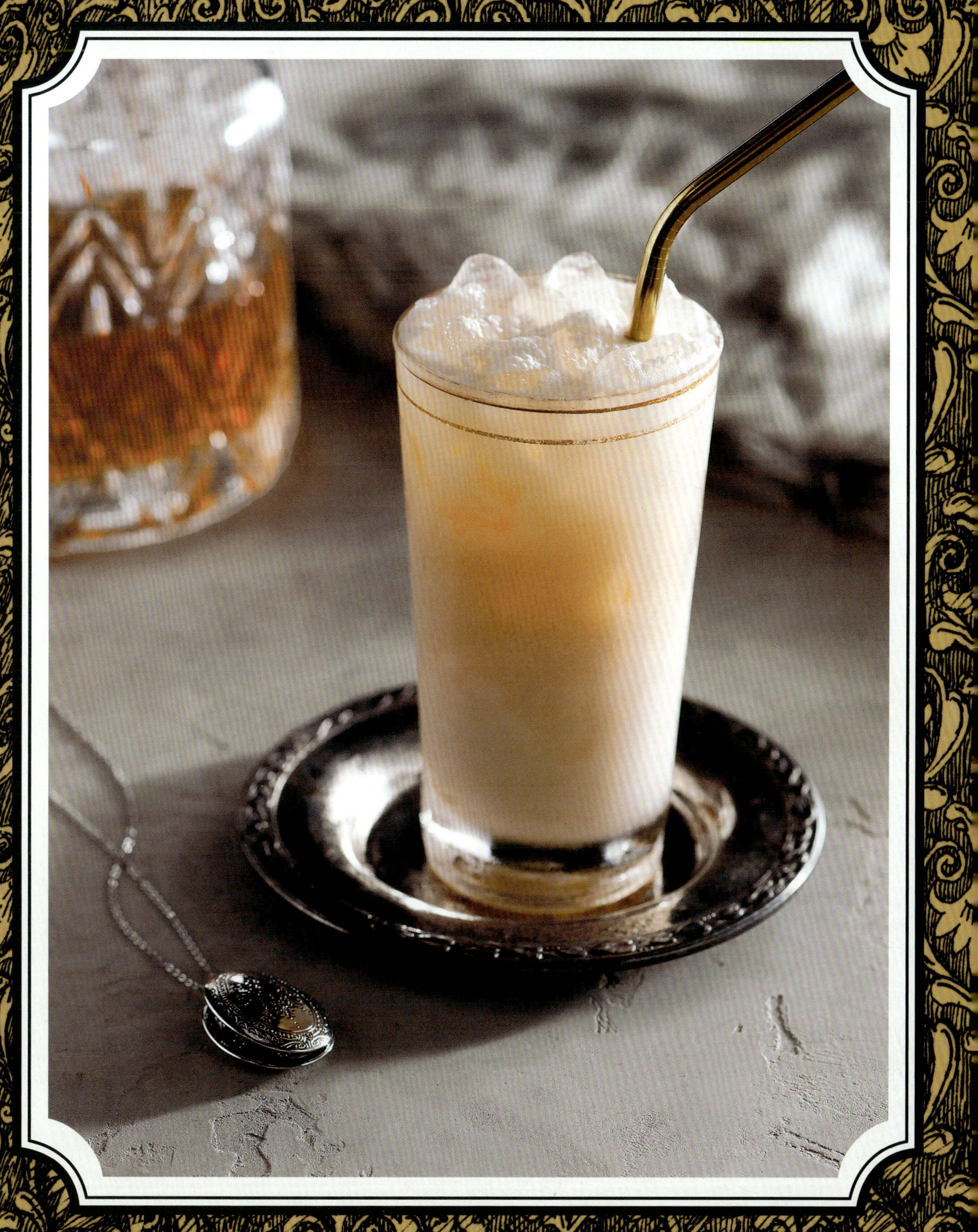

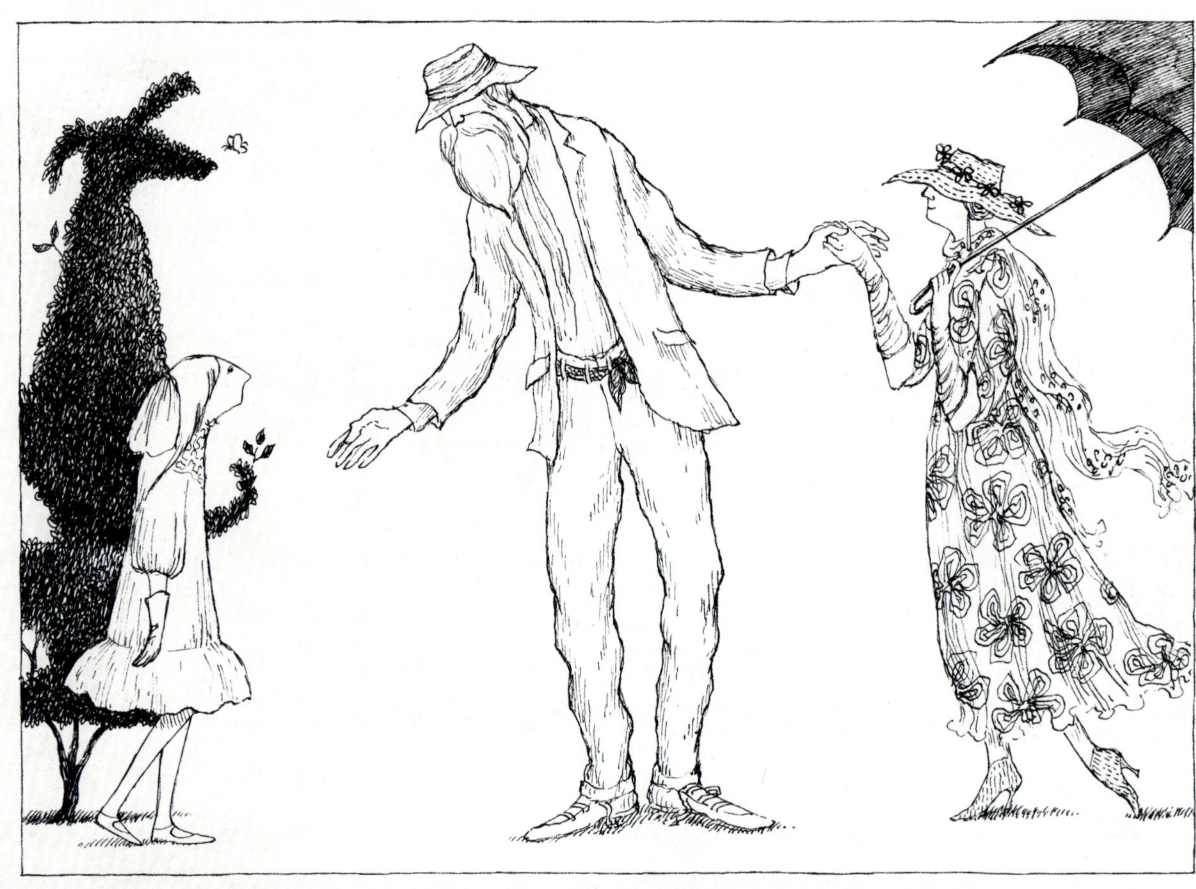

He kissed Miss Skrim-Pshaw's hand, and she presented Drusilla to him.

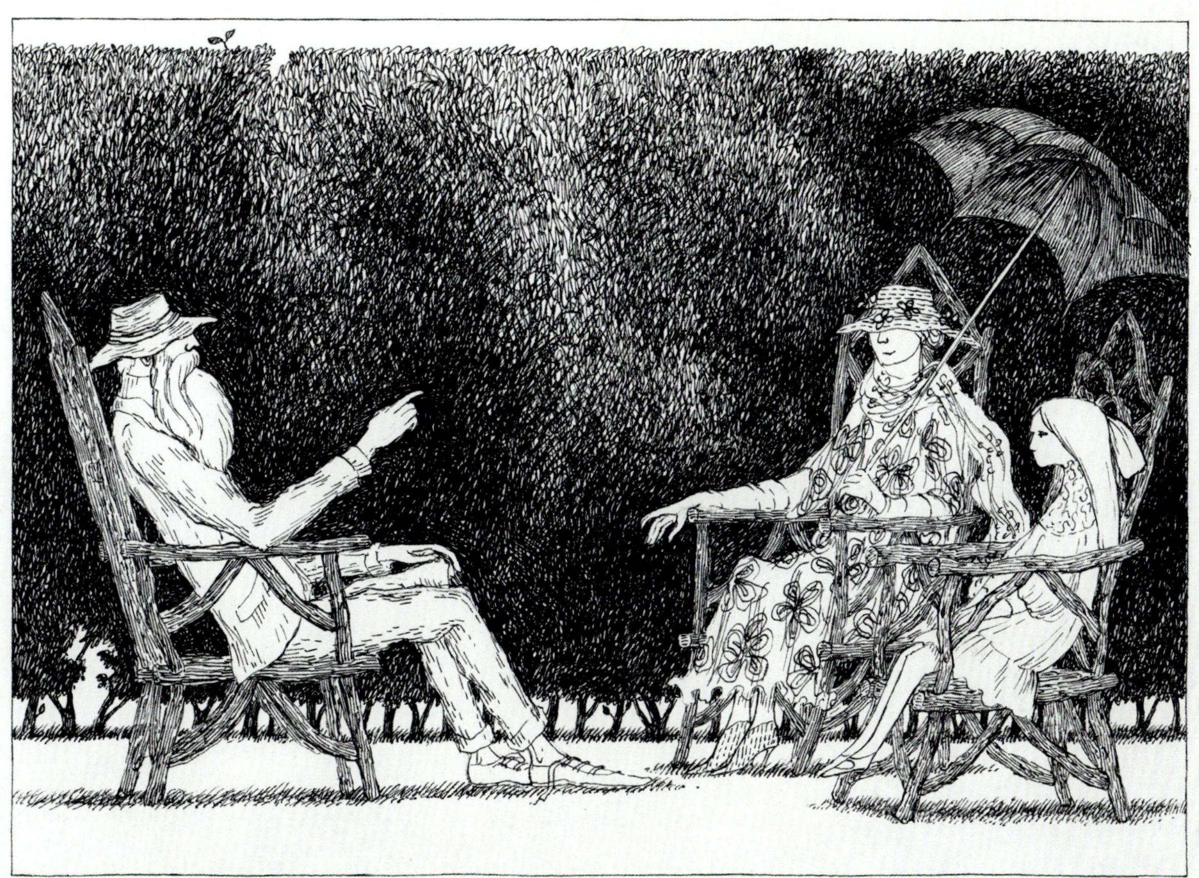

After they had sat down, Drusilla saw that Mr Crague wore no socks.

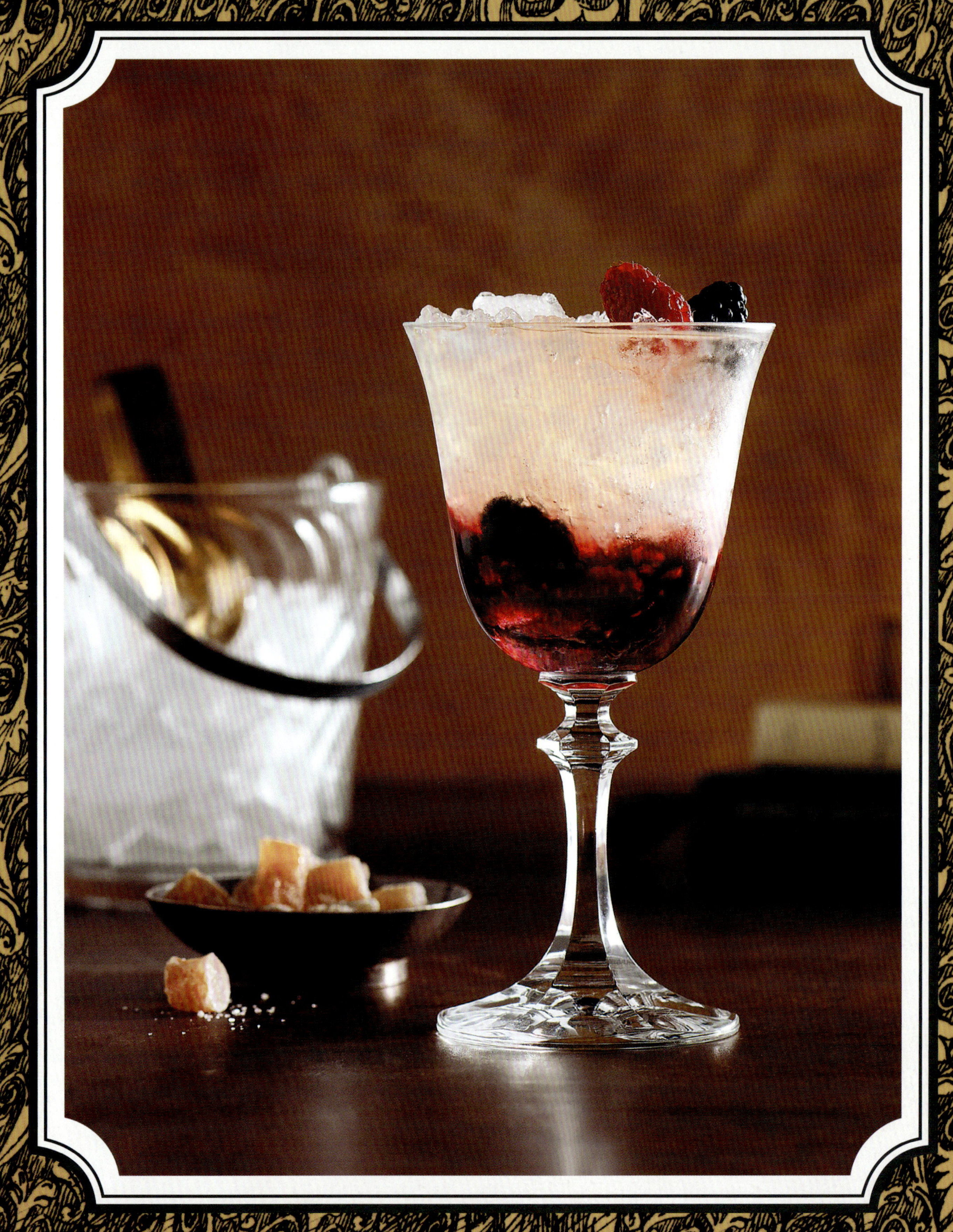

❦ INSPIRED BY *The Remembered Visit* ❦

DRUSILLA'S COBBLER

• MAKES 1 COCKTAIL • GLASS: COLLINS OR GOBLET •

The Remembered Visit is a sweet, sad, wistful story of forgotten promises put off until it's too late. It tells of an encounter between elderly Mr. Crague and the girl Drusilla, who visits him at "an inn called le Crapaud Bleu." Drusilla would not have indulged in drink and, in fact, they sipped "nearly colorless" tea with a plate of crystallized ginger. But we take inspiration from a classic Champagne cobbler, here adapted from Jerry Thomas's *How to Mix Drinks*, the first cocktail book ever published in 1862.

Cobblers are an entire cocktail category from the mid-1800s, a cousin of juleps, meant to cool and refresh. The Champagne cobbler is particularly simple but can be easily gussied up with berries or other seasonal fruit, balanced by dry brut Champagne or sparkling wine, with a touch of simple syrup to round it out. Try different simple syrups (infused with herbs, ginger, other fruits, etc.) to further mix up the drink. We garnish with crystallized ginger in keeping with the spirit of Drusilla and Mr. Crague's teatime reminisces over his "lofty and cultured" "dim past" and her envelope collection.

½ oz (15 ml) 1:1 Simple Syrup (page 142)

4-5 seasonal fresh berries

3–4 oz (90–120 ml) Champagne or sparkling wine, preferably brut

Garnish: Crystallized ginger, seasonal fresh berries or other fruit

---

In a Collins glass or goblet, combine the simple syrup and berries. Gently muddle at the bottom of the glass with a muddler or wooden pestle. Fill the glass with crushed ice and top with the Champagne. Garnish artfully with crystallized ginger and more berries. Serve with a straw.

Z IS FOR ZILLAH

• MAKES 1 COCKTAIL • GLASS: ROCKS •

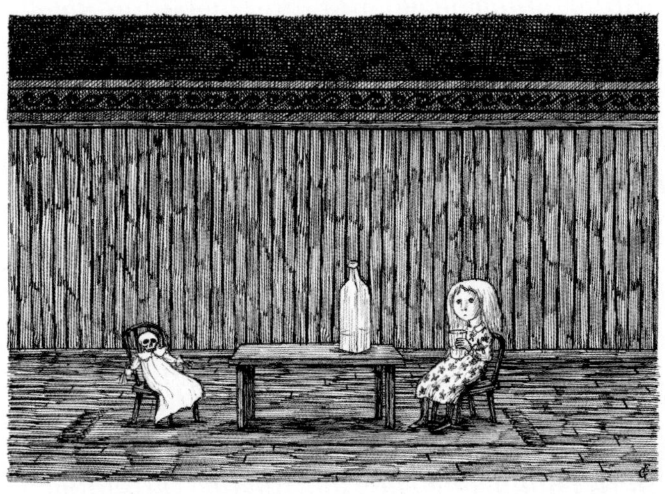

Z is for ZILLAH who drank too much gin

Poor little Zillah represents the letter *Z* in Gorey's iconic *The Gashlycrumb Tinies*. So though we love gin, we go in another direction here to help out dear Zillah by avoiding gin entirely in one of the most beloved cocktails in history, the Negroni.

The Kingston Negroni is a popular variation on the Italian gin, Campari, and sweet vermouth classic born in Italy. This version subs out gin for rum, an easy switch that transforms the cocktail from bittersweet and herbaceous to full, sweet, earthy, and tropically bitter, depending on the kind of rum used. Also called the Jamaican Negroni, this drink carries its own heft—and saves little Zillah from too much gin. The choice of rum completely affects the flavor profile. Many a great Jamaican rum will bring the robust funk and flavor that makes this cocktail sing. But you can also vary with a sweeter, rounder rum, if preferred. And If you prefer to drink like Zillah, you can swap the rum for gin to make a traditional Negroni.

---

1 oz (30 ml) Campari
1 oz (30 ml) sweet vermouth
1 oz (30 ml) aged rum
Garnish: Orange slice and pineapple frond

In a mixing glass with ice, combine the Campari, sweet vermouth, and rum. Stir with a barspoon for 20–30 seconds, until well chilled. Pour into a rocks glass over one large ice cube. Garnish with an orange slice and pineapple frond.

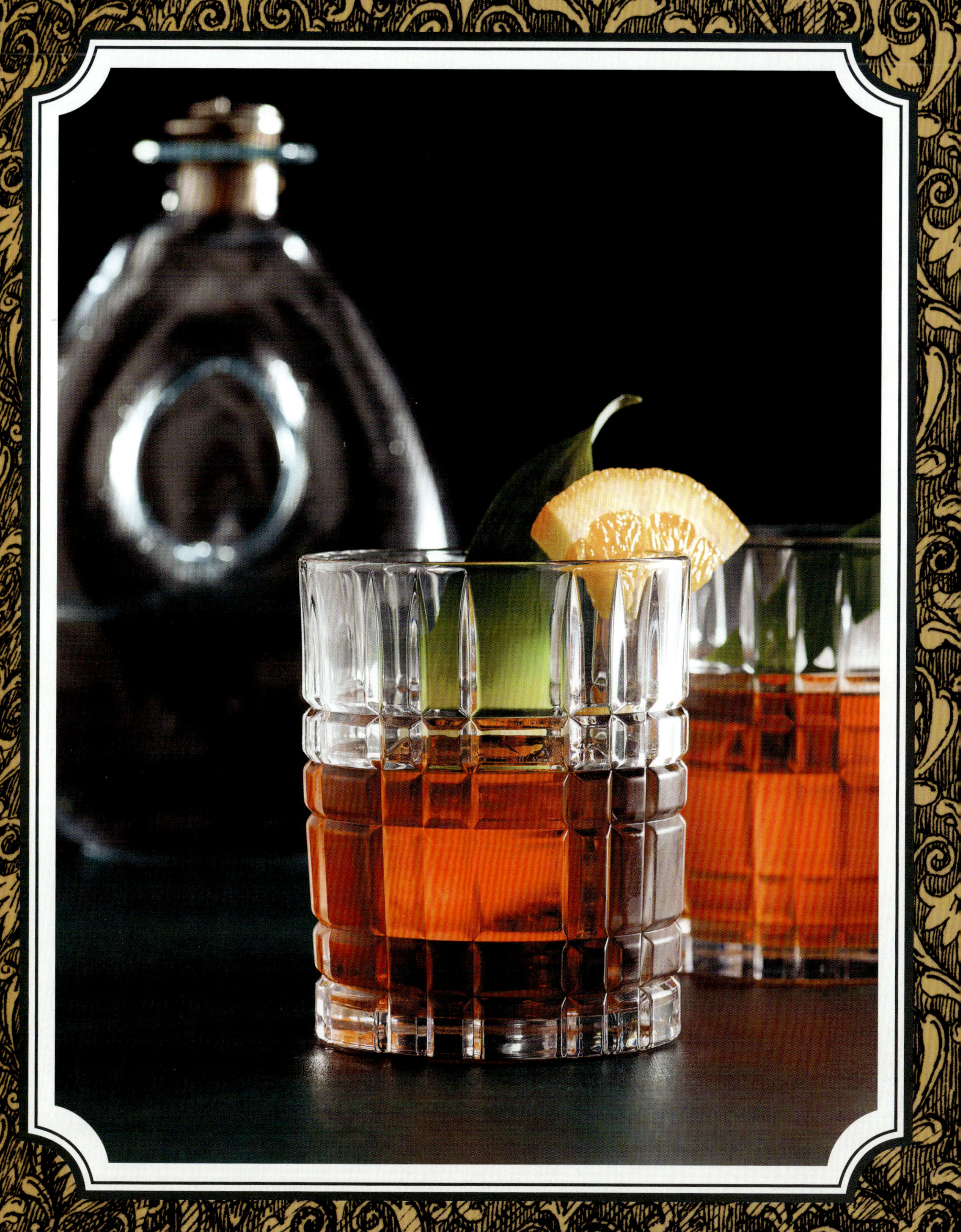

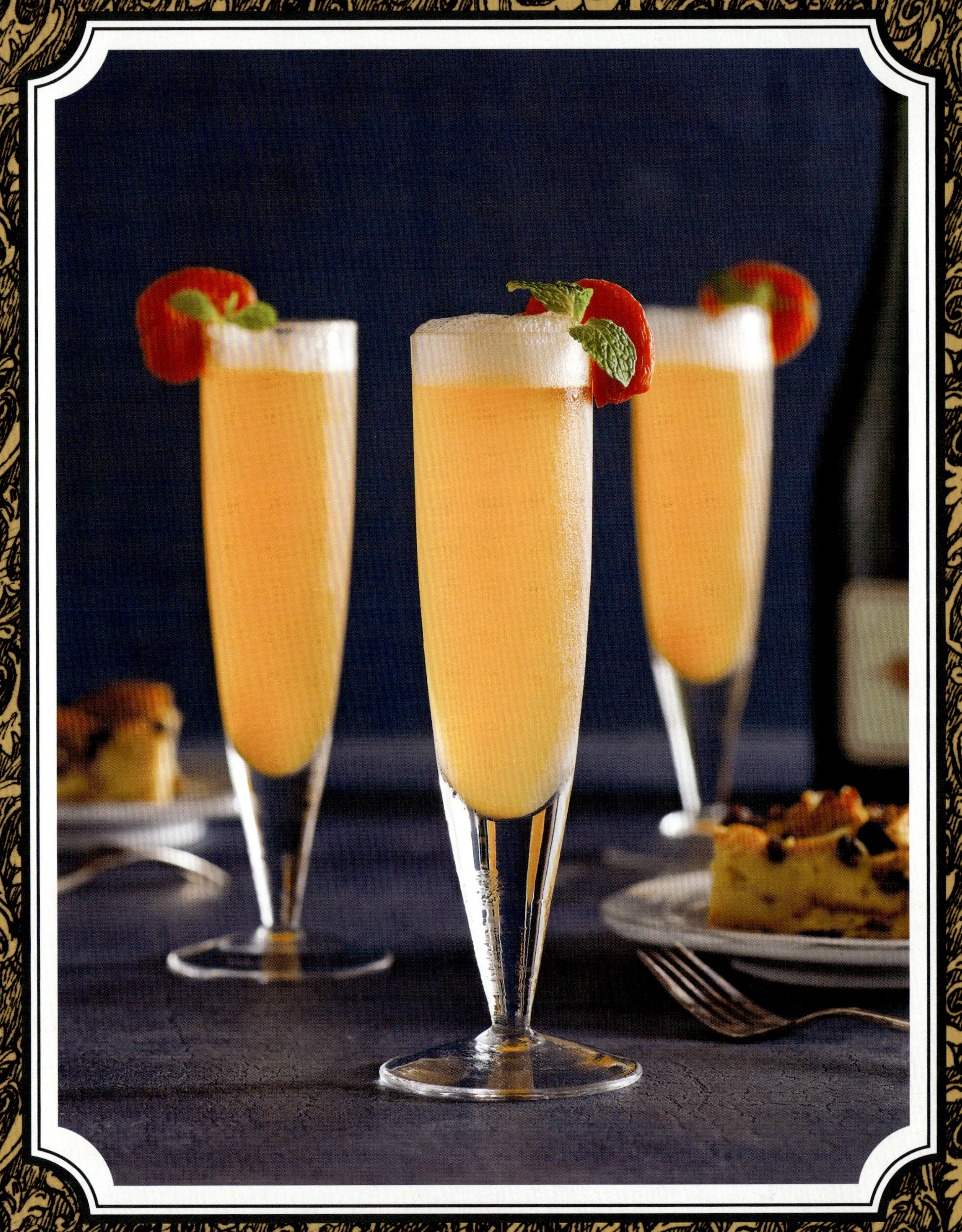

INSPIRED BY *The Pious Infant*

HENRY'S PIETY

• MAKES 1 COCKTAIL • GLASS: CHAMPAGNE FLUTE •

Little Henry Clump, the pious infant, found out when he was three years old "that his heart was wicked, but that God loved him nevertheless." Though "he was sometimes tempted by Satan," in the end, Henry was caught in a hailstorm, became fatally sick, and died. But with sins pardoned, his "little body turned to dust in the grave, but his soul went up to God."

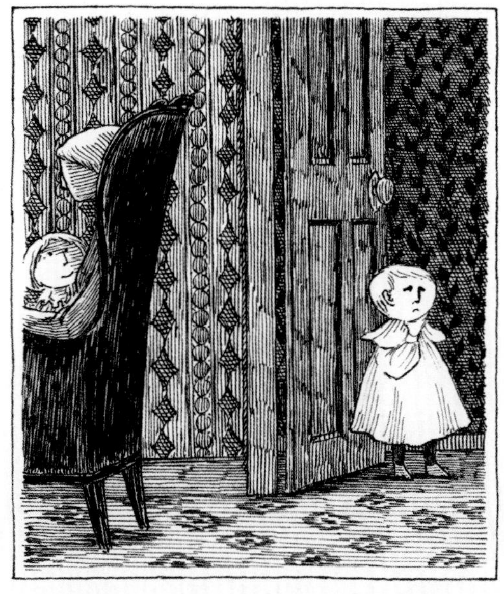

That night he had a sore throat, which by morning had turned into a fatal illness.

In a tribute to Henry, we allow him sweet things but keep it chaste and low proof in a variation on Italy's classic Bellini. All stone fruit works in this breezy brunch cocktail or afternoon aperitif. We go with apricot, recommending apricot brandies like The Bitter Truth apricot liqueur or Giffard apricot brandy, although this works equally well with Giffard mango or other fruit brandies.

1½ oz (45 ml) apricot nectar

1 oz (30 ml) apricot brandy

3 oz (90 ml) sparkling wine (Champagne, prosecco, cava, etc.)

Garnish: Fresh mint sprig, dried apricot or fresh apricot slice

---

Place a champagne flute in the freezer to chill completely. In a cocktail shaker with ice, combine the apricot nectar and apricot brandy. Cover and shake vigorously for 20–30 seconds, until well chilled. Strain into the chilled champagne flute. Add the sparkling wine and stir gently. Garnish with a mint sprig and apricot.

SARA'S COMFITS

• MAKES 1 COCKTAIL • GLASS: COUPE OR MARTINI •

A sly little cat walks off contentedly in Gorey's *Story for Sara*, while little Sara pays dearly for her treatment of the poor birds she once played with. In this low-proof sipper, we linger in the season of Sara's more carefree days before the "wicked thought" came to her to trap the birds in her little bag.

Nothing is trapped here. In fact, this low-proof drink showcases the light, clean silkiness of sake, one of the great rice beverage categories with hundreds of years of history in Japan. In this tropical, fresh cocktail, sake is married to a happy companion in the creamy, fleshy, sweet lychee fruit. A tart balance is achieved with lime and pomegranate-forward grenadine. This silky sipper hearkens to the simpler, brighter days when Sara and the birds were friends before her entrapment of the poor little creatures.

---

2 oz (60 ml) sake

1 oz (30 ml) lychee syrup, strained from the can

1 oz (30 ml) fresh lime juice

½ oz (15 ml) grenadine

Garnish: 1–2 lychees

Place a coupe or martini glass in the freezer to chill completely. In a cocktail shaker filled with ice, combine the sake, lychee syrup, lime juice, and grenadine. Cover and shake vigorously for 20–30 seconds, until well chilled. Strain into the chilled coupe or martini glass. Garnish with a lychee.

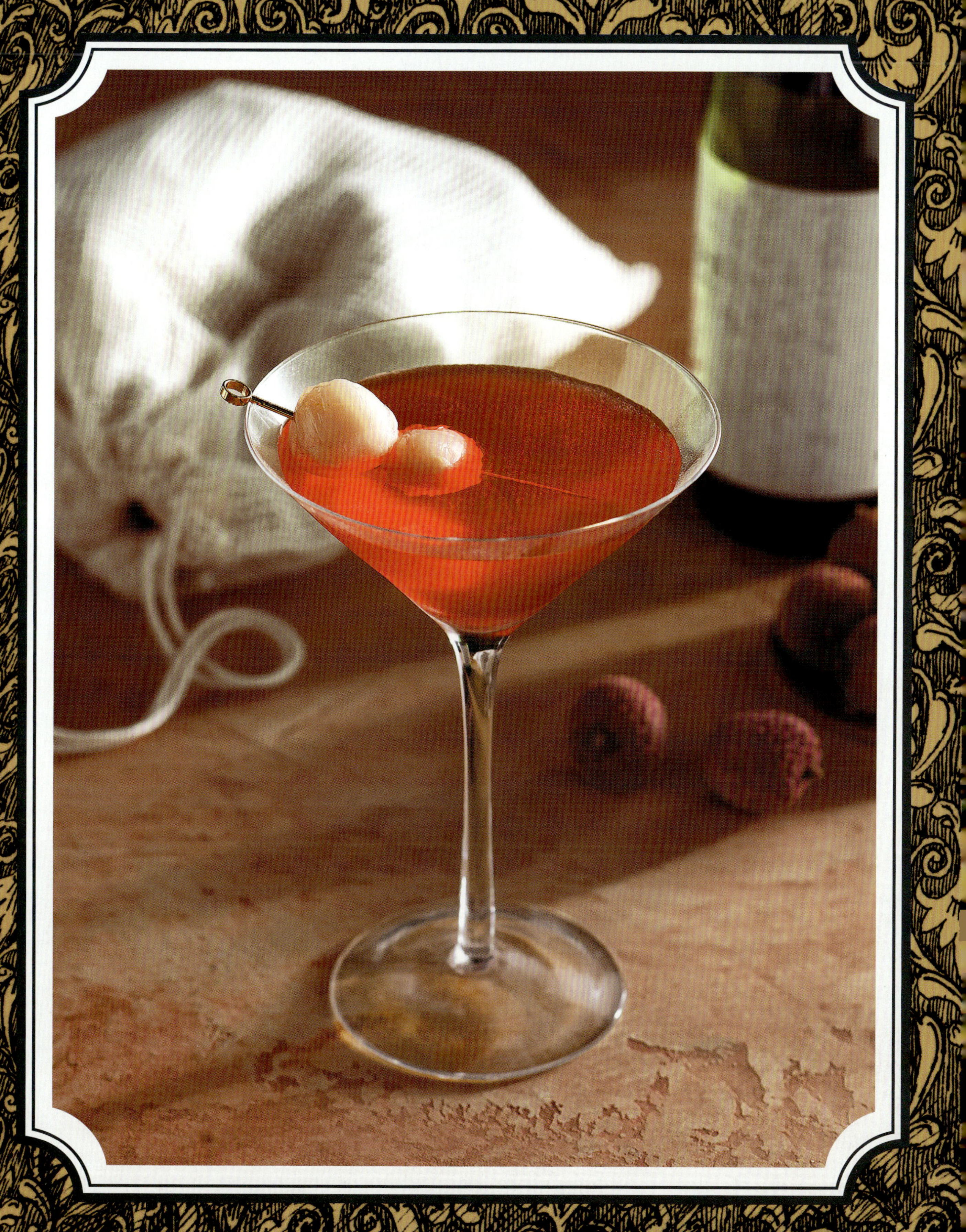

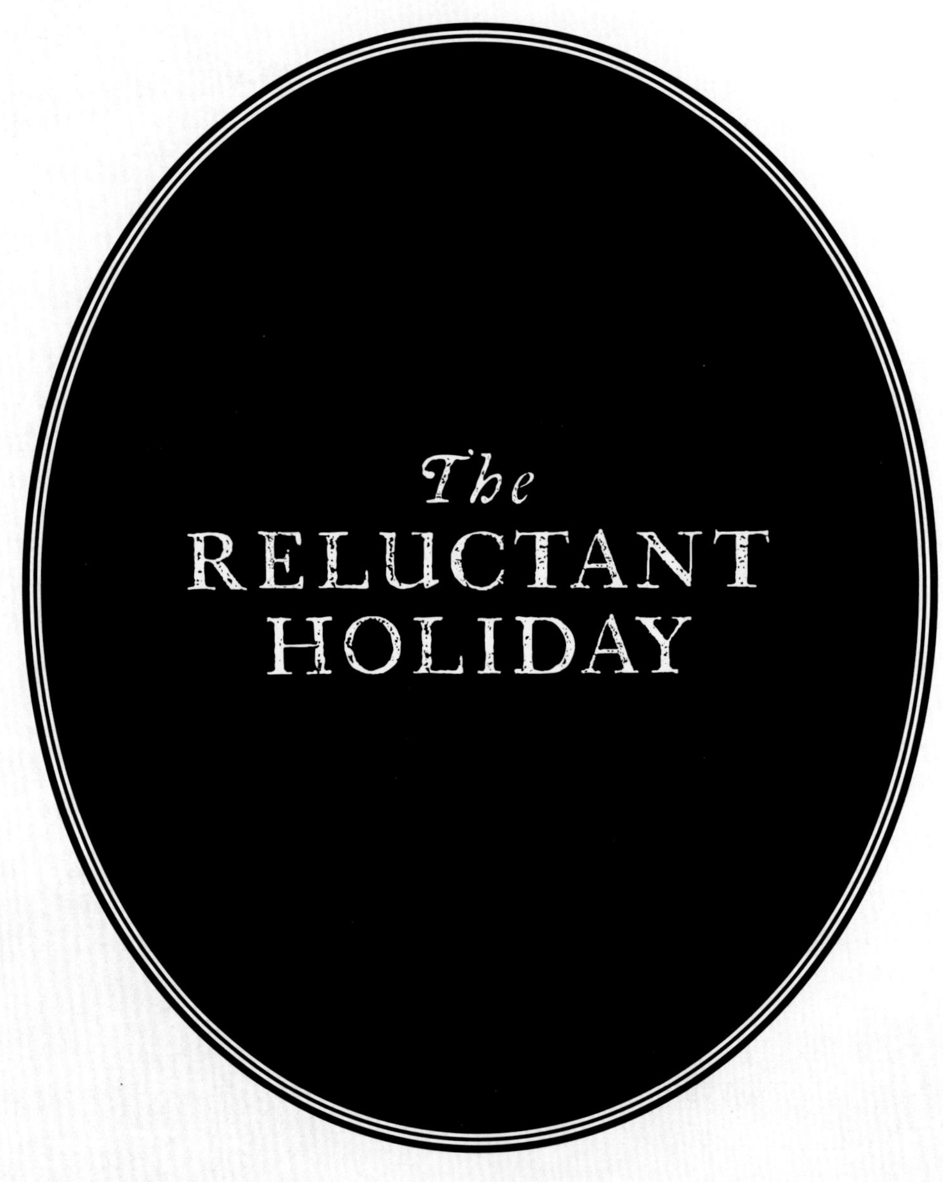

The RELUCTANT HOLIDAY

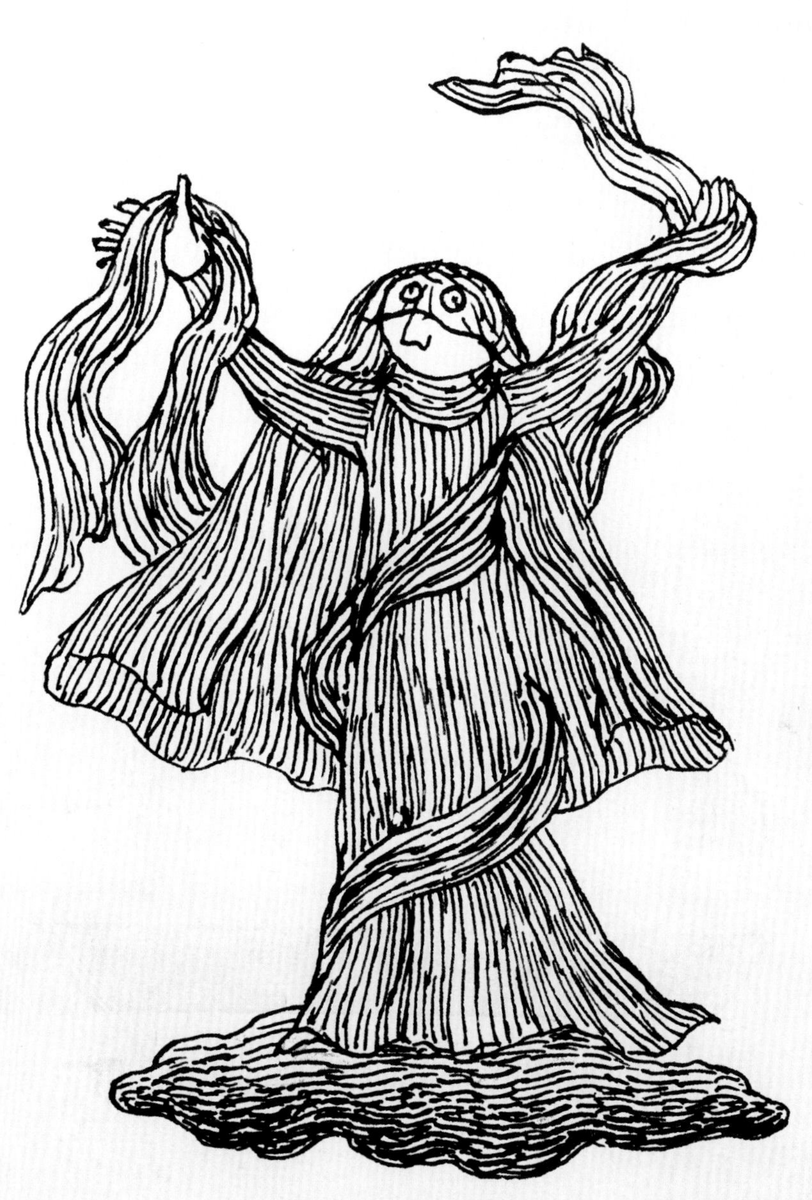

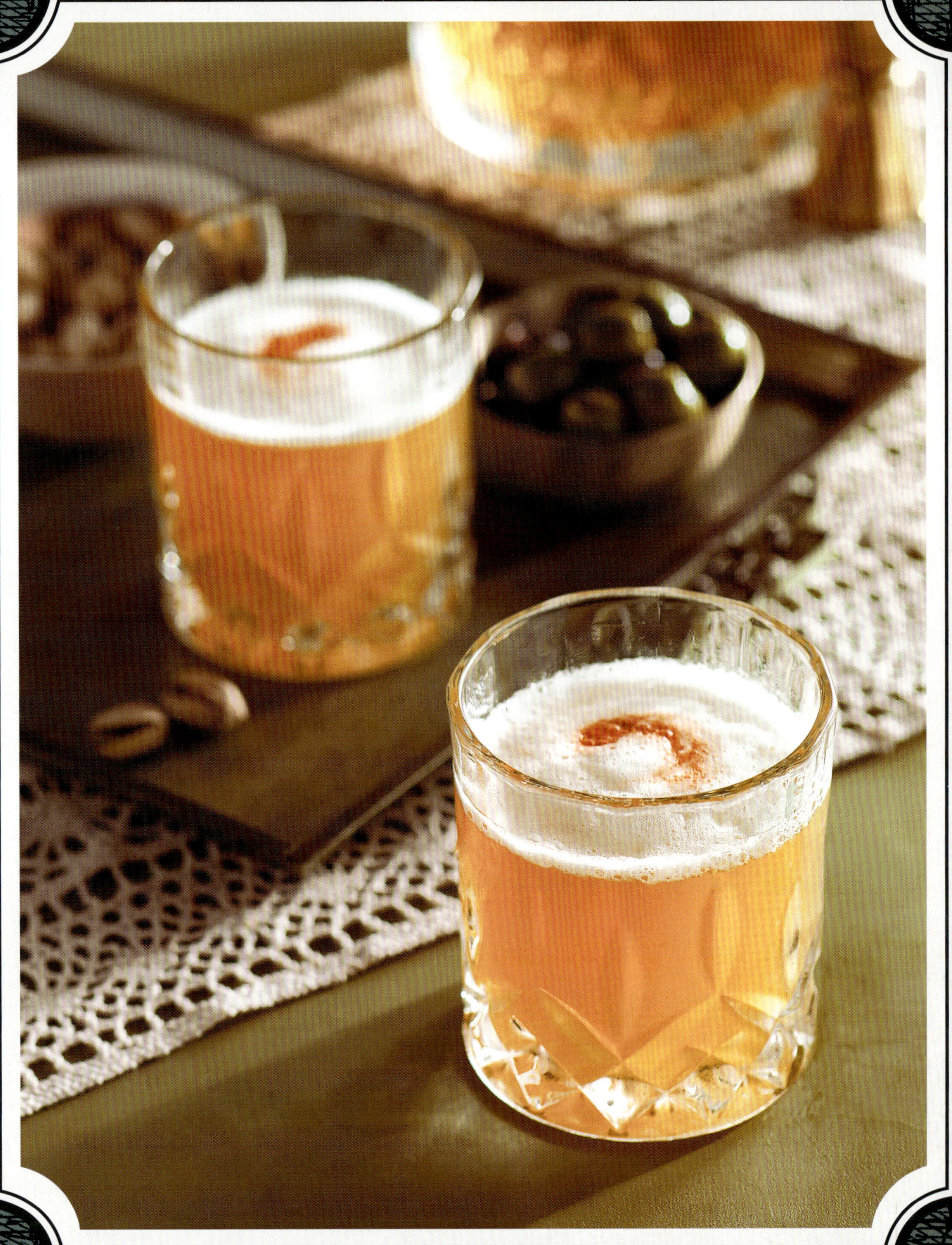

NATASHA'S PULVERIZED PASTE

• MAKES 1 COCKTAIL • GLASS: ROCKS •

Gorey's Neglected Murderesses series, *Dogear Wryde Postcards*, journeys through portraits of creative, crafty murderesses. Take, for example, Mrs. Daisy Sallow, who "eviscerated her daughter-in-law with a No. 1 hook, afterwards crocheting, over the course of three evenings, her shroud in a snowflake pattern." The least harmful to any human was Natasha Batti-Loupstein, who "pulverized a paste necklace and sprinkled it over a tray of canapés."

There is no "pulverized paste" here, only an autumnal version of a classic whiskey sour. This variation features ginger simple syrup, apple juice or cider, and egg white, keeping things frothy and light but with a cozy tribute to the twelve Neglected Murderesses.

---

1 egg white
2 oz (60 ml) whiskey (bourbon or rye)
½ oz (15 ml) fresh lemon juice
½ oz (15 ml) Ginger Simple Syrup (page 146)
½ oz (15 ml) apple juice or fresh apple cider
Garnish: Angostura bitters

Place a rocks glass in the freezer to chill completely. In a cocktail shaker, combine the egg white, whiskey, lemon juice, ginger simple syrup, and apple juice. Cover and dry shake, or shake the cocktail without ice, for 20–30 seconds, until frothy and foamy. Add a handful of ice to the shaker and shake again for about 20 seconds, until well chilled. Double-strain into the chilled glass. Dot the egg white with Angostura bitters.

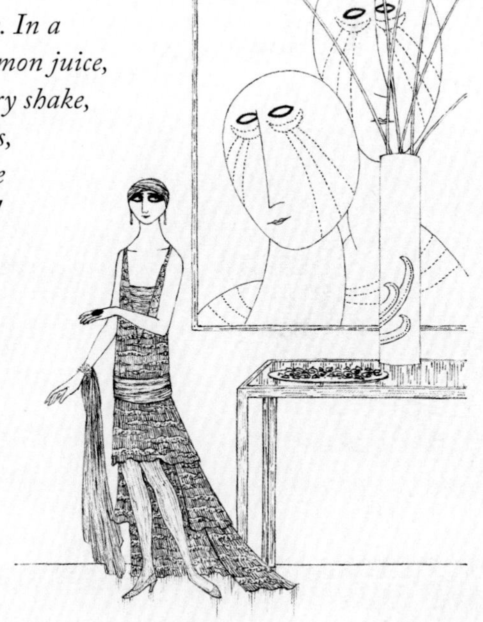

THE CHRISTMAS WRAP-UP

MAKES 1 COCKTAIL • GLASS: ROCKS

Gorey's macabre vibes work beautifully in his Christmas drawings. *The Christmas Wrap-Up* is one of his more colorful works. It showcases a whole crew wrapping a sparse, dark, Gorey-esque tree marked by leaves and lizard-like characters in place of ornaments. His usual black-and-white art is here punctuated by vibrant reds and greens. Red-and-green wrapping paper and ribbon, as well as a picture border of the green lizard-like figure over a red backdrop, impart a Halloween-meets-Christmas ambience.

This Manhattan offers a holiday variation on a classic, spirituous Manhattan with tart cherry juice and rosy-red hibiscus, also nodding to Gorey's choice of color and red in this sketch. The bracing goodness of an American whiskey—whether a sweeter bourbon or a spiced rye—is ruddy and bold. Angostura bitters tighten and sharpen the sweet grain flavors, while a large cherry ice cube slowly dissolves with a tart sigh into the cocktail.

---

2 oz (60 ml) whiskey (bourbon or rye whiskey)

½ oz (15 ml) sweet vermouth

½ oz (15 ml) Hibiscus Simple Syrup (page 143)

2 dashes Angostura bitters

1 Cherry Ice Cube (page 146)

In a mixing glass, combine the whiskey, sweet vermouth, hibiscus simple syrup, and Angostura bitters. Add regular ice and stir for 20–30 seconds, until well chilled. Place a cherry ice cube in a rocks glass. Strain the contents of the mixing glass into the rocks glass.

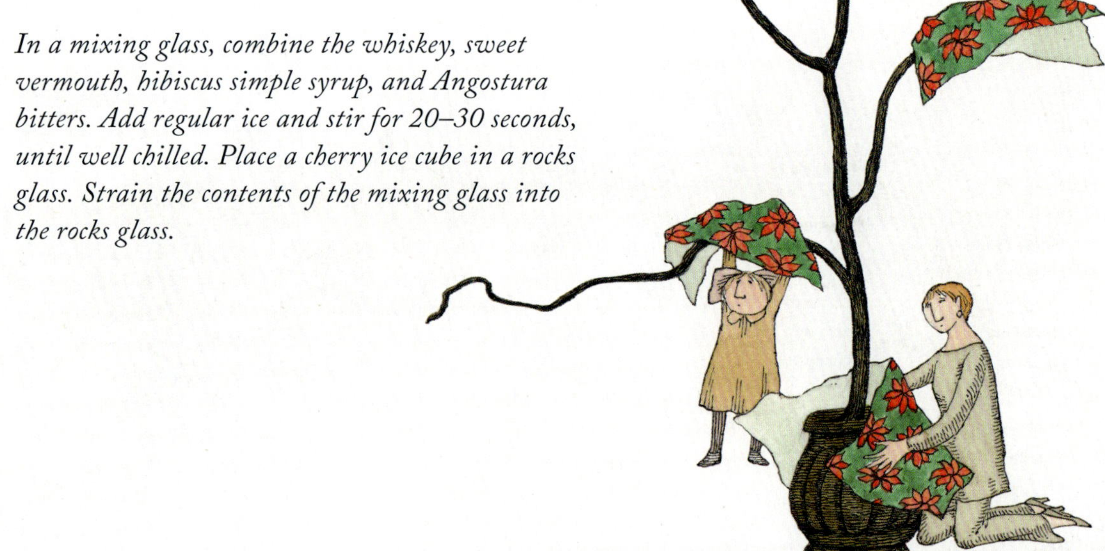

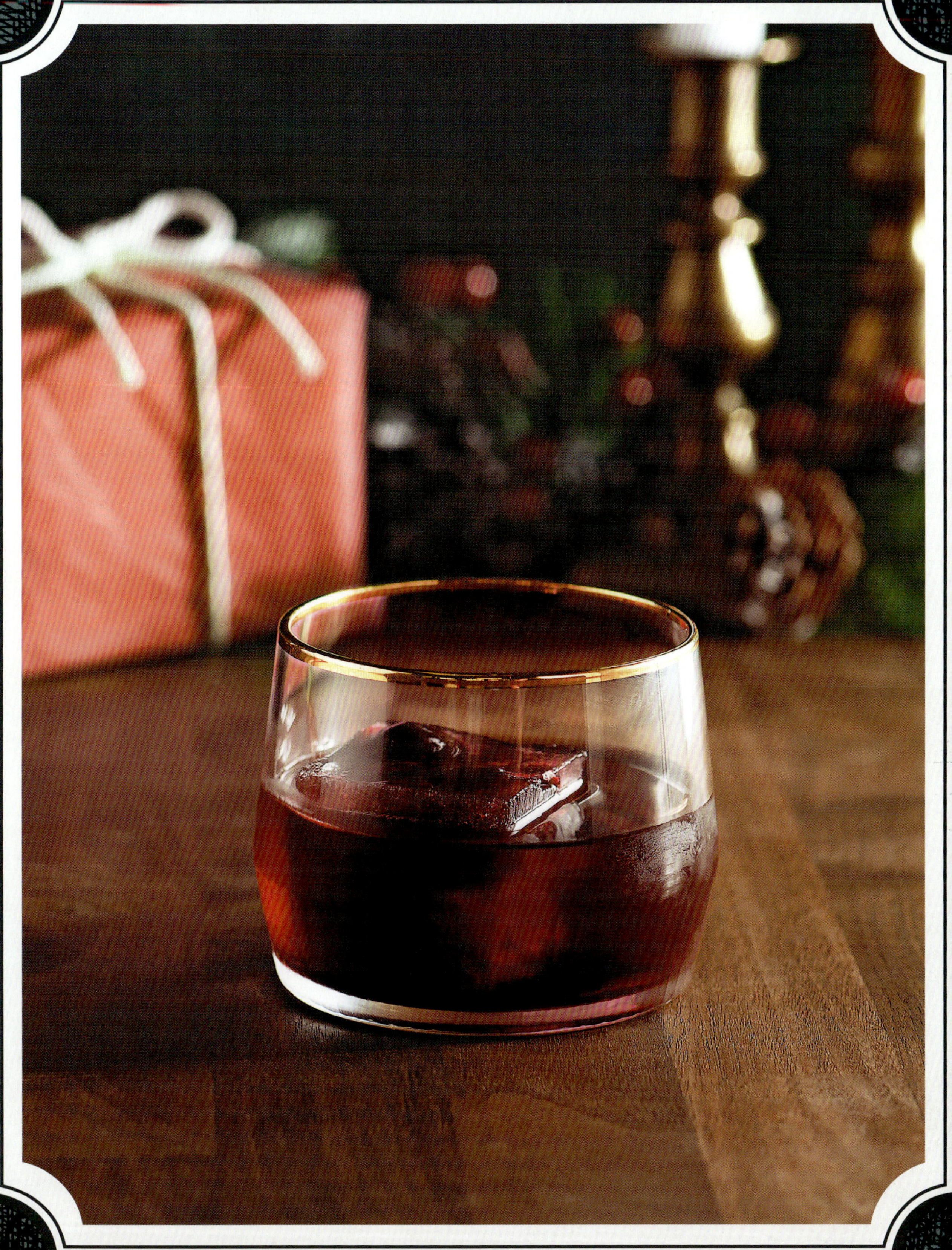

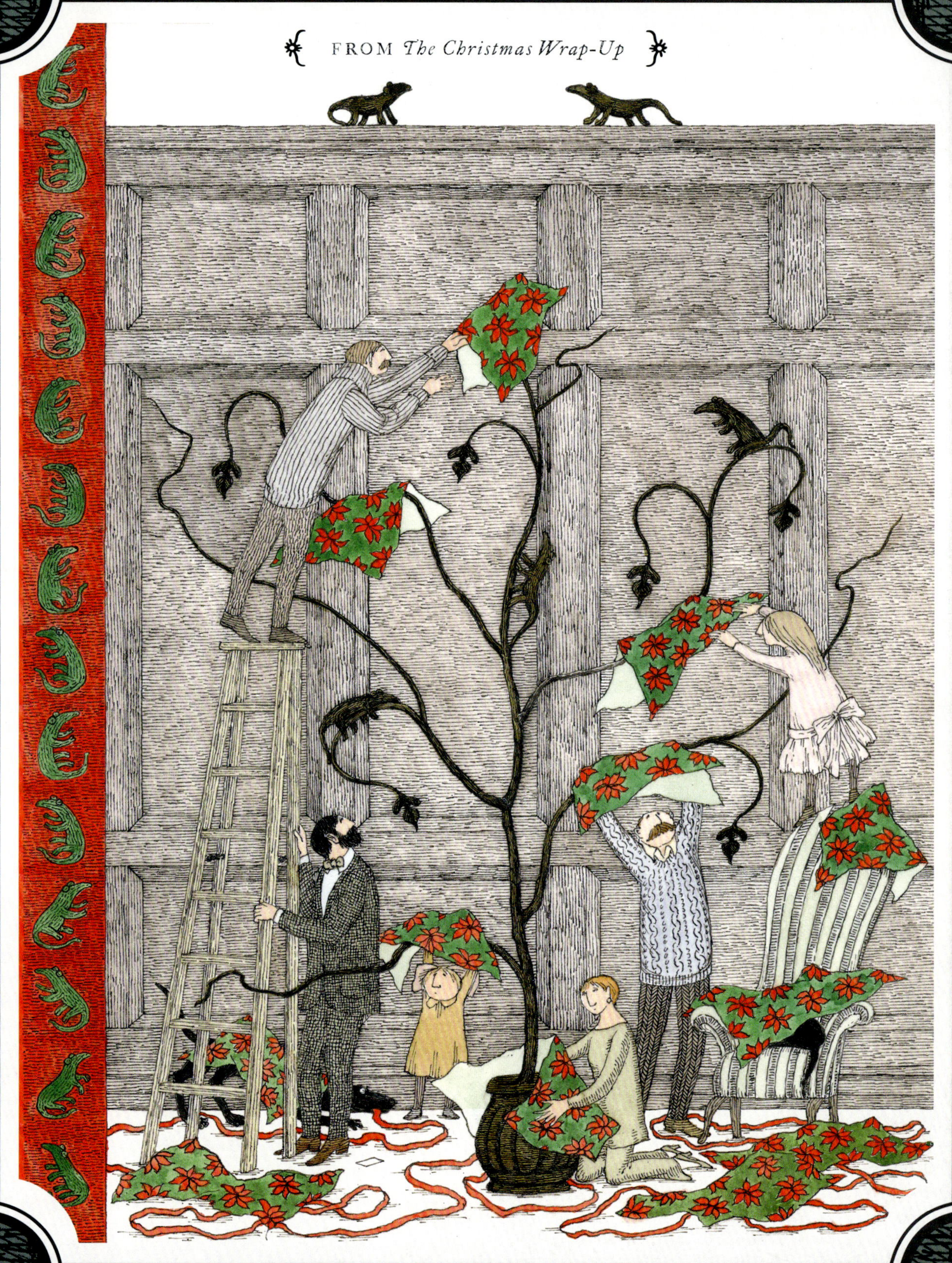

FROM *The Christmas Wrap-Up*

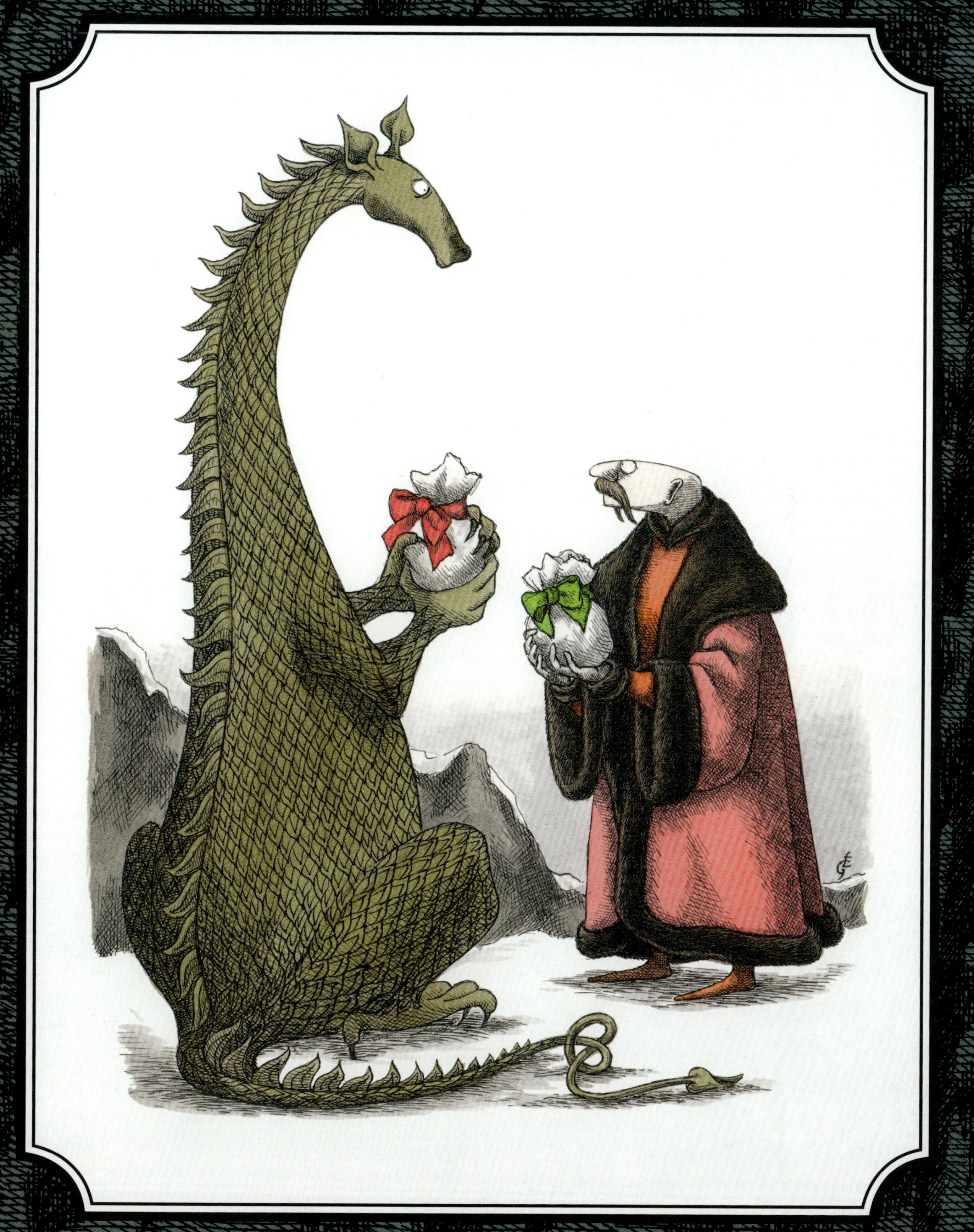

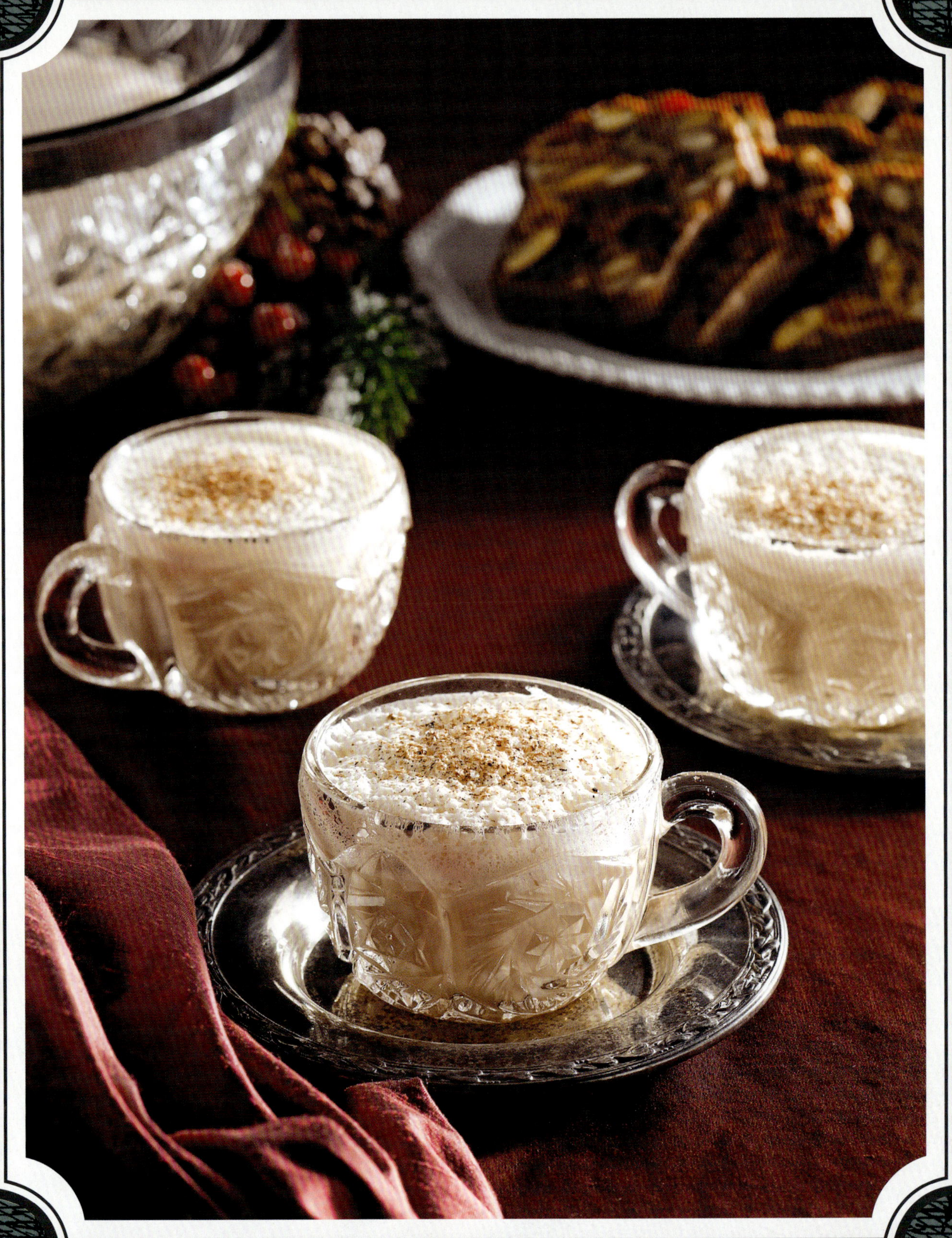

INSPIRED BY *The Haunted Tea-Cosy*

THE VERY EDGE OF UNSEEMLY

MAKES 1 COCKTAIL • GLASS: GOBLET OR MUG

In *The Haunted Tea-Cosy*, Edmund Gravel settles in to "take tea by himself on Christmas Eve" . . . with fruitcake. But then appears Bahhum Bug, who leaps from the tea-cosy to "diffuse the interests of didacticism," leading Gravel into *A Christmas Carol*-esque journey with the three Spectres of Christmas. This wild romp culminates in a holiday party so rowdy, there was declared to be "giggling, dancing, and shrieking . . . carried to the very edge of the unseemly."

Though we wish we could be invited to such a party, a proper, homemade eggnog could start the festivities, and maybe even lead to a "giggling, dancing, shrieking" party of your own. A creamy eggnog, essentially a classic flip (meaning a whole egg cocktail), is a robust tribute to these Christmas adventures.

---

1 egg, separated

1½ barspoons 1:1 Simple Syrup (page 142)

2 oz (60 ml) brandy (cognac, Armagnac, American brandy), dark rum, or a mixture of both

1 barspoon Madeira or port

4 oz (120 ml) whole milk

Garnish: Ground or freshly grated nutmeg

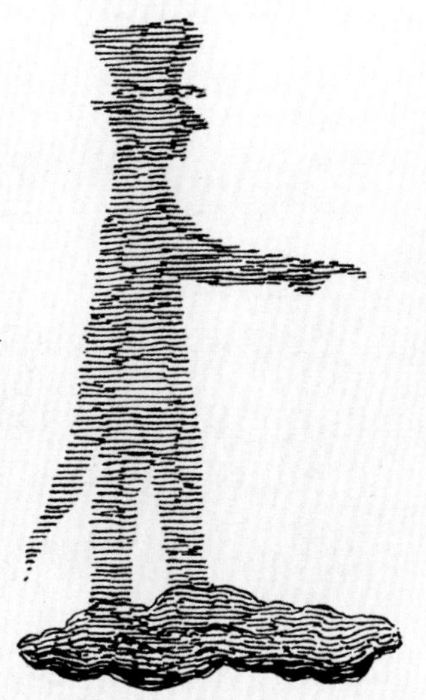

In a small bowl, using an electric mixer, beat the egg white until stiff peaks form. Set aside. In a separate small bowl, beat the egg yolk and simple syrup until combined. Add the brandy and Madeira and beat until blended. Add the milk and beat again. Finally, add the whipped egg white and beat briefly, just until combined. Transfer to a goblet or mug. Sprinkle with ground nutmeg.

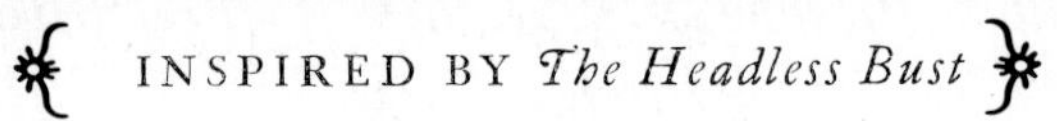

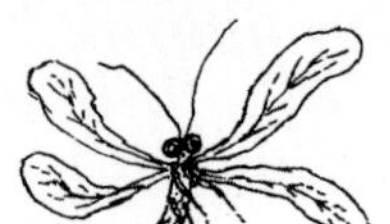

THE BAHHUM BUG

• MAKES 1 COCKTAIL • GLASS: COUPE OR NICK AND NORA •

The Bahhum Bug is back to wrap up the holidays and send Edmund into the New Year—specifically, the new millennium. But this time, a white flying bug called the Whatsit arrives to take them from "place to place / Where there is shame, also disgrace." They are dropped in a town with a curious cast of characters, but both Edmund and the Bahhum Bug have no idea why. When they question the Whatsit, he vanishes, leaving them back in Edmund's home to clean up after his holiday party. Edmund hacks an old fruitcake into pieces and sends it to Havens for the Indigent then sits down with the Bahhum Bug to sip tea and wait for the millennium to descend.

We take our own holiday spin with this spirituous cocktail and its own curious cast of characters. The chocolaty notes of the crème de cacao (white, as a nod to our Whatsit) sing with the sweet agave minerality of a blanco tequila and the herbaceous layers of génépy (aka génépi). The combination is subtle but bold, textured and layered. Just like Edmund's holiday adventures.

1½ oz (45 ml) blanco tequila
¾ oz (20 ml) white crème de cacao
¾ oz (20 ml) génépy
1 dash orange bitters

In a mixing glass with ice, combine the blanco tequila, white crème de cacao, génépy, and orange bitters. Stir for 20–30 seconds, until well chilled. Strain into a coupe or Nick and Nora glass.

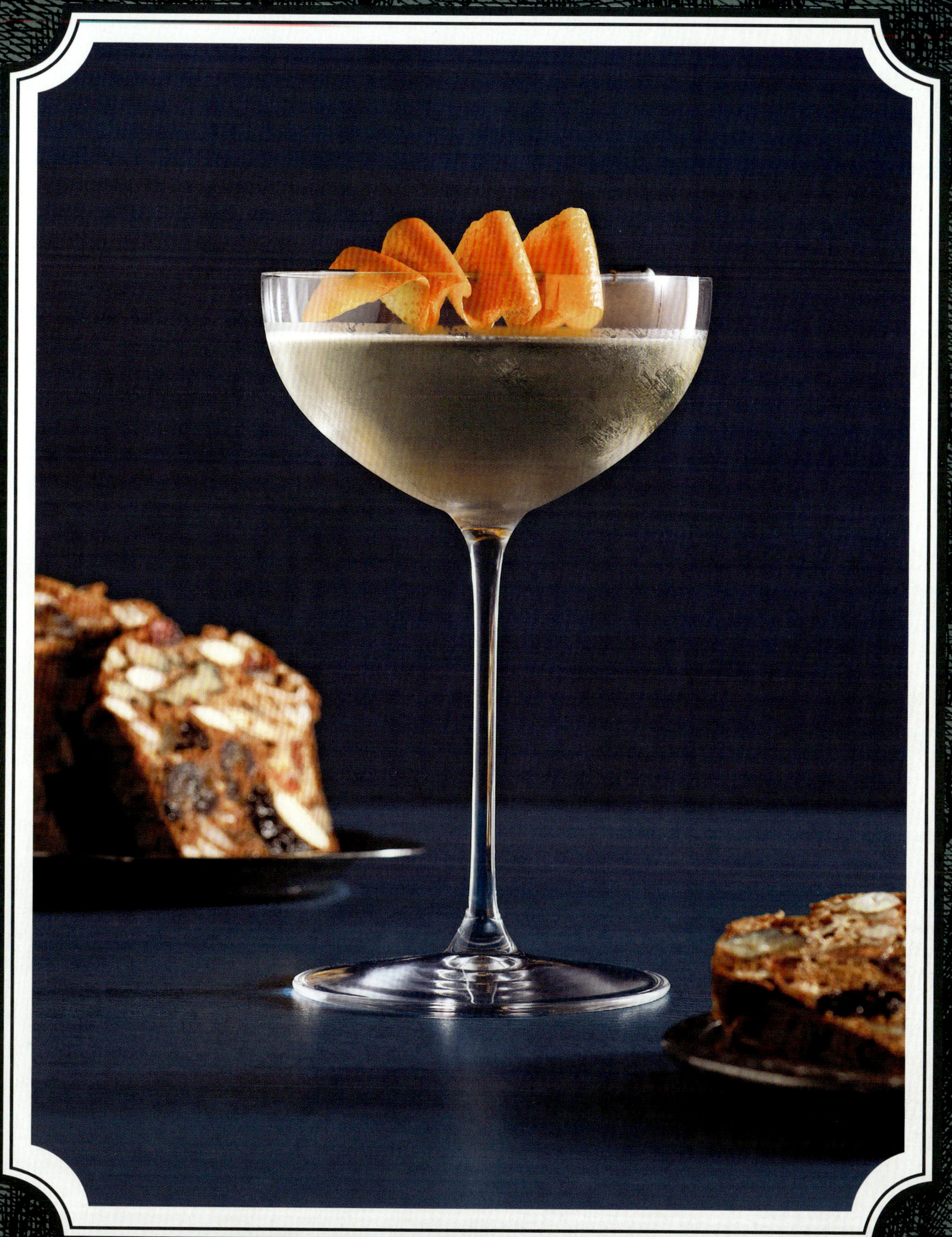

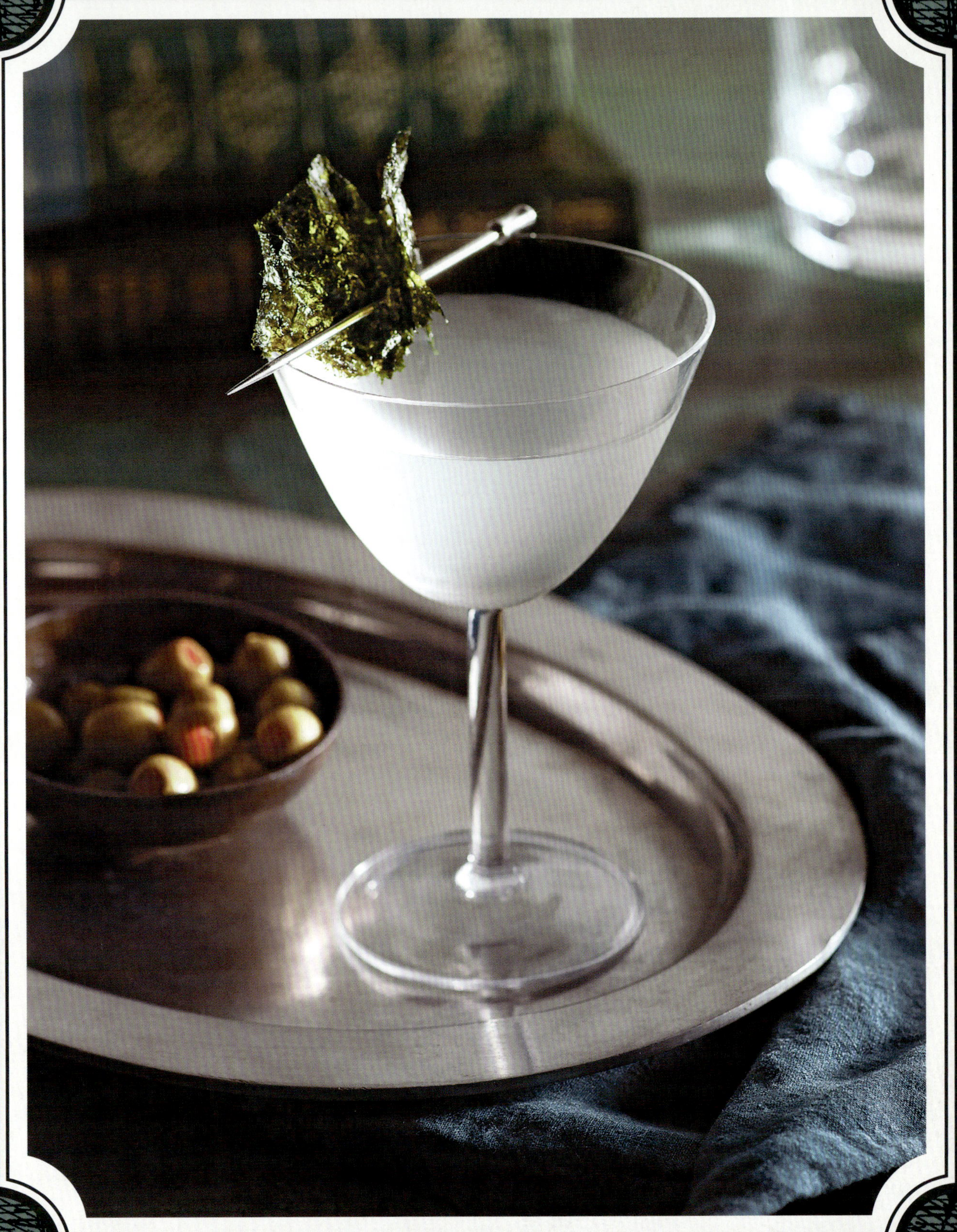

EDWARD'S COUNSEL

• MAKES 1 COCKTAIL • GLASS: MARTINI OR NICK AND NORA •

Verse Advice is a colorful Gorey drawing that offers proverbial wisdom like, "It's possible to pick up crumbs / By pressing on them with the thumbs." While more lighthearted than your typical Gorey tale, his dark humor still shows up in retorts like, "One cannot hope to end one's life / With nothing but a butter knife."

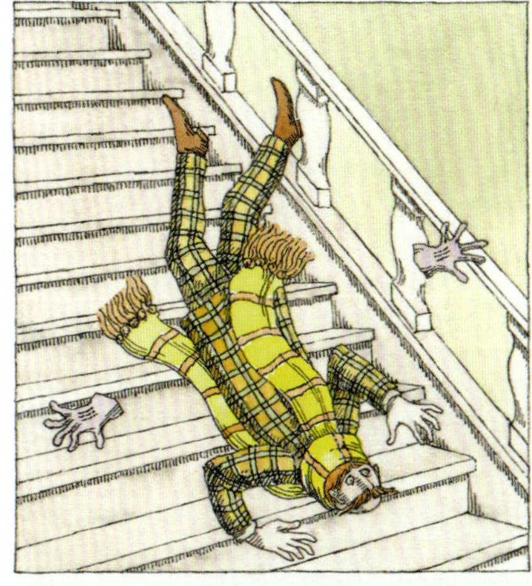

The one who wants to put on airs
Should not attempt them on the stairs.

The martini has always known what it's about, and an oceanic, mineral-forward martini variation is a thing of joy, whether infused with seaweed, dashi, oyster brine, or the like. It is ideal with food or for a pre-dinner sipper to stimulate the appetite, ideally paired with oysters, caviar, or another briny bite. Substitute vodka with gin for a more herbaceous version.

---

2 oz (60 ml) vodka

1 oz (30 ml) Seaweed-Infused Dry Vermouth (page 147)

1 dash celery or olive bitters

Garnish: Olive or small square of nori (seaweed)

In a mixing glass with ice, combine the vodka, seaweed vermouth, and celery bitters. Stir for 40–50 seconds, until icy cold. Strain into a martini or Nick and Nora glass. Garnish with an olive or a small square of nori.

NOTE

Based in Germany, The Bitter Truth produces an award-winning celery bitters and an olive bitters. Both work equally well in this martini.

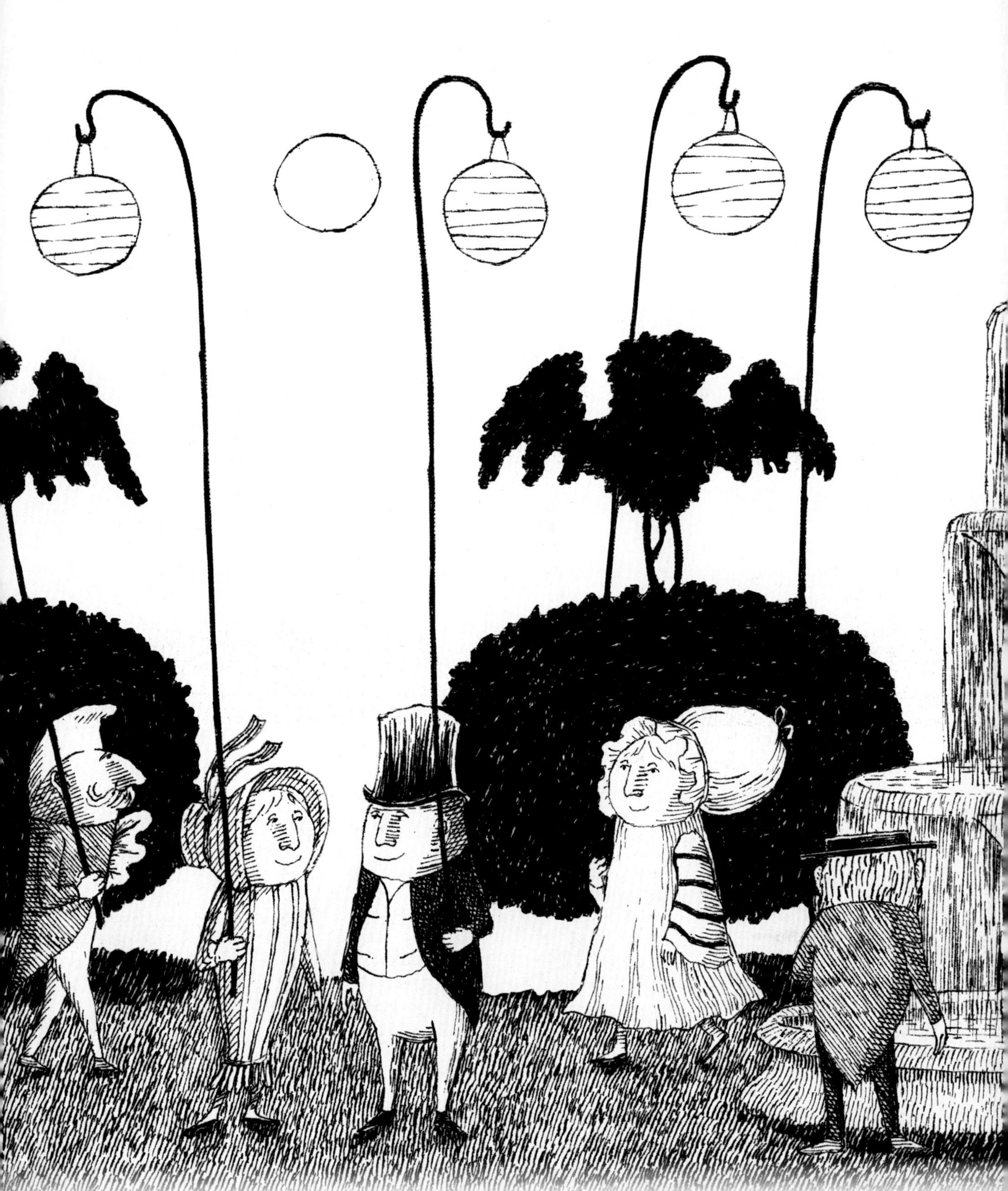

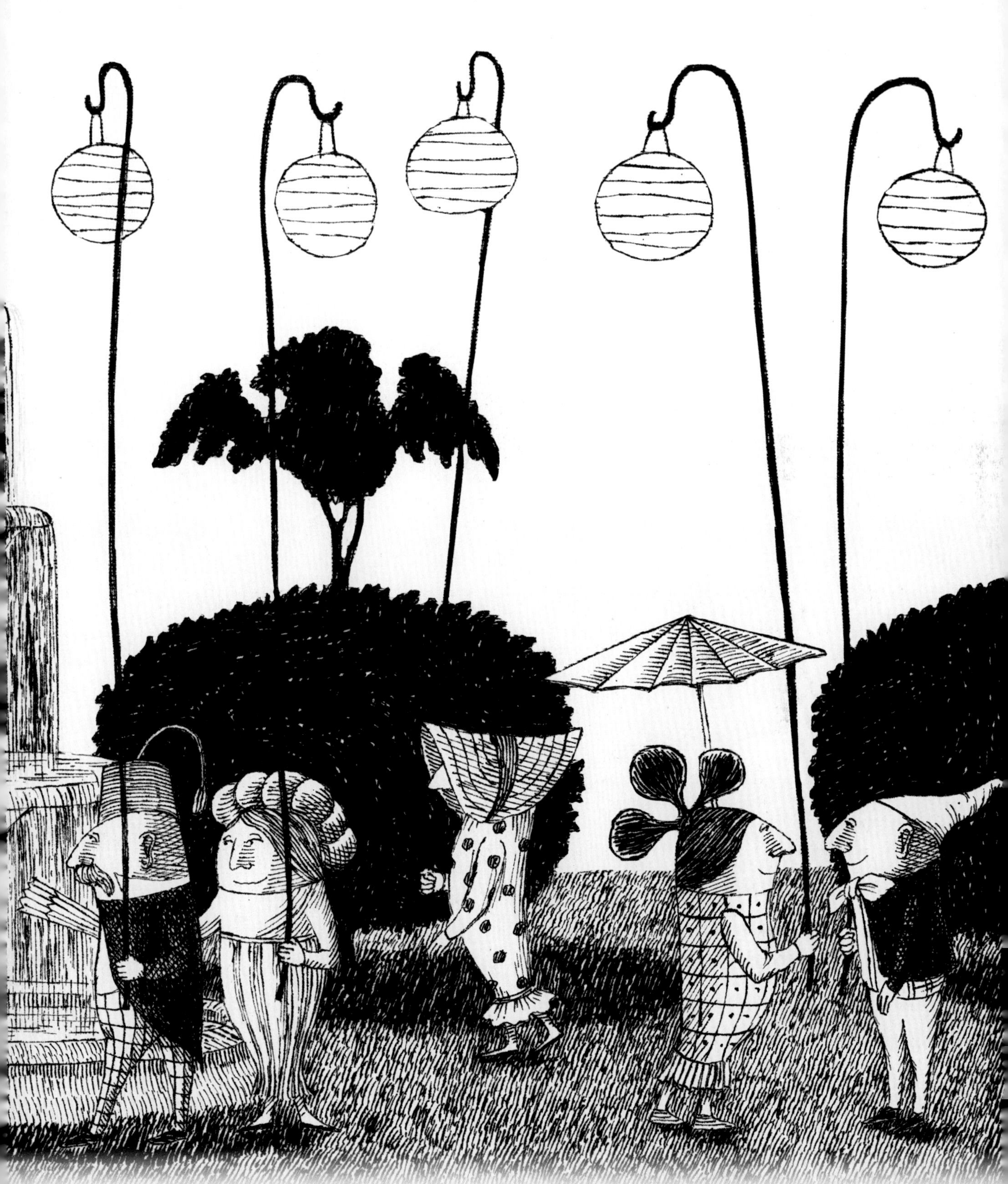

SYRUPS AND INFUSIONS

1:1 SIMPLE SYRUP

✦ MAKES ABOUT 1½ CUPS (360 ML) ✦

1 cup (240 ml) water

1 cup (200 g) sugar

In a small saucepan over medium-high heat, bring the water to a simmer. Add the sugar and stir until the sugar is dissolved. Remove from the heat and let cool. Pour into a clean container, cover, and refrigerate for up to 2 weeks.

MAKRUT LIME SIMPLE SYRUP

✦ MAKES ABOUT 1½ CUPS (360 ML) ✦

1 cup (240 ml) water

1 cup (200 g) sugar

6 fresh makrut lime leaves (or 1 lemongrass stalk, thinly sliced)

In a small saucepan over medium-high heat, bring the water to a simmer. Add the sugar and makrut lime leaves. Stir until the sugar is dissolved. Remove from the heat and let cool. Strain through a fine-mesh sieve into a clean container, cover, and refrigerate for up to 2 weeks.

MAKRUT LIME AND ROSEMARY OLEO SACCHARUM

• MAKES 7 OZ (210 ML) •

1 cup (220 g) superfine sugar

Zest of 8 makrut limes

4 fresh rosemary sprigs, leaves stripped and chopped

¼ cup (60 ml) hot water

Combine the sugar, lime zest, and rosemary in a bowl and massage together. Place the mixture in a bottle and let rest for 1 hour. Add the hot water and stir to dissolve the sugar. Strain through a fine-mesh sieve into a clean container, cover, and refrigerate for up to 2 weeks.

LAVENDER SIMPLE SYRUP

• MAKES ABOUT 1½ CUPS (360 ML) •

1 cup (240 ml) water

1 cup (200 g) sugar

1 tablespoon dried lavender

In a small saucepan over medium-high heat, bring the water to a simmer. Add the sugar and dried lavender. Stir until the sugar is dissolved. Remove from the heat and let cool. Strain through a cheesecloth into a clean container, cover, and refrigerate for up to 2 weeks.

HIBISCUS SIMPLE SYRUP

• MAKES ABOUT 1½ CUPS (360 ML) •

1 cup (240 ml) water

1 cup (200 g) sugar

½ cup (15 g) dried hibiscus flowers

In a small saucepan over medium-high heat, bring the water to a simmer. Add the sugar and dried hibiscus flowers. Stir until the sugar is dissolved. Remove from the heat and let cool. Strain through a fine-mesh sieve into a clean container, cover, and refrigerate for up to 2 weeks.

ROSEMARY SIMPLE SYRUP

✦ MAKES ABOUT 1½ CUPS (360 ML) ✦

1 cup (240 ml) water

1 cup (200 g) sugar

5 fresh rosemary sprigs, roughly chopped

In a small saucepan over medium-high heat, bring the water to a simmer. Add the sugar and chopped rosemary. Stir until the sugar is dissolved. Remove from the heat and let cool. Strain through a fine-mesh sieve into a clean container, cover, and refrigerate for up to 2 weeks.

SAGE SIMPLE SYRUP

✦ MAKES ABOUT 1½ CUPS (360 ML) ✦

1 cup (240 ml) water

1 cup (200 g) sugar

10 fresh sage leaves, roughly chopped

In a small saucepan over medium-high heat, bring the water to a simmer. Add the sugar and chopped sage. Stir until the sugar is dissolved. Remove from the heat and let cool. Strain through a fine-mesh sieve into a clean container, cover, and refrigerate for up to 2 weeks.

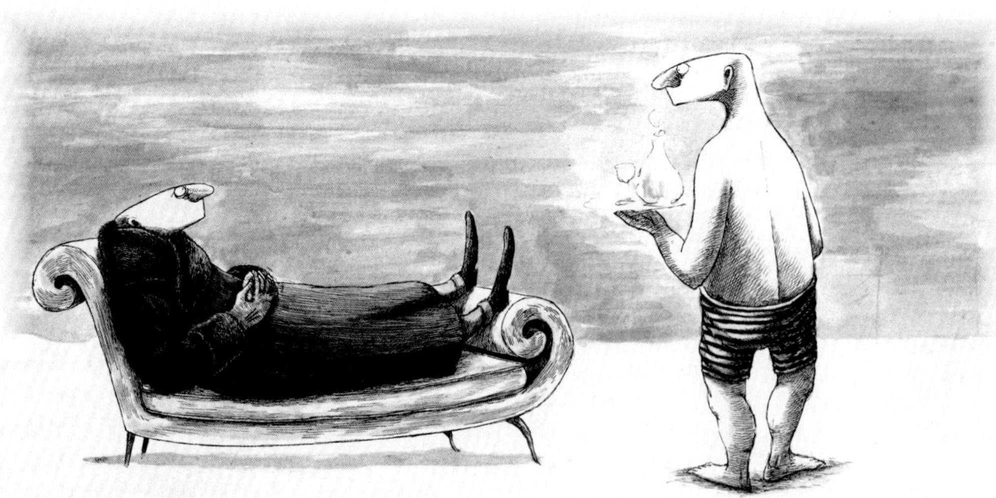

BASIL SIMPLE SYRUP

✦ MAKES ABOUT 1½ CUPS (360 ML) ✦

1 cup (240 ml) water

1 cup (200 g) sugar

15 fresh basil leaves, roughly chopped

In a small saucepan over medium-high heat, bring the water to a simmer. Add the sugar and basil leaves. Stir until the sugar is dissolved. Remove from the heat and let cool. Strain through a fine-mesh sieve into a clean container, cover, and refrigerate for up to 2 weeks.

TARRAGON SIMPLE SYRUP

✦ MAKES ABOUT 1½ CUPS (360 ML) ✦

1 cup (240 ml) water

1 cup (200 g) sugar

5 fresh tarragon sprigs, roughly chopped

In a small saucepan over medium-high heat, bring the water to a simmer. Add the sugar and chopped tarragon. Stir until the sugar is dissolved. Remove from the heat and let cool. Strain through a fine-mesh sieve into a clean container, cover, and refrigerate for up to 2 weeks.

GINGERBREAD SIMPLE SYRUP

✦ MAKES ABOUT 1½ CUPS (360 ML) ✦

1 cup (240 ml) water

1 cup (200 g) sugar

10 whole cloves

2-inch (5-cm) piece fresh ginger, peeled

2 cinnamon sticks

1 teaspoon ground cinnamon

1 teaspoon ground ginger

In a small saucepan over medium-high heat, bring the water to a simmer. Add the sugar and spices. Stir until the sugar is dissolved and let the ingredients simmer for 5–10 minutes, to the desired intensity. Remove from the heat and let cool. Strain through a fine-mesh sieve into a clean container, cover, and refrigerate for up to 2 weeks.

GINGER SIMPLE SYRUP

◆ MAKES ABOUT ¾ CUP (180 ML) ◆

½ cup (120 ml) water

½ cup (100 g) cane sugar

1-inch (2.5-cm) piece fresh ginger, peeled

In a small saucepan over medium-high heat, bring the water to a simmer. Add the sugar and ginger. Stir until the sugar is dissolved, for about 15 minutes, or longer for greater intensity of flavor. Remove from the heat and let cool. Strain through a fine-mesh sieve into a clean container, cover, and refrigerate for up to 2 weeks.

CHERRY ICE CUBES

◆ MAKES 6 LARGE ICE CUBES ◆

1 cup (240 ml) tart cherry juice

1 cup (240 ml) water

6 frozen or fresh cherries, pitted

In a large liquid measuring cup, stir together the cherry juice and water. Pour into six large ice cube molds. Add one cherry to each mold and freeze overnight or for up to 3 months.

VANILLA BEAN–INFUSED VODKA

◆ MAKES 2 CUPS (480 ML) ◆

2 cups (480 ml) vodka

1 whole vanilla bean

Add the vodka to a bottle or carafe. With a paring knife, split the vanilla bean down the center. With the knife, scrape the vanilla bean seeds into the bottle. Cut the bean in half, placing one half into the bottle and reserving the other half for garnish. Cap the bottle and shake. Let the vodka sit for 4–5 days for best results. Shake once more before straining the vodka into a clean bottle.

SEAWEED-INFUSED DRY VERMOUTH

✦ MAKES 1 CUP (240 ML) ✦

4–5 sheets dried nori

1 cup (240 ml) dry vermouth

Add the seaweed to the bottom of a container, like a mason jar. Fill the jar with the dry vermouth. Let sit for up to 2 days in the refrigerator to the desired intensity of flavor, then strain into a clean container. The infused vermouth will keep in the refrigerator for up to 2 months.

SALINE SOLUTION

✦ MAKES ABOUT 1½ TABLESPOONS (22 ML) ✦

1 tablespoon salt

1 tablespoon (15 ml) grappa

Combine the salt and grappa in a small glass and stir until fully dissolved. Used sparingly, 1–2 drops of saline solution will improve most cocktails. You can also make it with cognac, Armagnac, tequila, or even mezcal for a smoky flavor.

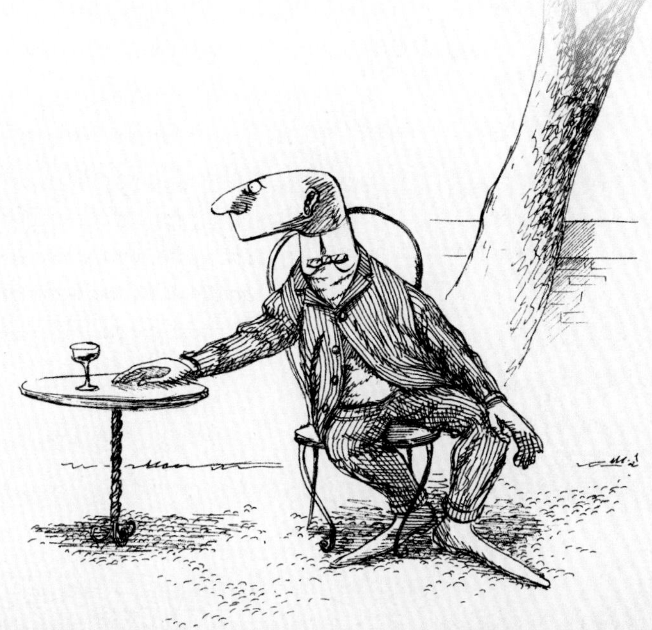

COCKTAILS BY MAIN INGREDIENT

AGAVE SPIRITS

BRANDY AND LIQUEUR

GIN AND AQUAVIT

HERBACEOUS SPIRITS

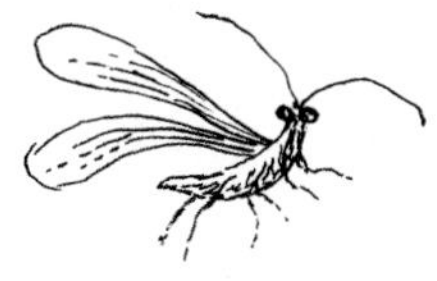

RUM

VODKA

WHISKEY

LOW PROOF

NON-ALCOHOLIC

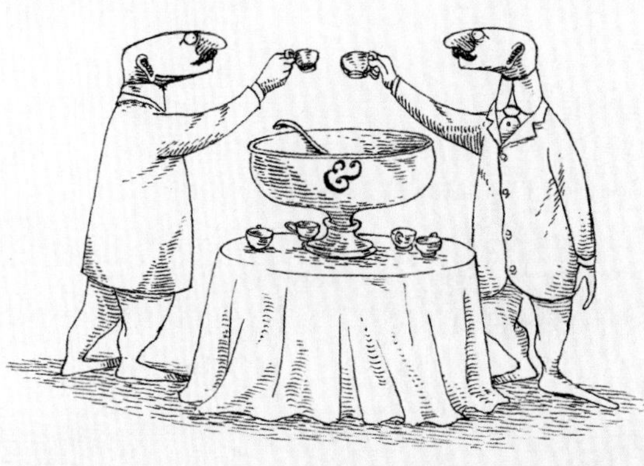

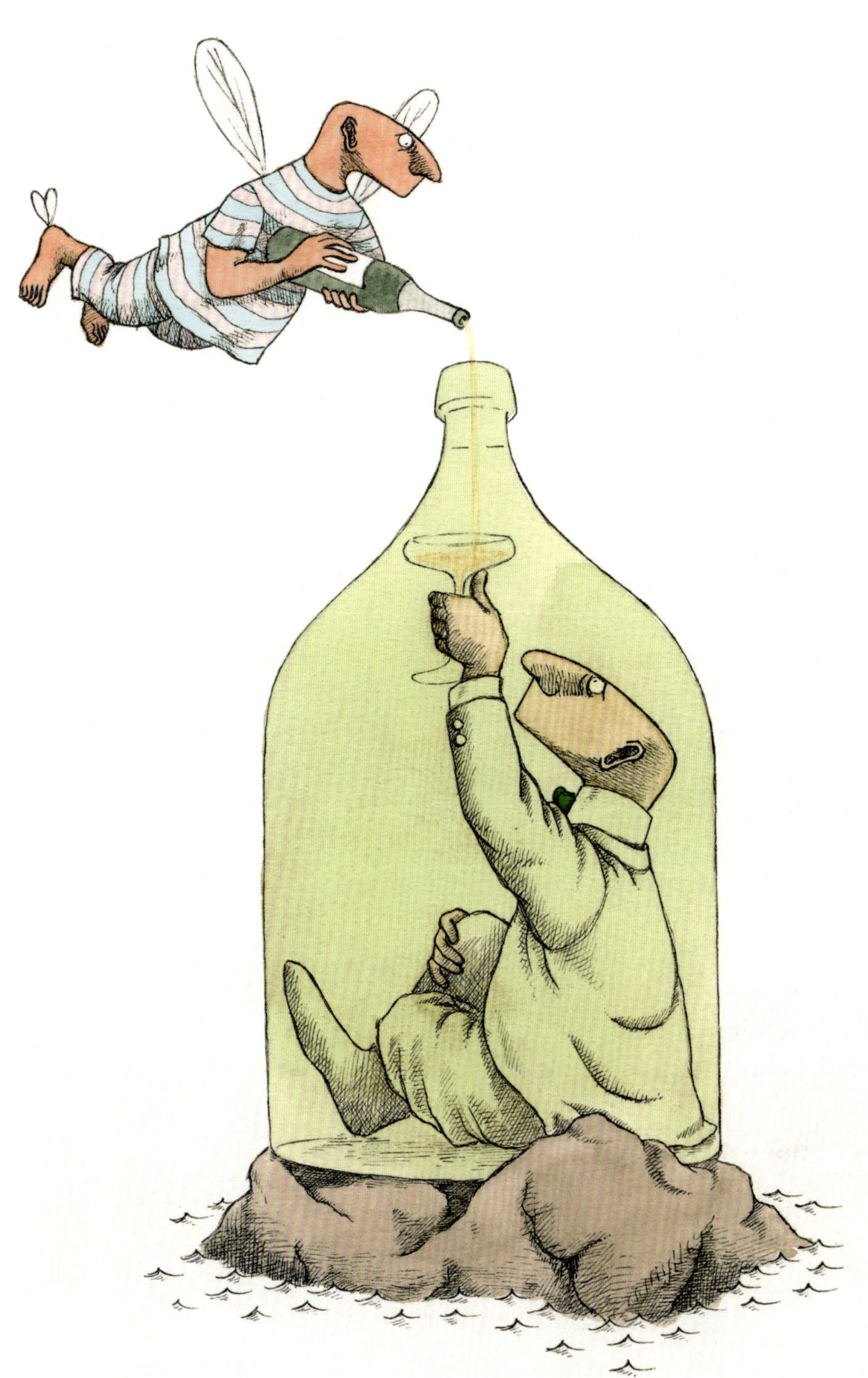

ABOUT THE AUTHOR

Born in Oklahoma with her first few years in Missouri, Virginia Miller mostly grew up on both coasts, in the suburbs of Los Angeles and New York City, until moving to San Francisco as she became an adult and finding her true home. She's been in the city ever since, where her career as a dining and drink writer began.

Founding The Perfect Spot in 2007 for sharing her top recommendations globally in food and drink, Virginia became the W. North America Academy Chair for The World's 50 Best Restaurants, part of the James Beard Foundation committee, and held roles as Zagat SF editor, *San Francisco Bay Guardian* restaurant critic, and Table8 National Editor/VP of Content. She's written about global dining, travel, spirits, cocktails, hotels, and bars for more than sixty international publications and is a regular columnist for multiple online and magazine sources, from *Bon Appetit* to *Time Out*, *Whisky Magazine* to *Distiller* magazine. She also wrote *The Official Emily in Paris Cocktail Book.*

Virginia consults in food and drink around the world, co-creating spirits with Pernod Ricard, consulting for multiple distilleries and brands, leading live and virtual tastings for businesses and private events, and educating on a range of spirits, cocktails, and food. Virginia advises on and has created menus for restaurants and bars, including creating the cocktail menu for three-Michelin-starred chef Dominique Crenn's Golden Poppy in Paris.

Virginia judges in many international dining, food, spirits, cocktails, wine, and bar competitions and awards (including SF World Spirits, ADI Craft Distilling, Tales of the Cocktail, Good Food Awards, IWSC in London, Nola Spirits Comp, and Whiskies of the World) and has visited more than 15,000 restaurants—and even more bars—around the world.

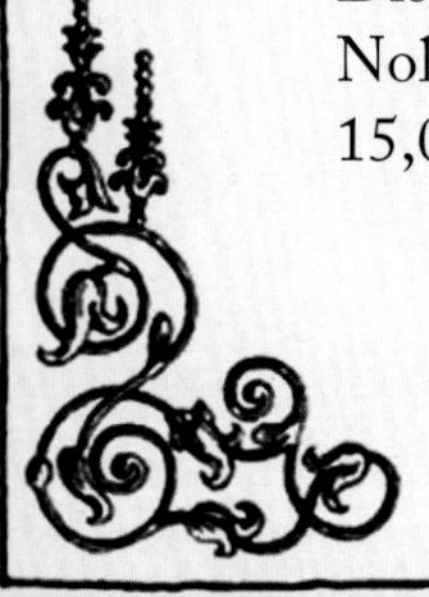

weldon**owen**
an imprint of Insight Editions
P.O. Box 3088
San Rafael, CA 94912
www.weldonowen.com

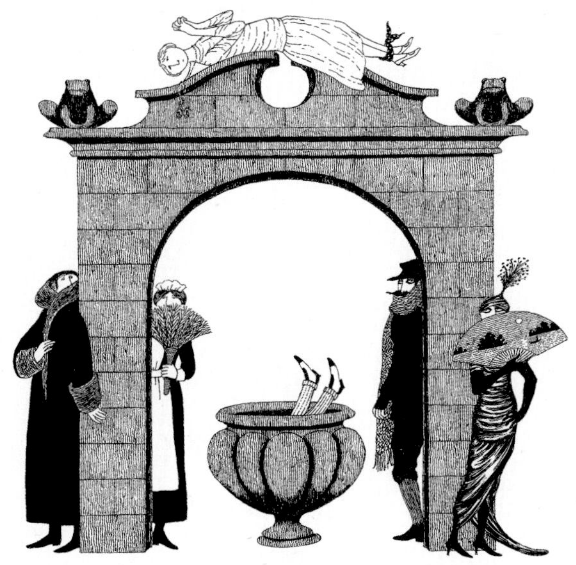

CEO *Raoul Goff*
SVP Group Publisher *Jeff McLaughlin*
VP Publisher *Roger Shaw*
Senior Editor *Karyn Gerhard*
Editorial Assistant *Jon Ellis*
VP Creative *Chrissy Kwasnik*
Art Director & Designer *Megan Sinead Bingham*
Production Design *Jean Hwang*
VP Managing Editorial Director *Katie Killebrew*
VP Manufacturing *Alix Nicholaeff*
Production Manager *Joshua Smith*
Strategic Production Planner *Lina s Palma-Temena*

Weldon Owen would also like to thank Karen Levy and Margaret Parrish for their work on this title. The editor would especially like to thank Raquel Serebrenik at 4Art Partners, Gorey archivist William Baker, and Eric Sherman at the Edward Gorey Charitable Trust; without their enthusiasm, guidance, and collaborative spirit, this book could not have been made.

Photography by Stacy Ventura
Food styling by Victoria Woollard
Prop styling by Megan Sinead Bingham

Pages 140–1: Gorey illustration for *The Dong with the Luminous Nose* by Edward Lear, 1969.

ISBN: 979-8-88674-239-8

Manufactured in China by Insight Editions
10 9 8 7 6 5 4 3 2 1

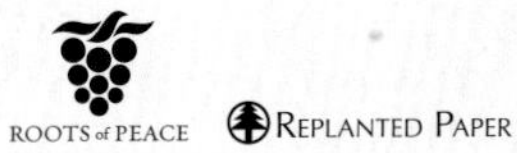

Insight Editions, in association with Roots of Peace, will plant two trees for each tree used in the manufacturing of this book. Roots of Peace is an internationally renowned humanitarian organization dedicated to eradicating land mines worldwide and converting war-torn lands into productive farms and wildlife habitats. Roots of Peace will plant two million fruit and nut trees in Afghanistan and provide farmers there with the skills and support necessary for sustainable land use.